Albion L

Albion Dreaming

A popular history of LSD in Britain

Andy Roberts

Designed and typeset by Phoenix Photosetting, Lordswood, Chatham, Kent
www.phoenixphotosetting.co.uk

Published in 2012 by Marshall Cavendish Editions
An imprint of Marshall Cavendish International

1 New Industrial Road, Singapore 536196
genrefsales@marshallcavendish.com
www.marshallcavendish.com/genref

Other Marshall Cavendish offices: Marshall Cavendish Corporation, 99 White Plains Road, Tarrytown, NY 10591 • Marshall Cavendish International (Thailand) Co Ltd. 253 Asoke, 12th Flr, Sukhumvit 21 Road, Klongtoey Nua, Wattana, Bangkok 10110, Thailand • Marshall Cavendish (Malaysia) Sdn Bhd, Times Subang, Lot 46, Subang Hi-Tech Industrial Park, Batu Tiga, 40000 Shah Alam, Selangor Darul Ehsan, Malaysia

A CIP record for this book is available from the British Library

ISBN 978 981 4382 16 8

Printed and bound in Great Britain by TJ International Limited, Padstow, Cornwall

To Gavin for charting the course,
Lindsay for being the imperfect guru and
Andy, Graeme, Chris and Helen, with whom I shared
adventures unfettered by time and space.
And for my Mountain Girl, blips!
What a long, strange, trip it's been.

CONTENTS

DRAMATIS PERSONAE

Steve Abrams	American parapsychologist who was at the heart of London's LSD counter culture
Jonathan Aitken	Journalist who took LSD, when still legal, for the Evening Standard; subsequently a disgraced Conservative MP
Richard Alpert	Colleague of Timothy Leary at Harvard and co-conspirator in the early promotion of LSD; subsequently eschewed drugs and became the spiritual teacher Baba Ram Dass
George Andrews	Poet and author of books on drugs
Paul Arnabaldi	Backer of Richard Kemp's Welsh LSD laboratory
Nigel Ayres	Attendee and recorder of many free festivals of the Seventies
Syd Barrett	Original Pink Floyd lead guitarist; LSD contributed to his descent into mental illness
Brian Barritt	Early LSD dealer in London; friend of Timothy Leary
Cecil Beaton	English fashion and portrait photographer
John Beresford	Paediatrician friend of Michael Hollinsghead

Christine Bott	Involved in Operation Julie conspiracy; common law wife of Richard Kemp
Joe Boyd	American record producer and co-founder of UFO club
Tara Browne	London socialite whose death possibly inspired the Beatles' *Day in the Life*
Richard Brunstrom	Chief Constable of North Wales; believes all drugs should be legalised and regulated
Julia Callan-Thompson	Occasional hippie prostitute; involved with the Kapur LSD conspiracy
Ernest Chain	Nobel winning biochemist who appeared for the defence in a 1967 LSD trial
Derek Channon	Naval rating who underwent LSD experiment at Porton Down in 1953
Harry Collumbine	Porton Down scientist
Sean Connery	James Bond actor who used LSD in psychotherapy
Julian Cope	Musician with a predilection for LSD
Francis Crick	Discovered DNA
Dave Cunliffe	LSD courier in late Fifties London
Paul Devereux	Author and researcher into prehistoric use of psychedelic drugs
Jeff Dexter	Legendary DJ at UFO club and 1971 Glastonbury Fair

Johnny Dolphin	American poet who spent time with Terry Taylor in Morocco
Bill (Ubi) Dwyer	LSD dealer in Australia and London; instigator behind the Windsor Free Festivals
Joel Elkes	Founder of Birmingham University's Department of Experimental Psychology; early LSD experimenter; linked to MOD LSD experiments
John Esam	London LSD dealer in the early Sixties
Harry Fainlight	Poet who read his LSD inspired poem at the 1965 Wholly Communion event
Mick Farren	Counter culture author and antagonist
Nigel (Leif) Fielding	Minor player in the Operation Julie LSD conspiracy
David Gale	Childhood friend of Pink Floyd's Syd Barrett
Christopher Gibb	London art dealer; friend of the Rolling Stones
Allen Ginsberg	American Beat poet with counter culture sympathies
Dave (Boss) Goodman	London LSD dealer in the Sixties
Eric Gow	RAF serviceman who underwent LSD test at Porton Down during the Fifties

Dennis Greenslade	Detective Superintendent in Operation Julie
Casey Hardison	American citizen sentenced to 20 years imprisonment in 2005 for manufacturing LSD in Lewes, Sussex
Lee Harris	Founder of London's first "head" shop; editor of *Home Grown*, Britain's first counter culture drug magazine
Gerald Heard	British expatriate philosopher; gave LSD to Alcoholics Anonymous founder Bill Wilson; instrumental in the development of early LSD philosophies
Bill Hicks	American satirist who campaigned against drug hypocrisy
Albert Hofmann	Chemist who discovered LSD in 1938
Michael Hollingshead	Introduced Timothy Leary to LSD; mover and shaker on early London psychedelic scene
Maxwell Hollyhock	MOD scientist who took LSD to examine its effects
John (Hoppy) Hopkins	Photographer and counter culture legend; co-founder of UFO club
Frankie Howerd	British comedian who underwent LSD psychotherapy
Chris Huhne	Liberal Democrat MP
Roger Hutchinson	Attendee and photographic recorder of many free festivals in the Seventies

Aldous Huxley	Intellectual and literary polymath; probably the finest writer on psychedelic drugs and their philosophy
Laura Huxley	Huxley's wife; administered LSD to Huxley as he died
Robert Hyde	American psychiatrist who took the first LSD trip in America
Mick Jagger	Singer in the Rolling Stones
Roy Jenkins	British Home Secretary 1965–67
Peter Jenner	Manager of Pink Floyd
Victor Kapur	The first man to be arrested in Britain for manufacturing LSD
Richard Kemp	LSD chemist; pivotal in the Operation Julie LSD conspiracy
Andrew Kerr	Instigator of the 1971 Glastonbury Fair, forerunner to the annual Glastonbury Festival
Ken Kesey	American author of *One Flew over the Cuckoo's Nest*; advocate of unstructured LSD use
Art Kleps	One of Timothy Leary's disciples
R.D. (Ronnie) Laing	Radical psychiatrist who used LSD personally and professionally
Timothy Leary	American academic, responsible for promulgating LSD as a spiritual tool

Richard (Dick) Lee	Detective Inspector in Operation Julie
Donovan Leitch	Folk rock musician involved in the early London LSD scene
Nigel Lesmoir-Gordon	Film maker and friend of Syd Barrett
Tim Lott	Author and journalist
Christopher Mayhew	British politician who took Mescaline as part of a 1955 televised experiment
Paul McCartney	The first member of the Beatles to publicly admit to taking LSD
Joey Mellen	Early London LSD facilitator, critical of Hollingshead's methods
Pete Mellor	Grass roots hippie with considerable experience of LSD
Ralph Metzner	American psychologist who participated in early LSD experiments at Harvard with Timothy Leary
John Michell	Author, researcher and philosopher; introduced many of the "mystical" ideas about Britain
Barry Miles	Author and chronicler of the Sixties
Monkey	Free festival attendee, LSD dealer and observer of the transition from free festivals to rave culture
Andy Munro	The chemist in the London part of the Operation Julie conspiracy

Simon Napier-Bell	Record producer
Jim Narg	First British person to mention LSD in song
Harry Nathan	Distributor of LSD for Victor Kapur
Desmond O'Brien	One of the backers behind Michael Hollingshead's World Psychedelic Centre
Humphrey Osmond	British psychiatrist who invented the word psychedelic
Anita Pallenberg	Actress and Rolling Stones' *femme fatale*
Clive Palmer	First person in Scotland to be charged with possession of LSD
Hugh Park	Judge at the main Operation Julie conspiracy trials
Paul Guest	Britain's leading Blotter art collector, expert and retailer
Norman Pilcher	British police officer who achieved notoriety by arresting pop stars for drugs; later convicted for conspiracy to pervert the course of justice
Sid Rawle	Early hippie, squatting veteran and free festival organiser
Max Rinkel	American psychiatrist who brought LSD to America in1949
Philip (Wally Hope) Russell	Charismatic hippie and LSD advocate who founded the Stonehenge Free Festivals

Greg Sams	American who, with brother Craig, was instrumental in setting up macrobiotic and whole food restaurants in Sixties London
Ronnie Sandison	Britain's first LSD psychotherapist
David Schneiderman	Enigmatic LSD dealer, briefly a member of the Rolling Stones' entourage
Ben Sessa	Contemporary British psychiatrist who believes there is a place for LSD in psychotherapy
Peter Simmons	Set up several LSD laboratories in the late Sixties
Ian Sinclair	London based author and psychogeographer, chronicler of Ginsberg's 1967 visit
David Solomon	American writer on drug issues; later became involved with the Operation Julie LSD conspiracy
Henry (Bing) Spear	Chief Inspector of the Dangerous Drugs Branch of the Home Office 1952–1986
Augustus (Bear) Owsley Stanley III	Legendary Californian LSD chemist
Ronald Stark	Enigmatic international LSD dealer; connected to international terrorism; suspected of working for various intelligence agencies
Arthur Stoll	Co-worker of Albert Hofmann

Terry Taylor	Beatnik author who went on to be an LSD dealer and to found LSD based magic cult in London
Vince Taylor	British rock and roll singer; Bowie's *Ziggy Stardust* was based on Taylor
Henry Todd	Key player in the Operation Julie LSD conspiracy
Dave Tomlin	Jazz musician and author; foot soldier of the psychedelic revolution
Alexander Trocchi	Poet and writer; dealt LSD in London during the Sixties
Alan Watts	British expatriate mystic and philosopher with an interest in psychedelic drugs; part of the scene around Aldous Huxley and Gerald Heard
Don Webb	Airman who took part in LSD experiment at Porton Down during the 1950s
Bernadette Whybrow	Occasional hippie prostitute and LSD dealer in the Kapur LSD conspiracy
Peter Wright	Former member of MI5; author of the controversial book *Spycatcher*

LIST OF ILLUSTRATIONS

GLOSSARY

Acid	LSD
Acidhead	One whose preferred drug is LSD
Blotter art	Non-LSD-containing sheets of blotter
Blotter	Dose of LSD on blotting paper
Bust	Police search, raid or arrest
Cap	LSD in capsule form
Coming down	The tailing off of an LSD experience, returning to "normal" consciousness
Counter culture	The culture, especially of young people who use drugs, with values or lifestyles in opposition to those of the established culture
Dig	Understand
Drop	To take LSD orally, i.e. to drop acid
Establishment	The matrix of political, legal, economic, religious, and social forces committed to maintaining the status quo
Freak	Early name for a hippie, member of the counter culture
Freak out	Adverse reaction to LSD, often in public
Happening	Spontaneous eruption of artistic display, often by amateurs
High	Under the influence of a drug
Hippie	Member of the counter culture
Mind blowing	Ecstasy producing experience or drug
Psychedelic	Mind expanding or mind manifesting
Scene	Any aspect of the counter culture, also used to describe a small part of it
Score	To buy drugs, i.e. "I went to score some acid"
Set	The mind set of the LSD user – their fundamental beliefs and values
Setting	The physical surroundings for an LSD experience

Stoned	Under the influence of a drug, usually cannabis
Straight	Someone who has not used LSD, a member of the Establishment
Tab	LSD in tablet form
Trip	LSD experience
Tripping	Under the influence of LSD
Turn on	To use LSD, to give someone else LSD
µg	Scientific symbol for microgram (one-millionth of a gram)
Underground	Another name for the counter culture

FOREWORD

I am so glad I took LSD. *Albion Dreaming* reminds me why, as well as telling me many things I never knew about the ultimate psychedelic and how its story played out here in Britain. This turns out to be quite a different story from the better-known tale of LSD in the USA. Acid was, after all, a European invention and there were many Englishmen involved in its early use, including Aldous Huxley who famously asked for it as he lay dying of cancer.

No wonder its discoverer, Albert Hoffman, called LSD 'My Problem Child'. More than any other drug I know, LSD has the capacity for the extremes of insight and joy as well as the bleakest and most fearful of depths. This may be why it can be such a great teacher and I guess this is the main reason I am glad. I was also very lucky to have good guides for my earliest trips and the opportunity to choose wonderful settings. For me the ideal has always been to take it early in the morning and spend a day on the cliff tops or the beach or the woods or even my own garden. I may have overindulged a bit in those early days in the 1970s – after all, it was all so exciting! But most of my life I have wanted it only once every few years when the time or the need seemed right.

In January 2006 I went to Basel in Switzerland for the symposium to celebrate Albert Hofmann's 100th birthday, and what an event that was and what an amazing man. I glimpsed him the first morning there as I was going up an escalator and looked round to see him halfway up. Crowds were hovering around him as though in awe or even worship. Part of me rebelled as I so dislike heroes turned into semi-religious figures but then I too was captivated as he stepped off at the top and I was looking into his bright, warm, intelligent eyes. He radiated a kind of presence that I have never seen before, and then moved steadily off amid an enormous crowd of admirers.

How can someone live to a hundred and be so fit and well? Did it have anything to do with the drugs he synthesised, tested and used? Perhaps it had more to do with his earlier spiritual or mystical experiences as a child, experiences that arguably led him to the 'mishap that was not a mishap' as he put it, to the intuition that the apparently innocuous 25th compound in the LSD series was worth a second look. Or was it, as he suggested, his daily breakfast of raw egg? We cannot know. Yet this hundred-year-old man participated fully in the three days of the conference. As he walked up onto the stage for the first time, he wobbled a little and steadied himself with his stick. Then he turned and apologised 'I'm sorry for being a little unsteady but I must remind myself that I'm no longer in my nineties'.

I was lucky enough to meet him briefly face to face. As well as just enjoying the event I was recording interviews with many of the people there, hoping to make a BBC radio programme and write articles on LSD. Like lots of other journalists and researchers I had asked for, and been politely refused, an interview with the great man himself. Then one afternoon, to avoid the melee, I had snuck away into a relatively quiet corner to interview Martin Lee, author of *Acid Dreams*. What I hadn't realised was that the innocuous looking door behind us was a secret way through from the conference centre to the hotel next door, and right in the middle of the interview I saw a small group coming towards us – the organisers escorting the birthday boy to this door. I was introduced right then and there to the centenarian who put aside his stick and warmly shook my hand. I went completely pathetic and mumbled what I tried to say in the most appalling German. Yet of course he understood for I was only saying what everyone else there wanted to say. Thank you Albert.

This deep gratitude is just one of many hints that LSD invokes something akin to mystical or spiritual experiences – leading to the vexed question of whether these experiences are really the same or ultimately different – whether a simple drug that affects the brain can really create true spirituality. Is laughing at the 'Cosmic joke' and delighting in sheer acid joy the same as mystical joy? Is the sudden understanding of the power of love the same as that met in prayer or contemplation? Is the involuntary review of who we are and all we have done, with its descent into fear or disgust at our own shortcomings, the same as the ultimately freeing acceptance reported in near-death experiences? Is the terror of letting go of self, or the joyful realisation that 'I' am not other than the universe, the same as the oneness reached in mystical experiences. Is this loss of self the nonduality that can take years of meditation practice to find? Or are these just tricks of the ultimate trickster drug? I cannot answer this deepest question about LSD any more than anyone else can, although my own intuition is that the answer is 'yes'.

The tragedy of LSD, as this and other books explore, is how it became abused, made illegal, and ultimately denied both to those who wanted to explore its spiritual dimensions and those could have benefited from its therapeutic potential. I get upset to think how differently things might have turned out. In my dream world I live in a society in which all recreational drugs are legally available, regulated and controlled; a society in which a culture of serious drug use rather than drug abuse grows up and matures. Just imagine being able to seek out experienced guides to take you, or your children, or your best friends, into that first trip. Just imagine a world in which professionals know how to guide people through bad trips and terrifying ordeals, and how to avoid the psychological damage that LSD can undoubtedly sometimes inflict. But I ask myself whether it could ever have been this way. Was the abuse and misunderstanding inevitable? Might we ever reach this dream world, and in my lifetime?

I do not know but I keep hoping. And in a country where more and more people want to see the end of the war on drugs, perhaps we can do it. I've read many histories of psychedelic drugs and met many of the characters involved, but *Albion Dreaming* gives us something new by showing how the history of LSD played out differently here in Britain from the way it did in the USA. This is one of the reasons I enjoyed it so much, and it may perhaps give us hope for LSD's future here in Britain.

Dr Susan Blackmore
Psychologist and author of *The Meme Machine* (1999), *Zen and the Art of Consciouness* (2011) and other books on consciousness, memes and anomalous experiences

Devon, February 2012

www.susanblackmore.co.uk
www.memetics.com

Albion Dreaming

1

TURN ON, TUNE IN, DROP OUT

> **LSD:** an abbreviation of the German term **L**ysergsäure-**D**iäthylamid for lysergic acid diethylamide: a semi synthetic illicit organic compound $C_{20}H_{25}N_3O$ derived from ergot that induces extreme sensory distortions, altered perceptions of reality, and intense emotional states, that may also produce delusions or paranoia, and that may sometimes cause panic reactions in response to the effects experienced.[1]

The American psychologist Dr. Timothy Leary once said LSD was the drug with the most unusual emotional and psychological effects when compared to any other. Why? Because just the *idea* of the drug has the power to cause terror among people who have never taken it. With this, Leary was referring to the worldwide moral panic that has attended LSD since the drug first became popular among the hippie counter culture in the Sixties.[2]

For politicians, the police, the media and the public, LSD represents and remains a powerful folk devil. The idea of LSD is freighted with fears that it is capable of causing insanity after a single dose. It is believed to contribute to the moral and social degradation of the individual and the development of a counter culture antithetical to the values of western materialism. In other words, the drug is perceived to be a serious threat to the individual and to society.

Yet there are fundamental differences in how different groups of people view LSD. Millions of individuals have taken LSD since its discovery in 1938 and its use has spawned a huge subculture. Devout supporters of the drug claim LSD is a beneficial tool for studying consciousness, with the potential of bestowing fundamental spiritual and personal insights on those who take it. Others simply laud the drug as being a powerful agent for altering consciousness and enhancing awareness, revealing the sensory world in all its glory. At the most mundane level, those who are not interested in LSD's spiritual or consciousness expanding possibilities speak of the sheer, boundless, multi-dimensional cosmic fun to be had using the drug recreationally: a Disneyland of the mind. There are innumerable reports from people who have taken LSD who testify to its beneficial effects on their lives, yet society has deemed it so dangerous that its manufacture, distribution or possession is punishable by lengthy prison sentences.

Of course, to those who have not taken LSD such claims might appear pretentious or deluded. They will refer to the handful of people who have died whilst under the influence of LSD. Alternatively, they will recount how some have been compelled to seek psychiatric help because the effects of the drug have been so overpowering. Everyone, whether they have taken LSD or not, has their own opinions, fuelled by a combination of experience and prejudice.

There is no way of adequately explaining the result of taking LSD other than through the accounts of those who have, and observation of how they have tried to integrate the experience into their lives. All of us are familiar with the effects of at least some drugs, from the lift that can be obtained from strong tea, coffee, cola, alcohol or tobacco, to currently illegal substances such as amphetamines, cannabis, ecstasy, cocaine or heroin. But the reactions to LSD are in a class of their own. To compound matters further, LSD, unlike other drugs, does not have a consistently predictable set of physiological or psychological reactions.

The effects of LSD on the body are minimal. On the mind, however, they are dramatic, complex, and inter-dependent on a variety of factors including purity, expectation, environment and dosage. The drug's potency is such that doses as small as 50-millionths of a gram (50 µg) can produce powerful effects, and even a significant dose is only 250 µg. How the interplay of dosage, expectation and environment creates different theories and reactions is a theme that runs throughout this book.[3]

Author, Tim Lott whose reaction to his first LSD trip can be found in Chapter 11, has written one of the most cogent and articulate explanations of what LSD means to him. It is a view shared, to varying degrees, by the majority of those who have taken LSD:

"I have many times tried to describe how simply taking a drug can change your whole perception of life, but it is rather like trying to explain colour to the blind. There are no terms of reference in ordinary life to help you to understand. And actually, I am torn between evangelising for the drug and warning everyone not to go within a million miles of it. I suppose the most simple and incredible fact about LSD is also the one that is hardest to believe: that what it reveals to you is not, as is popularly supposed, a hallucination, but an awe-inspiring glimpse of reality. Other drugs distort, but LSD gives you a reality far beyond words, or visual representation, or language. It is quite the reverse of seeing something that isn't there. LSD disables some chemical filter in the brain that, in order to keep the world manageable, limits the amount of reality you can experience with your senses. An LSD trip allows 'reality' – and if you have never questioned what that is, you would after taking LSD – to flood in untrammelled. The result may be terrifying and it may be wonderful, but it will be more 'real' than anything you experience in everyday life. LSD shows you that ordinary life is the hallucination. Or to put it another way, ordinary life is like listening to a record with fluff on the needle, and LSD removes the fluff. Psychotherapeutically speaking, it releases your subconscious into the conscious mind (or vice versa)."

Anyone who has not taken LSD might dismiss Lott's views as hyperbole to explain and justify the effects of a drug that actually mimic a form of temporary madness. But Lott has experienced mental illness, and is clear about the distinction between that and LSD, "... I've been mad – or at least severely mentally ill. And taking LSD is as different an experience as you can imagine."[4]

When LSD was discovered, the drug seemed loaded with potential. The problem was no one knew exactly what to do with it. LSD seemed to be the answer to a question that had not yet been formulated. And, like Tolkien's ring, LSD exerted a powerful force on individuals and institutions, leading several to assert it was the answer to *their* particular question. Firstly, the intelligence services and military laid claim to it, believing it could be the solution to the problems of interrogation, investigating its potential as, among other options, a "truth drug". The medical establishment also saw its possibilities for their profession, as a drug capable of unlocking and unblocking the unconscious mind. It was employed in experimental psychotherapy to cure obsessions and addictions, heal damaged psyches and to develop human potential. Both of these approaches yielded contradictory results, the experiments being curtailed long before any firm conclusions could be drawn or the way forward charted.

Inevitably, the secret leaked out and LSD became available to the public, slowly at first, building to a torrent after the mid-Sixties. LSD was legal in the early Sixties, those early psychedelic pioneers were awed, and astonished by the experience it provided. Travellers returned from LSD trips with tales of other dimensions, other ways of seeing, other ways of thinking and, most importantly, other ways of being. Small groups of psychonauts, often maverick professionals such as Timothy Leary, believed that LSD, if taken in the correct circumstances and with an experienced guide, could elevate consciousness to the spiritual heights tantalizingly offered by the world's major religions and spiritual disciplines. But unlike traditional spiritual practice, which offered no guarantees and demanded years, a lifetime even, of study and devotion, LSD, it was rumoured, could deliver enlightenment in just one dose. Use of LSD required no reliance on deity or scripture and the user was not required to be part of a spiritual hierarchy. The widespread belief was that by taking it an individual could be plugged into the hub of the Universe, to become one with everything, and could experience God directly. LSD soon became known as "the sacrament" and unsurprisingly, one popular badge in the Sixties bore the adage "God is alive in a sugar cube" – LSD soaked sugar cubes being a popular method of ingesting the drug in that decade.

Ultimately, the Establishment, that web of conservative social, political and religious ideologies, fought back. The idea of young people having access to a drug rumoured to confer instant enlightenment and spiritual freedom was abhorrent. The media, always looking for a new folk devil to exorcise, seized on LSD as the destroyer of youth, focusing only on the small number of personal disasters. Journalists, rather than exploring the success stories emanating from psychotherapists or the genuine and meaningful personality changes brought about by LSD, chose to amplify the possible dangers of a drug they knew little about.

The knock-on effect of the media offensive against LSD was that parents, with little knowledge of LSD, believed if their children took the drug they would be on the road to addiction or worse. Church leaders found the idea of instant enlightenment shallow and contrary to the ethics of Judeo-Christian religious belief, political administrations saw no purpose in a drug that encouraged people to live and think in a radically different way to that considered normal. The *idea* of LSD had grown out of all proportion to the substance itself and had, for the majority of society, become a demon, a barbarian at the doors of everyday consciousness and normality.

This intense barrage of ill-informed opinion and prejudice led to LSD being declared illegal in Britain in late 1966. Since then it has remained on the statute books as one of the most dangerous illegal drugs, ranked with heroin, cocaine and morphine. This contentious decision was based, as we will see, on the flimsiest of reasoning. LSD is not addictive and only a handful of deaths have been attributed to it. How the British Establishment has dealt with LSD is a prima face example of a society's inability to deal intelligently and consistently with consciousness-changing drugs.

Society's relationship with drugs is complex. Humans have used substances that alter consciousness for millennia. In his book *The Long Trip: a prehistory of psychedelia,* Paul Devereux traces the history of intoxicants into distant pre-history. The Sumerians recorded their use of opium as long ago as circa 5000 BC, predating the earliest record of humans' favourite drug, alcohol, which dates from 3500 BC. It seems that plants and fungi that cause hallucinatory phenomena have been used in every culture since the earliest times; the human desire to change consciousness has, it seems, always been a motivating factor in societies.[5]

Among shamanic, tribal cultures, plants and fungi that induce visions are frequently the centre of spiritual life and tradition. These substances are believed to be sentient beings, supernatural emissaries; the origins of music and medicine, cosmology and extensive botanical knowledge often attributed to the visions revealed under their influence. In such societies, rejection of the visionary knowledge offered by the botanical world would be a form of insanity. Yet in the twentieth and twenty-first centuries, these experiences are outlawed, often for no logical reason.

At various times throughout history governments have legislated for the use of drugs when they have been thought useful, and against when not. In Britain, for instance, prior to World War I, people often drank alcohol during the day because drinking water was full of impurities. While we were primarily an agricultural society this was not seen as a problem. The advent of industrialization saw drinking affecting production and so during World War I, licensing laws were changed to help increase productivity. Drugs were incorporated on the battlefield, troops being given a tot of rum to help boost the courage needed to walk into a hail of machine-gun fire. Cannabis, morphine and cocaine could all be purchased in chemists' shops until at least the 1920s, being recommended for complaints such as period pains, pain and depression. In World War II, amphetamines were issued to soldiers to increase alertness and enable them to fight for days at a time. In each of these cases, it has been the government who, for its own ends, has decided what drug its citizens should be able to legally take and in what circumstances they take it. By the 1960s all the drugs mentioned above, with the exception of alcohol, had been outlawed, with stringent fines and prison sentences for those who dared to experiment with their consciousness.[6]

All drugs are legal for many years before they are criminalised. This raises questions about the basis on which a drug is made illegal. Is the decision made from genuine, evidential research? Or is it merely due to public outcry, media pressure and political opportunism? Indeed, should any government have the right to tell individuals what they may or may not ingest? Those who believe LSD is dangerous claim it is illegal because of its potential dangers to the minds of those who take it. LSDs proponents argue it has been criminalised in order to deny access to it by those who seek to alter their consciousness for spiritual and personal reasons.

In most people's minds, the history of LSD is inextricably bound up with America. The drug was first widely used there, initially by the CIA and the military and later in a psychotherapeutic context. But it was the counter culture of the Sixties and Seventies, the hippies' flamboyant use of LSD that has been most visible and which has led to the identification of the drug with America. In addition, the vast majority of popular literature dealing with the drug has emanated from America including, of course, the drugs most famous proselytiser, Timothy Leary.[7]

This American bias has been at the expense of a much broader account of LSD's history in which Britain, with its own lengthy tradition of LSD use, plays a crucial role. In fact, LSD is a European export to America. The drug was discovered in Switzerland, the British pioneered LSD psychotherapy and military tests and much of the counter culture's underlying philosophy stems from British expatriates such as Aldous Huxley and Alan Watts. On a more fundamental level, at certain times the bulk of the world's LSD was manufactured in Britain. Nevertheless, when people think of LSD it is to American culture they turn for their knowledge.

Albion Dreaming seeks to redress the balance, tracing the history and use of LSD and restoring Britain's status as a major crucible of LSD culture. That process has already been started with a handful of books, notably Tony Melechi's *Psychedelia Britannica,* David Black's *Acid*, and Stewart Tendler and David May's *Brotherhood of Eternal Love*. These books are detailed and well researched but only cover certain narrow aspects of British LSD culture. *Albion Dreaming* takes a chronological and thematic overview of the drug's impact on individuals and society from its arrival here in 1952 until the present day. The book is intended to be a social history, reflecting how LSD has been viewed and used across all levels of society. It is, by no means, a comprehensive work. New information is constantly becoming available and there is more than enough material for an entire book devoted to each of the three main themes of this book; the military, medical and counter-cultural uses of LSD. The author hopes that his research will stimulate others into further investigation, leading to an even deeper understanding of the role LSD has played within British society.

Albion Dreaming has been compiled from a range of disparate, often obscure, sources spanning the period 1938–2007. Information about the military and medical use of LSD was sourced from a variety of government archives and augmented with information gleaned from new interviews with some of the individuals concerned. The fascinating saga of the counter culture's involvement with LSD, which forms the majority of the book, was pieced together from contemporary sources and new interviews with people crucial to the movement.

This aspect of the research has been the most frustrating. Some major players refused interviews. Others wish to minimise their involvement with LSD because of the drug's illegal status and an unwillingness to compromise themselves or their friends. Where this is the case, the interviewees have attempted to be as truthful as possible without betraying others in their trust. Some have been cautious because of their current jobs or because their families know little about their activities of forty or more years ago. However, over a hundred people have freely given of their memories, experiences and opinions with no constraints on how they are presented, with only one person requesting anonymity. As the LSD subculture evolved it has generated a specific jargon and to help clarify some of the language used a glossary of terms is provided.

Because LSD has permeated all levels of society, it has become fashionable to speculate that a conspiracy lies at the core of the worldwide LSD story. The arc of this conspiracy stretches from the belief the drug was created as part of an unspecified sinister plot, to belief that the CIA introduced LSD to post-war youth in order to dilute the desire for political and social change. Between these sketchy and unproven extremes flit real people to whom membership of these ill-defined conspiracies has been ascribed. However, the purpose of this book is not to pander to the fantasies of the counter culture. The reader must make up his or her own mind if there is evidence for any conspiracy surrounding LSD in Britain.

Ultimately, *Albion Dreaming* is not about LSD itself. It is about people's experiences of the drug, lifestyle choices made as result of LSD use, the drug's impact on society and the fundamental questions of whether an individual has the right to change their own consciousness in whatever way they choose and whether anyone has the right to prevent this.

The title of this book stems from Albion, the primeval giant from whom Britain took its first name, Alba. Albion has been described as having "... our native hills for his bones and our native forests for his beard ... a single figure outlined against the sea and a great face staring at the sky." William Blake drew on Albion as a symbol of man before the Biblical fall and historian Peter Ackroyd has used the term for the title of his book charting the origins of the English imagination. From the Sixties onwards sections of the counter culture used the term Albion to refer to their vision of a land, society and individual consciousness based on the insights offered by LSD. Thus, Albion embodies the mythological imagination of these Isles, a state akin to the aboriginal Dreamtime, to which everyone should have access. This, then, is Albion's dreaming.

2

HOFMANN'S POTION

> Would LSD become a blessing to humanity or a curse? This I often asked myself when I thought about my problem child.
>
> Albert Hofmann[1]

Unlike most drugs, it is known exactly when, where and by whom LSD and its effects were discovered. And, unlike most drugs, it is possible to trace the geographical spread and usage of LSD from the day the drug was first synthesised. The story of LSD in Britain, then, starts with its discovery in Switzerland in 1938. But to tell the full story of the drug's unique history and qualities we must go back to the childhood experiences of Albert Hofmann, the chemist responsible for the creation of LSD.

Hofmann recalls that as a child in Switzerland he had numerous experiences which defied rational explanation. These "enchantments", as he refers to them, were altered states in which his perceptions were greatly enhanced and the familiar became transformed into the strange. One such "enchantment" took place on a May morning while he was walking through the spring woods near his home: "As I strolled through the freshly greened woods filled with bird song and lit up by the morning sun, everything appeared in an uncommonly clear light ... It shone with the most beautiful radiance, speaking to the heart, as though it wanted to encompass me in its majesty. I was filled with an indescribable sensation of joy, oneness and blissful security."

Hofmann had similar transcendental experiences throughout his entire childhood. They helped formulate his world-view, persuading him of "the existence of a miraculous, powerful, unfathomable reality that was hidden from everyday sight." He reflected often on these enchantments, puzzled as to how he could carry them into adulthood and convey them to others.[2]

The young Hofmann eventually chose chemistry as a vocation because of his desire to "gain an insight into the structure and essence of matter." His choice of profession, driven by the mystery and wonder of his childhood enchantments, was to change the course of popular culture in the West irrevocably.

In 1929 Hofmann took a post as a research chemist with the Swiss pharmaceutical firm of Kern & Sandoz, based in Basel. Under the supervision of Professor Arthur Stoll he worked on extracting the active components of medicinal plants. After some years studying the chemical structure of the perennial herb Mediterranean Squill, Hofmann wanted a new challenge. He requested, and was granted, permission to investigate the ergot alkaloids. It was this decision that set Hofmann on the final path to discovering LSD.

Ergot is a parasitic fungus found on rye and other species of grain and wild grass and has a long and intriguing relationship with the human race. In the early Middle Ages, Europe was swept by epidemics and outbreaks of bizarre symptoms known as Holy Fire or St. Anthony's Fire. Though those suffering from it were unaware of the cause of the problem, it was ergot poisoning. Symptoms included painful burning sensations in the limbs, which caused the strange "dance" in those afflicted. In extreme cases the poisoning caused hallucinations, convulsions and a dry gangrene.

Several historical episodes have been directly linked with ergot poisoning. These include the 1692 witch trials at Salem, Massachusetts and the Great Fear that swept France in 1789 prior to the Revolution. In both these outbreaks the sufferers displayed the symptoms of ergot poisoning, their mental disturbances being ascribed to witchcraft and political paranoia respectively. In both outbreaks there was evidence that the weather leading up to the harvest had been wet, a prerequisite for the formation of ergot, and evidence that the condition of sufferers improved when fed on good quality bread. In her book *Poisons of the Past,* Mary Kilbourne Matossian makes a strong case for many other medieval bouts of hallucination or mental disturbance, such as the witch persecutions, being attributable to ergot poisoning. The last major outbreak of ergot poisoning took place during 1926–27 in parts of southern Russia.[3]

The first record of ergot in a medical capacity dates from 1582 when it is mentioned in a *Herbal,* or book of remedies, as being used to stimulate childbirth. Ergot was later widely used by midwives in Europe to induce abortions and to prevent post-partum bleeding. In common with other medicinal plants, the connection between the ergot fungus and human experience is an old one, presumably pre-dating the first written accounts of its use or poisoning.

Because of its unusual properties, chemists began to study ergot in depth and in 1918 Arthur Stoll isolated ergotamine from the fungus. This extract was marketed as Gynergen by Sandoz in 1921 and used in the same way medieval midwives had used the fungus. The majority of the ergot alkaloids have lysergic acid at their centre. By isolating lysergic acid and then re-combining it with other chemicals, new ergot derivatives could be created. Hofmann worked intensively on these combinations and in the process developed several successful new products for Sandoz. These included dihydroergotamine for the treatment of migraine, hydergine for the treatment of circulatory problems and methergine for post partum bleeding.

Hofmann created LSD-25, the twenty-fifth permutation of lysergic acid, in November 1938. In his search for a synthesis that might lead to the discovery of a circulatory and respiratory stimulant he combined lysergic acid with Coramine, a nicotinic acid diethylamide. But Hofmann was to be disappointed. Tests on animals indicated that LSD-25 had a strong effect on the uterus but this wasn't enough to warrant further investigation, so Hofmann abandoned further study of the compound.

If an experimental compound failed to yield results it was usually shelved and quickly forgotten. Yet there was *something* about LSD-25 that called Hofmann back to that particular chemical compound. Five years passed but Hofmann could not forget LSD-25. In his autobiography, he wrote that eventually: "A peculiar presentiment – the feeling that this substance could possess properties other than those established in the first synthesis – induced me, five years after the first synthesis, to produce LSD-25 once again so that a sample could be given to the pharmacological department for further tests."[4]

Hofmann's intuition led him to synthesise LSD-25 for the second time on Friday, 16 April 1943. As he entered the final stage of the process, the point at which the drug was purified and crystallised, he began to notice unusual physical and mental sensations. He recorded his experiences shortly afterwards in a note to his colleague Professor Stoll:

"Last Friday, April 16, 1943, I was forced to interrupt my work in the laboratory in the middle of the afternoon and proceed home, being affected by a remarkable dizziness. At home I lay down and sank into a not unpleasant intoxicated like condition, characterised by an extremely stimulated imagination. In a dreamlike state, with eyes closed (I found the sunlight to be unpleasantly glaring), I perceived an uninterrupted stream of fantastic pictures, extraordinary shapes with intense, kaleidoscopic play of colours. After some two hours, this condition faded away."[5]

Hofmann presumed that his odd experience had been caused by the drug he was working on at the time. He couldn't be sure how the substance had entered his system but he was certain of one thing: if LSD-25 was responsible for his symptoms it must be incredibly potent in minute dosages. As the drug hadn't caused an abreaction, Hofmann reasoned the most logical way to proceed was to try a scientific self-experiment.

In his laboratory, at 4.20 pm three days later Hofmann took 250 µg of LSD-25 dissolved in water. At 5.00 pm he noted in his laboratory journal: "17.00: beginning dizziness, feeling of anxiety, visual distortions, symptoms of paralysis, desire to laugh." That was the last entry in the journal that day. Hofmann was soon overwhelmed by the effects of the drug and had to ask his laboratory assistant to escort him home. As it was wartime they travelled by bicycle, Hofmann experiencing progressively more florid symptoms of the drug. The visual distortions increased in intensity and at one point he felt he was not making any headway on his bicycle, even though they were moving quite rapidly. When he arrived home he could barely stand, having just enough self awareness to ask a neighbour to call a doctor and bring him some milk as an antidote to the poisoning he believed he was suffering.

When the milk arrived Hofmann, now laid on a sofa, saw his neighbour as a masked witch bent on doing him harm. The room was spinning and the physical world was in a state of flux, once ordinary items such as furniture changing shape, size and perspective. Hofmann's internal world was in turmoil too. He believed he was possessed by a demon that was preventing him from exercising his will and this intensified his general anxiety. Then the thought struck him that the drug was causing him to go insane. He saw himself as if from outside his body, an impotent witness to the runaway psychological drama unfolding in his mind. What would his wife and children think? If he failed to return to sanity would they understand he had been trying a scientific experiment and not indiscriminately experimenting with drugs? All these thoughts were born and multiplied in ever more convoluted permutations in Hofmann's consciousness as he lay on the sofa. From the depths of his confusion Hofmann realised, somewhat wryly, that if he died as a result of his experiment it would be as a direct result of a drug he had discovered.

Though the drug's intensity had begun to wane by the time the doctor arrived Hofmann was still unable to formulate a coherent sentence. It was left to the laboratory assistant to give an account of what had happened as the doctor gave Hofmann a check up. Other than dilated pupils the doctor could find nothing wrong with his patient, who he ordered to bed. Once in bed, with the drug starting to wear off, Hofmann lost his fear of insanity and began to enjoy the experience. A state of synaesthesia ensued, with auditory sensations transforming into visual imagery of seemingly endless shape and colour. When his wife returned Hofmann was lucid enough to tell her what had happened after which, exhausted, he finally fell asleep.

When he awoke the following morning Hofmann was tired but suffused with a sensation of well-being. His senses appeared highly tuned: "When I later walked out into the garden, in which the sun shone now after a spring rain, everything glistened and sparkled in a fresh light. The world was as if newly created. All my senses vibrated in a condition of highest sensitivity, which persisted for the entire day."[6]

Hofmann reflected on his extraordinary experience for the next few days. He concluded that LSD-25 was a potent drug, highly active in infinitesimal doses. Hofmann was also impressed that despite the intense and overwhelming effect of the drug he was conscious throughout and afterwards able to clearly recall the details of the experience. Though he couldn't immediately foresee the uses to which LSD-25 would be put, he was certain the drug had a place in medical science, especially psychiatry. Hofmann's discovery also immediately re-connected him with his childhood enchantments: "Taking LSD reminded me of experiences I had as a child ... It came back to me taking that first LSD trip. It made me so sure of myself. It brought an inner joy, as well as a gratefulness for this internal sensitivity that few can experience. To be part of the miracle of Creation ..." Hofmann's connection of LSD and the religious experience would be repeated time and time again when LSD became widely available. It would be the subject of great debate between its proselityzers and those who believed it was naïve to ascribe religious experience to a chemical.[7]

Following Hofmann's discovery of the effects of LSD-25 an intense period of research into the drug's properties took place. Three of Hofmann's colleagues at Sandoz took the drug and even at a third of the dosage found the effects to be "impressive and quite fantastic." But for a drug to be used widely on humans it must first be subject to a range of clinical tests. The drug was tested on a variety of animals and it was obvious that some, such as the cat, experienced hallucinations. When given to one chimpanzee from a community the drug caused uproar, as the intoxicated chimp failed to adhere to the usual strict social hierarchy of the rest of the group. Yet there was no pattern of effects common to all the experimental subjects. In spiders low doses of LSD-25 affected their ability to weave webs, resulting in web structures of increased symmetry when compared to those woven by un-dosed spiders. High doses saw a reversal of this, the webs becoming very basic and asymmetrical.

Tests of LSD on animals sometimes exemplified the worst excesses of the scientific method. In a 1962 experiment to see if LSD-25 could induce madness in elephants, Tusko, a powerful male was given a dose of 297 mg. If this appears to be a low dose it should be borne in mind it would be enough to give 3000 adults a powerful LSD experience. An hour and forty minutes after being shot by a dart containing LSD, Tusko died. In an attempt to be positive about the experiment, its instigators noted, without a trace of irony: "It appears that the elephant is highly sensitive to the effects of LSD – a finding which may prove to be valuable in elephant-control work in Africa."[8]

Of course, laboratory experiments on animals and insects only give a narrow view of what the effects of a drug are. While testing drugs on animals might enable study of the physical effects, they tell us very little about the effects on the brain and personality of the subject. This becomes even more relevant when dealing with mind altering drugs such as LSD. Chemists at Sandoz were aware of this and after extensive tests on animals convinced them the drug was safe and unlikely to cause psychological or physiological harm, the next step was to test the drug on adults. A research programme run by Professor Stoll's son Werner was conducted in the psychiatric clinic of the University of Zurich. The participants were given dosages of between 2 and 13 µg. These dosages were very low compared to Hofmann's experimental dose of 250 µg, but the research subjects still reported euphoria as the principal effect of the drug. Everyone involved with the research was amazed at a drug that could have such powerful effects in miniscule quantities. Werner Stoll eventually tested the drug and took 60 µg. His lengthy report, the first published by a psychiatrist, detailed a stream of vibrant colourful imagery for which words were barely adequate. The psychological insights were startling. Stoll felt as though he understood abstract pictures, felt at one with all romanticists and dreamers and often "… seemed to stand at the pinnacle of artistic experience." Later in the experiment Stoll's euphoria changed to depression and he contemplated thoughts of suicide, but this passed and by the time he felt able to travel home he was euphoric again. "I had experienced unexpected, impressive things. It seemed to me that a great epoch of my life had been crowded into a few hours. I was tempted to repeat the experiment."[9]

Stoll's experiment took place mainly with his eyes closed or in a darkened room at his laboratory, with no preparation. Though several people had now taken LSD experimentally no consideration had been given to the two factors arguably most important when LSD is given to a person: set and setting. Set and setting, as will be seen throughout the story of LSD in Britain, are crucial and can make the difference between a positive and negative LSD experience. *Set* refers to the LSD taker's mind set, their personality, what and how firmly held are their moral, ethical and religious belief, what they know of LSD and what they expect from the LSD experience and so on. *Setting* refers to the physical location and type of surroundings in which LSD is taken. Later, recreational LSD users would find the combination and manipulation of these two factors could be decisive in how an LSD experience would develop.

Hofmann was uneasy about the controlled laboratory testing of LSD, believing it wasn't a satisfactory way of taking the drug. He seemed to have unconsciously grasped the principle of set and setting when he commented, "We used low doses – 50 μg – in a controlled setting with interviewers, Rorschach tests, written explanations of what we were going through. These weren't especially meaningful experiences; personally I thought it would be more interesting to see how it would work in an artistic surrounding."[10]

The chemist's notion that the LSD experience under laboratory conditions might differ from that of a more aesthetic environment was brought home to him when he "… arranged to explore these things in a non laboratory setting in 1951 with the pharmacologist, Herbert Knozett and the German novelist, Ernst Junger. I would say it was the first truly psychedelic experience, though it was a low dose and it didn't go very deep. But it was beautiful. I believed I was in North Africa among the Berber tribes. I saw all these beautiful, exotic landscapes, oases, while a Mozart record played like music from above."[11]

Hofmann went on to take LSD numerous times and had many religious experiences and insights which deepened his personal philosophy. Though his initial statements about LSD were reserved, in his old age he had become more outspoken about the positive effects of LSD, eventually accepting his place as the elder statesman of the psychedelic generation.

In 1947 Sandoz had enough confidence in its controlled LSD tests to market it as Delysid, a name proposed by Hofmann. Initially the drug was provided free of charge to research institutes in return for their data being shared with Sandoz. Delysid was available as sugar-coated tablets containing 25 μg or ampoules containing 100 μg. The prospectus issued by Sandoz distilled their findings as: "The administration of very small doses of Delysid (half to 2 micrograms per kg of body weight) results in transitory disturbances of affect, hallucinations, depersonalization, reliving of repressed memories and mild neurovegatative symptoms."

Sandoz suggested that LSD could be used to good effect in two specific areas. Laboratory tests had indicated that LSD might be useful in analytical psychotherapy, where the psychiatrist may want access to material repressed by a patient suffering from anxiety and obsessional neuroses. The second use recommended by Sandoz was more surprising. They advocated LSD should be taken by those investigating the nature of psychoses noting, "By taking Delysid himself, the psychiatrist is able to gain an insight into the world of ideas and sensations of mental patients." Sandoz' summing up of LSD's possible effects noted that the drug should not be given to those who were unstable or suffered from suicidal tendencies and advised the drug only be taken under medical supervision.[12]

Sandoz' decision to make LSD publicly available was a key factor in the chain of events, which led to it becoming the most contentious drug of the twentieth century. Though Hofmann had lived through two bloody world wars, a new conflict was already on the horizon. Its weapon – the nuclear bomb – was developed just months before the discovery of LSD. In the space of five months two discoveries had been made, both of which changed millions of lives and which altered the course of popular culture forever. LSD evangelists would later suggest this was no coincidence, that one discovery was the counter-balance to the other. In 1966 poet and author of several books on drugs, George Andrews, published the poem "Amsterdam Reflection" which contained the lines: "Soldiers, take orders only from the rainbow alliance! Peace to the world LSD is the only answer to the atom bomb."[13]

By the early 1950s, the Cold War was raging across the political landscape of the northern hemisphere. Both sides in this war of ideologies believed the other held technological secrets. Espionage rather than overt aggression was now the name of the game and intelligence gathering was being honed to a fine art. It was no longer acceptable to use physical torture to extract information. Subtler, more devious methods were required and a scientific race was on to see who could find the perfect "truth drug".

The Nazis had used the hallucinogenic drug mescaline, derived from the peyote cactus, on captured allied agents in World War II as well as in the concentration camps. But while mescaline made interrogation subjects talk, it proved impossible to control the content of the grilling. The US Office of Strategic Services, predecessor to the CIA, had also begun a wartime search for the perfect interrogation drug. But the OSS soon discovered, as the Nazis had, that none of the drugs, even peyote, gave them the results they required.

When the CIA was formed in 1947 they redoubled their efforts to find a chemical which would act as the perfect "truth drug". In the same year the US Navy instigated Project Chatter which revisited mescaline on this basis. Results with the drug were inconclusive and Project Chatter was discontinued five years later. The CIA's search for the elusive drug that would loosen tongues demonstrates just how little was known in the Forties about the workings of the human mind. No such drug existed then or now. But the Cold War was a kaleidoscope of rumour and counter rumour. It was believed the Russians already possessed, or were on the brink of discovering, the ultimate truth drug; therefore the West had to develop its own lest they fall behind in the drugs race. Whether the Russians really were exploring LSD's potential uses during the Cold War is unclear. At the height of the Cold War, CIA psychologist John Gittlinger commented, "I'm sure they were, but if you ask me to prove it, I've never seen any direct proof of it." Nonetheless, as soon as the CIA became aware of LSD and its potential as a truth drug they plunged large amounts of money into research.

Despite the CIA's later obsession with LSD, they initially seemed ignorant of the drug. LSD arrived in America courtesy of the psychiatric profession who heard about it from Viennese doctor Otto Kauders. Kauders, in America in search of research funding, held a conference at Boston Psychopathic Hospital in 1949, where he spoke about the new experimental drug. The hospital's research director Milton Greenblatt was keenly interested in Kauders' account of how a barely measurable dose of LSD had convinced Hofmann he was going insane. "We were very interested in anything that could make someone schizophrenic," he recalls. The possibility that LSD mimicked schizophrenia and psychoses greatly intrigued psychiatrists everywhere and was the key driver in the spread of LSD among the medical community during the Fifties.[14]

Research psychiatrist Max Rinkel, a delegate at the conference, immediately ordered some LSD from Sandoz and gave a 100 µg dose to his enthusiastic colleague Dr. Robert Hyde, who became the first person on American soil to have the LSD experience. Hyde and Rinkel tested it on a hundred volunteers at Harvard University's affiliate Boston Psychopathic Institute, discovering it produced "a transitory psychotic disturbance". This was in line with conclusions drawn by the Sandoz chemists and led the American psychiatrists to believe LSD could be used to induce mental illness in otherwise sane people for the purposes of objective study.

It was during the CIA's early investigations into LSD that one of the most enduring legends about the drug was born. Before the Agency started testing the drug they contacted Los Angeles psychiatrist Nick Bercel, the first medical professional in the USA to work with LSD, and asked him a bizarre question. What would happen, they queried, if the Russians were able to introduce a large amount of LSD into the water supply of a major American city? Bercel told them nothing would happen because the chlorine would make the drug ineffective. Although the CIA toyed with altering the chemistry of LSD to create a variant that wouldn't be destroyed in chlorinated water the idea was soon abandoned. But the notion that terrorists could put enough LSD into a city or country's water supply became one of the first LSD scare stories and was often repeated by the media, as we will see later in this book.

Early success with initial trials using LSD suggested to the CIA that the drug held promise. Military personnel were dosed with up to 150 µg and given a "secret", which they were asked not to disclose. In at least one case the officer revealed all and was unable afterwards to recall what he had divulged. This was just the kind of result the CIA was looking for from a drug, and from 1953 onward they began many years of contentious experimentation with LSD. The history of the CIA's involvement with LSD is fascinating but appears to have had little direct impact on the history of the drug in Britain. The interested reader is referred to Martin Lee and Bruce Shlain's *Acid Dreams,* as the most comprehensive book on the matter to date.

In the early Fifties the British psychiatric and military establishment was aware of the effects and potential uses of LSD; however, the drug was still to be used on British soil. This situation was to change in September 1952 when psychiatrist Ronnie Sandison set off from England on a study tour of Swiss mental hospitals.

3

LSD: THE CURE OF SOULS?

> There are good reasons for believing that the LSD experience is a manifestation of the psychic unconscious.
>
> R. Sandison[1]

Until its closure and demolition in the closing decades of the twentieth century, Worcester's Powick Hospital stood in the long shadow of the Malvern Hills. The Victorian hospital, originally the Worcestershire County Pauper and Lunatic Asylum, was built in 1852 to house the mentally ill from across the county. In its early years, the hospital practised an enlightened regime, encouraging patients to work in its various workshops and to play in the hospital band. The composer Edward Elgar was bandmaster there in 1879 and exercised a powerful influence over the artistic life of the hospital; from his tenure until the 1940s it was a requirement that all male nurses must be able to play a musical instrument.

Until 1907 Powick was a model of hospital treatment for the mentally ill. Then Dr. Fenton took over as medical superintendent. Fenton's miserly ways soon led to services and treatment at Powick being determined purely by how much money could be saved. The result of this style of management was the hospital's slow deterioration from mental health flagship to depressing and run down institution. It was in this state that Dr. Ronnie Sandison, the newly appointed Consultant Psychiatrist found the hospital when he started work there in September 1951.[2]

In an interview Sandison recalled: "When I first arrived at Powick, Arthur Spencer the Medical Superintendent, said something like: 'I'll run the administration if you will run the clinical side of the hospital.' That suited me perfectly."[3] With this agreement in place, Sandison and Spencer worked hard to return the hospital to its former glory. In the space of a year the hospital, its staff and systems had been overhauled and it was once again a fit place in which to treat the mentally ill. Most importantly Sandison introduced psychotherapy to the treatment regime. In doing so he set the hospital on course to be internationally regarded as a centre of excellence and, later, controversy.

Following a wartime career as a physiologist with the RAF, Sandison trained as a psychiatrist at Warlingham Park Hospital in Surrey. There he came across Freudian and Jungian analysts and decided on a career in psychotherapy. Analysts practiced Depth Psychology, a psychology of the unconscious, in which conscious recollection as well as the content of dreams is analysed for clues to the origin or stimuli of a patient's mental health symptoms. While Freudian and Jungian analysts differed in their interpretation the principles of analysis between the two schools were similar, the technique becoming known as psychoanalysis. Psychoanalysis is one of the methods that fall under the wider heading of psychotherapy, and is based on the experiential relationship between patient and therapist using dialogue, communication and behaviour modification to deal with certain types of mental health issues.

Sandison became intrigued by the process of psychoanalysis while at Warlingham noting: "My colleagues regarded the utterances of psychotic patients as something to record in their notes and thus justify their continued detention in hospital. I saw them as priceless material in my understanding of madness." [4]

The problem with any form of analysis was that it relied on the therapist's ability to elicit information from the patient. Some were extremely resistant to the process and could be in analysis for months or even years before a breakthrough was made. This meant that psychoanalysis was a time consuming and expensive treatment available to the few who could afford it. If a chemical could be found that made the patient more receptive to the therapist's skill, then psychotherapeutic practice could be speeded up considerably. In theory, this would mean that more patients could be treated effectively over a shorter timescale.

Freud had considered this problem in 1938 speculating: "The future may teach us how to exercise a direct influence, by means of particular chemical substances, upon the amounts of energy and their distribution in the apparatus of the mind. It may be that there are other still undreamt of possibilities of therapy."[5] Freud had no idea that LSD had been synthesised that same year and would come to play a major role in psychotherapy within fifteen years.

In September 1952, at the end of his first year at Powick, Sandison accepted an invitation to join a study tour of Swiss mental hospitals. He accepted, not knowing just how important his visit would prove. Recalling the trip in 2001, Sandison remarked, "It was a journey into the unknown, but it was to have far reaching consequences both for me and the lives of many future patients."

During the trip Sandison visited the Sandoz laboratories in Basel. He found the chemists there in a state of great excitement. Sandison "… knew nothing about LSD before (my) visit to the Sandoz labs …" but found the chemists there to be "… absolutely a-buzz with LSD, they weren't doing anything else at that particular time." [6]

While at Sandoz, Sandison met Albert Hofmann and they discussed the effects of the drug on the small group of people who had experimented with it so far. Sandison was excited with the possibilities it offered and returned to Powick with the drug very much in his thoughts. He re-visited the Sandoz laboratories two months later, returning to England with a box of ampoules. These were a gift from Hofmann, each containing 100 µg of LSD, under the trade name Delysid. Sandison did not know it, but he was the first person to bring LSD to Britain.

At that moment in time there was, as Sandison states, "… no theoretical basis for supposing that LSD could be used as a practical tool in combination with psychotherapy, but it was clear … it produced a loosening of mental associations, that it facilitated the transference, and that forgotten and sometimes painful memories could be released." The few studies that had already been done with LSD suggested the drug had potential in psychoanalysis because it improved the contact between therapist and patient, thus speeding up the process of psychotherapy. So, on his return to Powick, and after discussions with colleagues, Sandison began the clinical use of LSD, incorporating it into the psychotherapeutic regime there.[7]

New drugs are now extensively trialled before their use is allowed on humans. In the Fifties, this was not the case and Sandison was able to use the drug without any interference. Although some laboratory tests had been carried out on the effect of LSD on humans, use of the drug was still very much in its infancy. If LSD were to be discovered in the twenty-first century it would have to undergo years of testing on animals, followed by an equal number of years of rigorous tests on human subjects before its use would be permitted in psychotherapy. But the early 1950s were, according to Sandison: "… before the Royal College and the Committee of Safety in Medicines. …There were no ethical committees and no concepts such as Evidence Based Medicine whatsoever. One was left to get on with it, if one felt a treatment was right."[8]

Sandoz supplied LSD to Sandison free of charge until he left Powick in 1964. Dr. Harold Holgate, the company's London-based Chief Medical Officer gave him a great deal of assistance and Sandoz asked for nothing in return, though Sandison sent them copies of his published papers out of courtesy.

The results of the first year of LSD psychotherapy at Powick were published in a 1954 paper in the *Journal of Mental Science*. This groundbreaking paper was the first article about LSD to be published in Britain and effectively set down the ground rules for its clinical use. In the paper Sandison and his colleagues Spencer and Whitelaw gave the results of the psychotherapeutic use of the drug on thirty-six patients over the course of a year.

The thirty-six patients of Sandison's study were regarded as being: "… very difficult psychiatric problems … all in danger of becoming permanent mental invalids, life-long neurotics or of ending their lives by suicide." These were individuals at the end of their mental tether, all suffering from extreme mental tension. Sandison believed that most of the thirty-six patients would have been considered suitable candidates for lobotomy.

The scientific paper also outlined the history of LSD and the early experiments that had taken place on the Continent and in America, before summing up the effects noted in the therapy at Powick. In less than a year of clinical practice with LSD, Sandison and his team had defined the characteristics of its effects on humans and related them to a specific form of treatment. Most notably Sandison and colleagues isolated three major experiences manifested by the patient's unconscious which were often revealed at the height of the LSD session. These were:

1. the hallucinatory experiences resulting from a general non-selective disturbance of the unconscious;
2. the reliving of repressed personal memories; and
3. the appearance of impersonal images.

The paper also discussed the nature of the patients' hallucinatory experiences and expanded on how these were elaborated as forms of Identification Phenomena and Projection Phenomena. The former is the experience whereby the patient identifies themselves with another person or object, believing them to have become that person or object. The latter involves the patient projecting images or personalities onto other people or objects. Thus, a patient undergoing LSD therapy might identify with a snake for instance and "become" that creature.[9]

In the clinical setting at Powick, identification and projection phenomena were observed and occasionally guided by the doctors and nurses. Later this information would be framed in a psychoanalytical context and used to help with the patients' resolution of mental health issues. In non-western cultures where indigenous people use hallucinogenic materials as part of their spiritual practice, identification and projection phenomena become the vehicle by which the shaman or tribal member contacts gods and spirits. In both western LSD psychotherapy and tribal culture there is a structured framework for the use of hallucinogenic drugs. This structure makes their use purposeful and meaningful and less likely to cause psychological trauma. Later, when LSD became widely used by the public, and despite the best efforts of the counter culture's drug advocates, the LSD experience often had little structure. The result was that while the effect of the drug was just as powerful and revelatory as it had been in psychotherapeutic use people could not always extract useful meaning from the drug trip. In many cases the lack of purpose and structure led to mental confusion, "bad trips" or in extreme cases longer term personality problems.

The conclusion drawn by Sandison from this initial study was that LSD therapy was useful and had potential. Of the thirty-six patients, twenty had been in a variety of treatments prior to the LSD therapy. Sandison notes that: "... we think it reasonable to suppose that all of these would at best have been left with chronic neurotic disabilities had they not received LSD-25 therapy." Of those twenty, fourteen recovered from their illness, three showed moderate improvement, two were not improved and one could not be assessed. Though it was the first paper dealing with the LSD therapy treatment in Britain the results, on paper at least, were impressive.

Prospective candidates for LSD therapy were seen four or five times as out-patients as part of a holistic assessment process which took "... a complete history and established rapport with the patient and his relatives". Once accepted for treatment the patient was admitted to Powick and introduced to drug therapy. This was done by giving injections of Sodium Pentothal, a rapid-onset, short-acting anaesthetic. If there were no problems at this stage the patient moved on to being given LSD as part of their therapy. The dosage of LSD given to patients varied. In researching the most appropriate dosage levels Sandison's team became aware of one of LSD's many contradictory effects: "100 micrograms given on one day may produce the most dramatic upsurge of unconscious material. The same dose repeated the following day may be without effect." Though Sandison never pursued the reasons for this, it is obvious that set and setting are just as important for a patient in a clinical setting as they are when the drug is used recreationally.[10]

Patients selected for LSD therapy might have been told they were taking a drug called LSD, but in the early Fifties the initials would have meant nothing to them. There was no public awareness of the drug at that time, no knowledge of the drug's effects or potential for causing permanent changes in belief and behaviour. Nor were patients asked to sign any documentation acknowledging or agreeing to LSD therapy. As Sandison notes: "We operated in a climate of openness rather than secrecy ... in 1954 patients and doctors operated in an atmosphere of mutual trust and, of course, patients were much more compliant and less questioning than today. On the whole, written consent did not fit the culture of the day."[11] In the Fifties the actions of doctors and other professionals such as teachers, the police and the judiciary were rarely questioned and they were regarded with respect by the majority of the population.

When LSD was first embraced by the counter culture, a guide was deemed to be crucial to the well being of the LSD user, particularly those taking the drug for the first time. Sandison and his team of professionals also understood the need to have someone acting as a guide for the duration of the patient's LSD experience. In their case the nurse assumed this role: "She has to understand and yet not comment on the patient's experience; she must not trespass on a delicate situation with bright and diverting remarks; she may answer but not ask questions; she must be prepared to be at the patient's side if needed and to play an intuitive, passive, vigilant part."[12]

Publication of Sandison's scientific paper alerted the media to what was taking place at Powick. The *Sunday Mercury* reported that the new therapy "... consists of administering a new drug to the patient which transports him, in thought, back to his early childhood. The patient acts, speaks and thinks like a child and in this state is led step by step through buried memories until the incidents which may be causing his mental condition are reached. Once the source of the sickness is uncovered the work of the psychiatrist becomes comparatively easy." The *News Chronicle* headlined with "Science has Alice-in-Wonderland Drug" and gave a sober, informed view of the possibilities of LSD treatment.[13]

The reference to Alice in Wonderland was an allusion to the pills given to Alice by the White Rabbit, which made her perceive she was of different sizes. The Alice in Wonderland theme in relation to LSD would be repeated time and time again throughout the media and the counter culture over subsequent years; most notably in the song "White Rabbit" by Jefferson Airplane in which Grace Slick, over a slowly building Bolero beat, chants a paean to the perceptual shifts offered by LSD, culminating with the operatic exhortation to: "Remember what the dormouse said, 'Feed your Head.'"

In British Prime Minister Harold Macmillan's "never had it so good" decade of the Fifties, the media were naïve about drugs and much more interested in scientific potential than sensationalism. They saw LSD as a product of the scientific process and in the Fifties it was widely believed that science was the answer to all medical problems, so all the newspaper reports about the new therapy at Powick were positive. The media's tacit reassurance that LSD was both harmless and useful would have gone a long way in encouraging patients to accept LSD therapy as being the conventional thing to do were it offered. Over the next twenty years the media would slowly change their mind about LSD and would embark on a witch-hunt to vilify not only the drug, but also those who worked with it or took it in any capacity, medical or recreational.

Sandison's 1954 paper set the scene for LSD therapy in the UK for the next two decades. The paper's summary placed emphasis on what became the central tenet of psychotherapists who used LSD, which was: "... the property possessed by the drug of disturbing the unconscious so that repressed memories are relived with remarkable clarity and a change to an infantile body image."[14] As we will see while this was *one* way of addressing and using the LSD experience, it was not, by any means, the *only* way of using the drug. To an extent the medical profession were trapped in a narrow way of thinking about the use of LSD and within twenty years had been scared off exploring the drug's potential by the media and disapproving governments.

For the first two years of LSD psychotherapy at Powick patients were treated in the main hospital building. This wasn't ideal and so in 1956 Sandison approached the Birmingham Regional Hospital Board with a request to fund a specialised LSD unit. Funding was granted immediately and the LSD unit was operational within two years. The unit cost the taxpayer £50,000, the equivalent of over £1,000,000 in 2008: an unprecedented amount to spend on a new, controversial and barely tested treatment.

The speed with which the funding for this unusual project was granted, together with the high cost and the rapid completion of the building itself has led to speculation that there was more to the LSD unit than history has so far revealed. Documents held at London's National Archives suggest that official bodies other than the Birmingham Regional Hospital Board had a covert interest in Sandison's LSD research.

Dr. Joel Elkes, one of Sandison's colleagues outside Powick, had also come into contact with LSD in the early 1950s. In 1951 he had founded Birmingham University's Department of Experimental Psychology and had a special interest in the effects of drugs on consciousness. Elkes became fascinated with LSD after reading it was effective in doses of millionths of a gram. At first he believed this was a misprint, for no drug could be effective at such a miniscule dosage. After checking the article's reliability and finding that LSD *was* effective in infinitesimal quantities, Elkes immediately sourced a quantity of LSD and ingested it: "The personal experience was intense and exquisite, and gave one an insight never to be forgotten of the full, mysterious sensation of the full psychedelic experience."

Elkes' interest in LSD grew and a few years later he attended a lecture on LSD given by Sandison at Powick, remarking: "I had the feeling I had listened to something important."[15] The pair became friends and Sandison soon realised that Elkes was an intelligent and outgoing individual with the ability to influence decision makers. Sandison recalls, when funding for the LSD unit was being applied for, "Joel Elkes gave the plan every possible help". Sandison firmly believes Elkes was instrumental in paving the way for funding of the LSD unit but never questioned his motives.

Yet though they were good friends, Elkes kept concealed a great secret from Sandison: his close connections with the Ministry of Defence. By 1955, long before the planning and funding application for the LSD unit, Elkes had attended high level meetings at the MOD. These meetings were convened specifically to discuss LSD and Elkes played a key role in them, being recognised by the MOD as an expert in the field. Sandison admits he had no idea of Elkes' links with the MOD, aware only that he was a signatory to the Official Secrets Act.

The MOD's involvement with LSD will be clarified in the next chapter but Elkes' interest in Sandison's LSD research at Powick begs many questions. Writing in the medical journal the *Lancet* in 1955, Elkes voiced his concerns about the rapidly expanding use of LSD by psychotherapists, counselling: "Until more is known about its mode of action, we urge those interested to refrain from using the drug in out-patients or in day-hospital patients, and restrict its use to in patients – and then only when constant supervision by trained personnel is available."[16] This would have been an admirably cautious statement were it not for the fact that within a year Elkes was actively supporting the development of Sandison's research at Powick. The vast majority of those treated with LSD were day patients. Why had Elkes changed his mind in such a short space of time?

Was Elkes' support of Sandison based purely on a shared professional interest? Alternatively, was he keen to see the LSD unit operational so he could share the results of Sandison's research on civilians, feeding it back to his contacts at the MOD? If that was Elkes' plan then Sandison fell for it completely: "Elkes knew as much as I could tell him about LSD as I believe it is the function of researchers to share their findings with others in the same field."[17] And what could the MOD learn from Sandison that they could not from their own research? Elkes' mutually exclusive involvement with the MOD and Sandison is just one of the many puzzles scattered through LSD's history that hint at the possibility of a bigger, possibly conspiratorial, picture.

But in 1956 all Sandison was aware of was that Elkes, a fellow professional who shared his interest in LSD, had friends in high places. When completed, the brick built single storey LSD unit stood in stark contrast to the imposing stone built Victorian mental hospital in whose grounds it stood. The specially designed building was designed so that up to five LSD sessions could be run at any one time, with two doctors and three nurses in attendance. The unit allowed the numbers treated with LSD to be increased and there was no shortage of those wishing to take up the new therapy.

While some patients who opted for LSD treatment were already in traditional psychotherapy, others were new patients and the decision to invite patients to try the new form of psychotherapy had no set criteria. Though there was no shortage of patients wanting to try LSD in the hope it would relieve their mental torment, Sandison didn't believe in treating just anyone. There had to be an engagement between doctor and patient: "You don't really choose people for therapy by diagnosis, you treat them by a kind of feel you have, 'I think I could help this chap or this woman' … and then you discover they've got an anxiety state or depression or whatever. Worldwide I think every known condition has been treated. I think LSD gives people hope and it gives them an access to a part of themselves they never thought existed."[18]

Sandison recognised that some types of mental disorder, such as psychosis, were not appropriate subjects for LSD therapy. But there were plenty of patients displaying neurosis, anxiety or depression for whom the drug was suitable. Initially Sandison had no real idea of the optimum dosages for patients and this was determined on a trial and error, "purely experimental" basis. Sandison wasn't worried about the drug's physiological effects, believing it to be "incredibly safe" and having only relatively mild effects on the body.

Most of those treated were day patients. Volunteer drivers would pick them up from home in the early morning and deliver them to Powick by 9.00 am. After a group meeting with the others who were having LSD psychotherapy that day, each patient would be given a dose of LSD dissolved in water. The dosage varied and could be as little as 20 μg or as much as 150 μg. Some patients were given up to 400 μg, a very strong dose, and a few were given much higher doses. Dosages tended to start low and were increased in subsequent sessions until some advancement in their condition was noted. After the patients had been led to their rooms they were left alone for the next few hours, with doctors or nurses checking on them at intervals.

The treatment rooms were quite stark, simply furnished with a bed and a chair. Though the room was plain there was nothing about it to suggest a medical setting and patients felt quite comfortable taking LSD in those surroundings. The only "props" to aid the patient's experience were often just a teddy bear, a blackboard and a record player. Photographs in Sandison's collection show patients involved in various activities as the LSD coursed through their system; one young girl is curled in a foetal position on the bed, holding a teddy bear and staring into the middle distance, another shows a woman drawing what appears to be a monster on the blackboard provided. But props and attendant medical professionals notwithstanding, once in the treatment room and under the influence of LSD each patient was alone with the contents of their subconscious.

By closely monitoring the experiences of the LSD patients both during their experience and in analysis afterwards Sandison was able to help them direct their visual and mental images. Imposing this structure on the potentially chaotic nature of the LSD experience enabled patients to work through their problems, going deep into their subconscious, often back to their childhood and to traumas that had been suppressed and which were the root cause of the present symptoms. Artistic representation played a part in helping patients to externalise and resolve these issues. One patient's painting done under LSD was originally a crossroads. A later session added a lighthouse to the scene. Another was of a spider which was later resolved into a flower, and so on. All of these images had meaning for the individuals concerned and Sandison found the images recalled and painted by his patients to contain a lot of archetypal material. This led him to believe: "… LSD opens up a high road to some of the deeper and collective aspects of the unconscious."[19]

Following suggestions made in 1958 by visiting American psychologist Betty Eisner, Sandison noted that his LSD patients liked music. But rather than the swirling washes of electronic sound which would later characterise the music of the counter culture, Sandison's patients preferred folk music over classical or pop. Patients were asked what their favourite type of music or artiste was and the LSD Unit's staff would endeavour to provide it from their large collection.

LSD treatments could be frequent, often once a week and sometimes twice. Some therapists went so far as to administer LSD to their patients every day. However, Sandison believed that up to a week was needed between sessions to allow the patient to absorb and reflect on the experience. Sometimes a gap of several weeks was needed. Most of Sandison's patients received some follow up psychotherapeutic sessions after they'd finished their LSD treatment to allow some form of closure to the experiences.

As the afternoon drew to a close and the effects of LSD were tapering off the patients would re-group to discuss their day's experience prior to being driven home again. In retrospect this way of dealing with people under the influence of LSD might seem irresponsible. The doses of LSD that were administered, even the low doses, were enough to cause significant effects long after the patients had returned home. Sandison was very much aware of this and encouraged the volunteer drivers to talk to the patients as they drove them home. For some patients the transition from the colourful mental kaleidoscope of the LSD experience to the relative drabness of home life must have been quite disorientating. Barbiturates were available if needed to help patients "come down" from their LSD experience, but generally speaking most returned to normal consciousness without any problems. Patients were also told they could phone the unit at any hour of day or night if the effects of the LSD were causing problems.

Despite the potential for serious psychic trauma Sandison claims that few patients were distressed by their LSD experiences. He did, however, recognise that during a course of LSD treatment the patient "... may be tempted to make major alterations in his environment and way of life". Sandison wrote that the patient should be allowed to make some minor changes but "... any major alterations, particularly where these involve the question of marriage, marital separation or divorce, should be decided on only after the LSD phase of treatment has concluded." One of the many perceptions reported by LSD users is that it enables them to see people as they really are. The potential for devastation in a relationship in which discord has been suppressed or not properly resolved when one partner has used LSD and "sees through" the other is immense. Later, recreational LSD users would also note that often after taking a dose of LSD they changed their entire way of living. Sandison reported in his 1964 paper that: "We have found that about one half of our cases required extensive rehabilitation involving the establishment of a new set of conditioned social responses." Another way of saying they had their minds blown and needed to take a long hard look at their beliefs and relationships.[20]

Decades later some patients would challenge Sandison's opinion that long lasting deleterious effects from LSD therapy were rare. Driven by their personal demons and fuelled by the prevailing compensation culture a number of those who had been treated with LSD would eventually seek redress through the courts.

At the heart of Sandison's LSD psychotherapy was the relationship between two people, the patient and the therapist. To ensure that relationship was as effective as possible Sandison, intensely curious about the effects of LSD, decided that he should take the drug. That way he would have an inkling of what his patients were going through, the better to engage in the psychoanalytic relationship. "I think it is important that the therapist should have taken LSD himself, but it is essential he or she has a proper training in psychodynamics and have themselves had a training analysis."[21]

Sandison took LSD just once: "… I learnt something about myself and about what the patients were experiencing. What I did learn was firstly you should never take LSD alone; you could get into all sorts of difficulties if you do. You need to have a trusted person with you; I had Sister Hopkin with me. We did it one Sunday, we were both off duty and she was just there, it was very helpful. It was part of the work of getting to know LSD. A number of the registrars took it as well."[22]

Ronnie Sandison's work at Powick is well documented, but by the mid-Fifties many other doctors in Britain were also treating their patients with LSD. Sandison believes there might have been more than ten centres where LSD psychotherapy was practised. Hospitals that offered LSD therapy included Roffey Park in Surrey, the Marlborough Day Hospital and Guy's Hospital in London, Netley Hospital in Southampton, Bromley Psychiatric clinic and several other locations. Many psychiatrists also offered LSD treatment at their clinics or in private practice. The majority of the LSD therapy practised at hospitals and clinics around Britain during the Fifties and Sixties was similar if not identical to that carried out at Powick. Sandison, by dint of his chance visit to Switzerland, had set the ball rolling and others followed in his wake.

Among the thousands of people who underwent LSD therapy in the Fifties and Sixties were several well-known show business personalities. Comedian Frankie Howerd was one of them. As can often be the case with successful comedians Howerd's humour masked a depressive personality and his life was a constant search for meaning. In his search for inner peace he tried a wide range of therapies including psychiatry and psychoanalysis.

Following the death of his mother, Howerd believed LSD therapy might be a solution for his problems and contacted Thomas Ling at the Marlborough Day Hospital. Ling was one of the first doctors other than Sandison to use LSD therapy, both in the hospital and in private practice. Ling's belief that LSD "… helps the patient see himself as he really is", was just what Howerd wanted. After an initial meeting Ling undertook to treat Howerd and they began regular fortnightly LSD psychotherapy sessions.

Howerd's manager and lover, Dennis Heymer recalls one of his jobs was to drive Howerd to see his LSD psychotherapist at the Marlborough Day Hospital. According to Heymer the sessions followed a set pattern. At 6.00 pm, Howerd was taken to a darkened room where he was injected with 80–120 µg of LSD. As the drug began to take effect Howerd was injected with a small dose of Ritalin to stimulate his central nervous system. Then, alone in the locked room, Howerd was left to recall and write down his earliest childhood memories. Props such as teddy bears, mirrors, family photographs, dummies and other reminders were supplied so Howerd could act out his childhood repressions. At the two-hour stage another dose of Ritalin was administered to inspire "penetrating understanding" and reflection on the experience.

The LSD session was terminated at 11.00 pm by a mixture of Largactil and Sodium Amytal which caused Howerd to drift from psychedelic awareness into a deep sleep. On waking he would write a report of his LSD experience which Ling would then use as the basis for psychoanalysis. Howerd had many LSD sessions under Ling's guidance and believed they left him a calmer person, more capable of understanding the impact his father had had on him and with more insight into his strengths and weaknesses. Heymer, however, wasn't convinced that LSD therapy was useful for Howerd, "It didn't do him any good. I wouldn't recommend it at all."[23]

Michael Horsley-Millman remembers the LSD therapists at the Marlborough as being highly competent at putting the traumatised human psyche back together as they: "... led one on and on, through doors off corridors of one's self built haunted house ... down stairways that Hitchcock's *Psycho* never knew existed. Far beyond any hallucination that today's drug culture imposes ... an outward beyondness that says 'before birth, before mother's breast, before, before', in pretty pictures in blue and gold, the heightened aura blocking out the persistent everyday thinking about thoughts which themselves don't exist, but lay low like clutter on the floor of some dismal hovel."[24]

Most of those who used LSD as a psychotherapeutic tool did so quietly and without fuss. Publicity wasn't actively courted but was accepted when it became necessary as a means to secure or maintain funding. There was however one flamboyant exception: R.D. "Ronnie" Laing.

Once Laing had qualified as a psychoanalyst he opened a practice in London's Wimpole Street. In the burgeoning liberalism of the Sixties, Laing's idiosyncratic approach to therapy meant he was instantly popular and patients flocked to him. LSD fascinated him and he first used it in 1960 when it was given to him by Dr. Richard

Gelfer. In line with many other medical professionals, Gelfer mistakenly believed LSD mimicked psychoses and introduced it to Laing as such. Laing's experience however was that "... it was an experience of extraordinary familiarity ... enhancement of multi-levels of association that one can simultaneously bring to bear in a way that one only glimpses in a usual state of consciousness."[25]

The LSD experience firmly imprinted itself on Laing's psyche. Laing had three precepts for anyone who wanted to become a psychoanalyst. The first was the person should undergo personal analysis, the second that they should read the standard edition of Freud and the third was that they should ingest LSD.

Laing soon included LSD in his psychoanalytical toolbox and his son and biographer, Adrian recalls former patients confiding: "... dropping acid with R.D. Laing was both exhilarating and liberating." Some individuals reported that a six-hour LSD session with Laing was more effective than several years of traditional psychoanalysis. Unlike his colleagues in traditional LSD psychotherapy Laing preferred to take LSD with his patient, but took a smaller dose so he could exercise some control over the experience.[26]

In 1966, Laing gave a presentation to the annual conference of the prestigious National Association for Mental Health. It consisted of a bold speech on the therapeutic benefits of LSD and mescaline. In it he demonstrated he knew exactly what the potential of LSD was and how it related to therapy: "An LSD or mescaline session in one person, with one set in one setting may occasion a psychotic experience. Another person, with a different set and different setting, may experience a period of super-sanity ... The aim of therapy will be to enhance consciousness rather than to diminish it. Drugs of choice, if any are to be used, will be predominantly consciousness expanding drugs, rather than consciousness constrictors – the psychic energisers, not the tranquillisers."[27]

Laing's reputation as a therapist spread rapidly among London's artistic crowd, leading him to have some very high profile, and unlikely, patients.

Diane Cilento, first wife of actor Sean Connery, wrote that

following his success in 1964's *Goldfinger* the second James Bond film, Connery felt insecure and spiritually blocked; he was convinced he wouldn't feel "safe" until he had a million pounds in the bank. Cilento met Laing and was impressed with his radical ideas about LSD therapy, which meant patients could be helped without spending years on the analyst's couch. Cilento eventually arranged a consultation for Connery and Laing accepted the Bond star for treatment. In keeping with the times Laing didn't believe in selling himself short and demanded: "... a great deal of money, complete privacy, a limo to transport him to and from the meeting and a bottle of the best single malt Scotch at each session."

At their first session Laing gave Connery a full dose of LSD, taking a much smaller amount himself to enable him to act as guide during the session. Cilento claims the initial session didn't go too well. Connery couldn't "let go" and resisted the drug, having to spend several days recovering in bed as a result. But the LSD had worked its magic in loosening Connery's tightly wrapped subconscious: "This initial trip opened a Pandora's box ... Suddenly, Sean began to remember challenging childhood scenes with his mother or father. Buried anger, victories or defeats came tumbling out without warning."[28]

Laing moved easily between the tight-knit world of psychotherapy and the night-life of swinging London, becoming a frequent sight at counter culture events. When Pink Floyd's Syd Barrett was undergoing his LSD induced nervous breakdown bassist Roger Waters tried to arrange treatment for him with Laing. After some persuasion Barrett eventually agreed to meet Laing and they took a taxi to his flat, but at the last moment he wouldn't get out of the cab. A few months later they tried again but Barrett wouldn't even leave his flat when the taxi arrived.[29]

Laing remained a staunch advocate of the personal and professional use of LSD to his death, his writings making a considerable impact on the Sixties and Seventies counter culture.

Ronnie Sandison left Powick in 1964. He had worked with LSD for twelve years and wanted a break and running LSD psychotherapy sessions on a daily basis was a time consuming, physically and mentally draining, experience. Powick was changing too, becoming more a centre for community psychiatry. Two new consultants had recently joined the staff team, both of whom had no interest in pursuing LSD psychotherapy. For Sandison these were all signs that it was time to move on and he took an appointment as Consultant Psychiatrist at Knowle Hospital, near Southampton, in Hampshire. Though he used the drug with a few patients in 1965 after leaving Powick his days of practising LSD psychotherapy were behind him.

LSD psychotherapy was slowly but surely coming to an end in Britain. From early 1966 onwards the British and American media regularly featured lurid stories and exposés about the social use of LSD. Though LSD had caused no fatalities and there had been a surprisingly low number of episodes of mental illness, for the media LSD had become a social panic. Privately, medical professionals who were practising LSD psychotherapy became concerned that LSD was going to face trial by media. This would bring their activities into the public eye and they realised that if that were the case the notoriously conservative medical establishment would try to distance itself from the drug even though it was still legal to use in a medical context. As legislation to outlaw the drug other than for medical use loomed large, a number of those working with LSD began to openly express their concerns in the medical press.

Following Sandoz' decision in 1966 to cease the supply of LSD, Powick Hospital's Chief Medical Superintendent Arthur Spencer wrote a strongly worded letter to the *British Medical Journal*. Spencer railed against Sandoz, claiming that their action to terminate the supply of LSD without notice had left many patients midway through a course of treatment. A Dr. S.E. Browne wrote to the *BMJ* to point out that LSD therapy was the only form of psychotherapy available to those on a limited income. Browne wrote: "Some patients being treated with lysergic acid are, in fact, fighting for their lives; treatment has already been stopped of patients who were responding very well to lysergic acid after all possible forms of physical therapy had failed."

Browne's final paragraph starkly highlighted what many have seen as the essential inequality of the laws against LSD, "What seems to me an extraordinary state of affairs is that any doctor can (and some still do) prescribe amphetamines, the use of which is therapeutically unjustifiable because of the danger of addiction and psychosis, while a potentially life-saving drug is withdrawn." These feelings were echoed by a trio of doctors who wrote to the *BMJ* from West Park Hospital in Surrey, who claimed: "It will be unfortunate if LSD becomes available only for 'kicks' and not for serious psychotherapeutic endeavour."[30]

These pleas notwithstanding, the era of LSD psychotherapy in Britain was rapidly ending. After Ronnie Sandison left Powick, Spencer found a new source of the drug and continued working with it until the mid-1970s. A few other therapists continued work with LSD but the constant media vilification made its use as a psychotherapeutic tool increasingly unfashionable, if not professionally untenable. A CV that boasted years of LSD aided psychotherapy was unlikely to help anyone's career in the climate engendered by the media's vigorous defamation of psychedelic drugs. Psychiatric medicine was moving away from what it considered to be contentious, possibly unreliable therapies. The aggressive marketing of the large pharmaceutical companies was funnelling psychiatry towards a culture of prescribing other drugs for depression, anxiety and conditions for which LSD therapy had proved effective.

Though high profile medical practitioners such as Ronnie Laing, who arguably had other agendas to pursue on the back of his personal and professional LSD use, continued to use and champion LSD, by the mid-Seventies therapy with LSD had ceased completely in Britain, its use quickly regarded as something of an archaic curio. It wouldn't be until the first decade of the twenty-first century that the idea of LSD as a viable therapeutic tool would be taken seriously again.

The heyday of LSD therapy in Britain had spanned fourteen years. During that time large sums of taxpayers' money had been used to fund what amounted to a unique experiment. Throughout those halcyon years the LSD psychotherapists believed they were alone in their use of the consciousness altering drug. But Sandison and his colleagues had been unaware that another strand of work with LSD had been running parallel, but completely separate, to theirs. At the same time as the psychotherapists were using LSD to heal aberrant mental states; the British intelligence services and the Ministry of Defence were also using taxpayers' money to fund LSD research. But rather than a tool for healing, they hoped LSD would provide them with a new weapon with which to destroy the will of combatants on and off the battlefield.

4

LSD: A CURE FOR THE COMMON COLD?

They stick to the old maxim:
never apologise, never explain.
Don Webb[1]

In the early 1950s, the future for peace looked bleak. With World War II still a raw memory, the world was now rapidly descending into the Cold War, America and Britain teetering on the brink of hostilities with Russia and the Eastern Bloc countries. We are now all too familiar with the key weapons of the Cold War: nuclear bombs and warheads, supersonic jet fighters and bombers and the concept of mutually assured destruction. Throughout the twentieth century, governments were keen to parade these and other weapons before their citizens, the physical displays of strength intended as reassurance and warning to friend and foe. However, behind the public face of Britain's military hardware lay a much more sinister cache of armaments, one that the government wanted to remain hidden from the public. These were chemical and biological weapons, one of which was LSD.

Unfortunately, the government's refusal to open its files to the general public means the full story of Britain's LSD tests might well remain hidden forever. Decades of institutional secrecy and an unwillingness to be accountable to the taxpayer have ensured information about this most sensitive of subjects has been withheld at all costs. In recent years, however, a combination of the Freedom of Information Act and persistent lobbying from ex-Forces personnel has lifted the lid on the secrecy surrounding these sinister experiments.

Exactly what prompted the British government to initiate LSD testing is unclear, although it can be inferred from a number of sources. The CIA took an immediate interest in LSD following World War II and began tests with the drug on military and civilian personnel in 1947. The American and British intelligence services were both convinced that Russia was experimenting with LSD or its analogues to produce a "truth drug" for use in interrogations, and this seems to have been the driving force behind Britain's decision to carry out experiments with LSD.

A 1956 MOD report titled "Abreactive Drugs", prepared for the Defence Research Policy Committee, notes LSD first came to the attention of the Joint Intelligence Bureau (JIB) "some 4 years ago". This formal discussion about LSD took place during Professor Henry Beecher's visit to Britain in the spring of 1952. The Harvard Professor of Anaesthesiology had a controversial involvement with psychedelic drugs, having first been involved in secret CIA mescaline experiments in Germany after World War II. Beecher saw a role for these drugs and wanted to spread the word among the Allied intelligence agencies.[2]

The British intelligence community were intrigued by the drug but unsure of its potential, and so for further information they contacted one of the only two men in Britain who had any real knowledge of LSD. Joel Elkes was not a member of the intelligence services, but was closely connected to them. During World War II, he had researched human nerve conduction, which placed him at the forefront of research into how chemicals were assimilated in the brain. After the war, scientists at the British Chemical Defence Experimental Establishment at Porton Down supplied Elkes with a variety of chemicals for him to map how they worked within the brain. Elkes already had the necessary scientific background and direct experience of LSD, so it was logical for the JIB to approach him for advice.

Elkes had founded Birmingham University's Department of Experimental Psychiatry in 1951. A mercurial character, in the Fifties Elkes acted as both advisor to the intelligence services, while also being instrumental in the developing field of LSD psychotherapy, playing a crucial role in assisting Ronnie Sandison to obtain funding for the LSD therapy unit at Powick Hospital in 1956 (see Chapter 3). The JIB could have approached Sandison, but he did not have Elkes' research credentials or any previous experience of working with the intelligence services. Whatever Elkes told the JIB, it gave them the confidence to investigate LSD further and, later in 1952, the Porton Down military facility was commissioned by the Secret Intelligence Services (SIS), better known as MI6, to run Britain's first military LSD tests.

Porton Down, home to Britain's Defence Science and Technology Laboratory, lies on Salisbury Plain in Wiltshire. Since opening in 1916, the top secret, secure establishment has carried out research into a wide variety of chemical weapons on behalf of Britain's military and intelligence agencies. At the close of World War II, the Allies discovered that the Germans were far more advanced in chemical weapon development than was thought and had developed several nerve agents. On the basis that some of this knowledge would have been discovered and developed by Russian intelligence services, the thrust of work at Porton during the Fifties was on nerve agents such as Sarin and the riot control chemical, CS. A battery of tests was designed to measure the effects and resistance of these chemicals agents on service personnel who were attracted to the facility as volunteers, with the promise of extra pay and time off from their normal duties. It was against this broader backdrop of chemical warfare research, that the MI6 LSD tests at Porton Down were organised.[3]

Porton scientists realised the only way to observe LSD's effect on humans was to administer the drug to volunteers and monitor the results. Basic information about the action of LSD on human physiology and psychology was required to act as terms of reference for the tests and an early summary of the drug's effects on the human body appeared in a March 1953 paper prepared by the MOD's Chemical Defence Advisory Board. The report cites research done in America by Rinkel which predates the earliest human LSD experiments in Britain.[4]

Using the term "volunteer" to describe those who took part in LSD experiments at Porton Down is actually a misnomer. None of the participants was told what drug they would be taking, or what its effects might be. In reality the "volunteers" were all dupes, conned into taking a powerful mind-altering chemical in strange and unfamiliar circumstances. Porton Down scientists seem to have chosen to ignore the Nuremberg Code for human experimentation, failing to ensure that the volunteers gave informed consent before the tests.

The source of the LSD used in the 1953–54 trials at Porton Down is unknown. In 1953, the only known manufacturer of the drug was Sandoz in Basel, Switzerland. Porton Down now claims to have no record of the source of the LSD used in these early tests, stating, "The Defence Science and Technology Laboratory has reviewed its archive holdings and has been unable to locate any information relating to the manufacture or supply of LSD during the time period to which you refer."[5]

Initial tests on human subjects at Porton Down began sometime in early 1953, and were carried out "… in the context of the cold war". Thirty-seven volunteers, all ordinary ranks from various branches of the armed services took part in LSD trials at Porton in 1953, each being given varying doses of the drug of between 50–100 μg. Volunteers underwent medical examinations prior to the tests but their psychological fitness was not assessed. This might seem odd, considering the nature of the drug they were to be given, but it merely reflects the paucity of knowledge even Porton Down scientists had about the effects of LSD.[6]

Naval rating Derek Channon was 23 in 1953 when he volunteered for the tests at Porton. All he knew was that he was to be a human "guinea pig". On the morning of the trial Channon was given an LSD-soaked sugar cube to swallow, though the Porton Down scientists omitted to tell him what drug he was taking. He then "…

sat in a darkened room where they showed a kaleidoscope on the wall. I could see tigers and God knows what in this thing. They were coming at you like a 3-D cinema. It was quite vivid. It was frightening. I will never forget it."[7]

In 1954, a second series of LSD trials was carried out on service personnel and Porton Down staff to establish whether the drug could be useful as a "truth drug". Five servicemen volunteered for tests at Porton. None were told at any time what drug would be tested on them.

For nineteen-year-old Royal Navy radio operator Eric Gow, the offer on the poster on the wall of the canteen at Devonport's Royal Navy Signal School seemed too good to be true. The poster was recruiting volunteers to take part in a research programme to find a cure for the common cold. "It stated we would receive leave and additional pay of ten shillings" remembered Gow. He immediately volunteered, and in January 1954 found himself at Porton Down.

When he and his colleagues arrived they were asked to sign the Official Secrets Act, but nothing was said about the nature of the research programme for which they had volunteered. Gow and his friend were separated from the other sixteen volunteers and taken to an office in the main building. There, they were introduced to a man they took to be a doctor. He said he would like them to carry out some tests, after which he would give them something to drink and they could repeat the tests. The only hint of what was to come was the doctor's comment that they might find the second round of tests "difficult". Gow, young and cocky, thought: That's what you think.

He found the first set of tests simple and quickly completed them. All he had to do was write his name and address on a sheet of paper, add three sets of numbers and walk in a pattern around some chairs in another room. This was almost too easy, he thought. Then the doctor "... pushed two sherry glasses towards us across the desk and I remember he used the expression 'bottoms up'. We both drank the clear liquid (it had a peculiar taste)."

The effects of the drug came on fast, dramatically affecting Gow's perception of the world. He remembers a kaleidoscope of imagery: "I suddenly saw the large old-fashioned radiator behind the man start to shrink and expand like a concertina. The brown lino of the office had heel marks that were spinning like Catherine wheels." Gow tried to do the simple tests again. This time his name and address filled a whole sheet of foolscap writing paper. Adding three sets of numbers together posed another problem. He could add the first two easily enough but no matter how hard he tried, he could not factor in the third number.

Gow isn't sure if he managed to do the third test with the chairs because his next memory is of him and his friend on a bicycle, "giggling like mad and riding up and down the corridors of the building". There seemed to be little control over the experiment and nor were there any further questions from the doctor, who appeared to have just vanished. Later that day Gow and his friend were sitting in the canteen, still hallucinating, his friend "... laughing his head off at a packet of soap powder dancing along the shelf". Left to their own devices the hallucinating duo went into a telephone box to phone a taxi, Gow noticing that each of the little windows had technicoloured pictures in them: "There were cowboys chasing Indians in one, just like a film. Others were kaleidoscopic in nature."

Gow's next recollection is that they were at a dance, in nearby Salisbury, in their Wellingtons: "I don't think we got a date that night." Later in the trip, after walking along country roads lobbing snowballs at signs, they wandered into the RAF camp at Old Sarum where they were put up for the night in the cells, given breakfast in the morning and driven back to Porton Down. Other than the first few minutes of the experience Gow believes they were unsupervised, allowed to wander where they wanted, even leaving Porton Down unchallenged.

In retrospect, their escape from the LSD experiment probably saved them from having a much worse experience. As Gow puts it, "I do not think I had any fear, it was more like being completely free and wild," a feeling many LSD users in the counter culture would soon come to know.[8]

The exact reason for Gow's time at Porton was omitted from his official Navy records. Indeed, although he served in the Navy until 1960, no one ever mentioned what had happened to him.

It was as though his disorientating experience had never taken place. For the next five decades, though, it would rarely be far from his thoughts.

The refusal by MI6 to release their files on the 1953–54 LSD tests has made it difficult to obtain a full picture of how the tests were structured and what conclusions were reached. Nor has there been any official statement to explain why these early tests were discontinued. However, a significant clue exists in the unpublished autobiography of Porton Down scientist Harry Collumbine, who wrote of the Fifties experiments: "We stopped the trials ... when it was reported that in a few people it might produce suicidal tendencies."[9]

The existence of the Porton Down LSD tests in the Fifties was hidden from the British public until 2002. The government's obsession with secrecy for its own sake led at first to a complete denial the tests had ever taken place, a denial that was only withdrawn when legal pressure was brought to bear. Despite the denials, there was already evidence in the public domain that the tests took place. When ex-MI5 operative Peter Wright's memoir *Spycatcher* was published in 1985, it was immediately banned in Britain. In the book, Wright had revealed: "The whole area of chemical research was an active field in the 1950s. I was co-operating with MI6 in a joint programme to investigate how far the hallucinatory drug LSD could be used in interrogations, and extensive trials took place at Porton. I even volunteered as a guinea pig on one occasion."[10]

When the MOD was confronted with Wright's allegation in 1997 they claimed staff at Porton Down could not find any record of the 1953–54 tests. This was most probably because the SIS had removed all files pertaining to the early LSD trials carried out at their behest. However, they cleverly anticipated any future problems by referring to another document which they said "... indicates that some work on LSD may have occurred prior to 1961."[11]

Wright and his colleagues in the intelligence services appear to have concluded that LSD was of little use as an aid to interrogation or as a "truth drug", and MI6 sponsored tests were abandoned in

1954. The MOD's interest, though, continued and the subject of LSD was once again on the agenda in 1955. The discussion paper referred to a report made by the Canadian Directorate of Scientific Intelligence, which suggested that "... LSD 25 had a marked effect which might be a factor of some importance in war and it was suggested that this substance might be used in the role of a more or less conventional CW (Chemical Warfare) agent." In view of this, a meeting held on 7 July agreed to pursue the matter and the JIB held further meetings in July and November 1955.[12]

Professor Joel Elkes attended the 23 November meeting, once again indicating the depth of his involvement with, and influence on, the British intelligence community. Elkes described the reactions to a dose of 50–100 μg of LSD in subjects, "quite unaware they had been given anything". Oddly, there is no mention in the archives of Elkes' Department of Experimental Psychiatry to suggest that LSD was tested on unwitting subjects, yet Elkes' statement indicates such tests took place. One possibility is that he could have been referring to the 1953–54 SIS tests or making an oblique reference to tests run at the Department of Experimental Psychiatry.

Porton scientist Harry Collumbine also attended the meeting, apparently in support of the idea that LSD could be used as a drug for interrogation purposes. The minutes record: "Dr. Collumbine was of the opinion that subjects to whom the drug had been administered without their knowledge were affected to the extent that their reactions were beyond their control when subjected to interrogation by a skilled interrogator experienced in the application of this drug." Collumbine's faith in LSD as a possible interrogation agent does not appear to have been followed up, presumably because of his concerns about the potential for mental disturbance in test subjects.[13]

The meeting went on to discuss various theories of LSD application in warfare. These included dispensing the drug in an aerosol for use against targets such as battleships or aircraft, or against key civil defence personnel such as firefighters. It was even speculated that the effects of LSD on a small number of combatants might cause mass hysteria, the afflicted mimicking LSD symptoms though they hadn't been directly exposed to the drug. The report cited a case from World War I when large numbers of troops fled the front line in the belief they had been gassed when they were in fact entirely unaffected. The counter culture would come to know this phenomenon as a "contact high", in which people who had not taken LSD found themselves in an altered state of consciousness after spending time with those who had.

The report recommended that further investigation of LSD and its analogues could prove fruitful and made several recommendations. The most significant was: "Its potential as a large scale Chemical Warfare agent required expert examination." The report ended: "In view of the above conclusions, the panel strongly recommend that. 'The necessary action should be taken to bring its views to the notice of the appropriate authorities.'" The implication was LSD tests with military personnel in simulated battlefield conditions were required, and there were several internal discussions at Porton in the late Fifties about the ethics of such trials.

Porton scientist Roger Brimblecombe made the situation perfectly clear at a meeting of the Porton advisory committee when he said the only way to determine if a drug might be of use in battle was "... by tests on humans, but there were many objections to that". Professor Rydon speculated whether permission would even be granted for human experimentation of this type and thought it pointless even applying unless it could be shown "... whether the effect of psychomimetic drugs was always temporary and entirely reversible, even in persons liable to develop psychoses without the administration of drugs". Professor Gaddum thought that the effect of a few doses was not a barrier to human tests but "... if repeated doses were given, an irreversible effect might be produced".[14] In his book *Gassed,* Rob Evans quotes an anonymous former Porton Down scientist as saying that since "... quite a lot was known about LSD, it was thought to be potentially safe to expose people to it".[15]

A compromise was reached and it was agreed that future tests on humans would be buffered by a series of tests to screen out those who might react badly to LSD so that "... only normal people would be used". This seemed to satisfy the higher echelons of the MOD and tests on humans resumed in late 1961. At first, it was only Porton scientists who were administered the drug, intravenously and under the supervision of medical staff. The doses were low, 50 µg, enough to precipitate psychological effects but not enough for a full-blown hallucinatory journey. One of the scientists involved was Maxwell Hollyhock, who would later write up his experiences for the popular science journal *New Scientist*.[16]

Further tests on volunteers took place in 1962, with the dosage remaining at 50 µg of LSD. Then, in November 1962, following the results of a working party chaired by Nobel Prize winner Sir Alexander Todd, the Chiefs of Staff decided that chemical weapons should form a part of Britain's armoury. This reasoning was based on the revived belief that Russia held large stocks of poisonous gas and other chemical and biological agents. In addition, the nature of warfare was changing and the Chiefs argued that creating battlefield incapacitants fulfilled a variety of hitherto unrealised needs. For instance, chemical weapons could be employed as a delaying tactic, preventing the enemy from immediate nuclear retaliation. Alternatively, chemical warfare agents could be used to incapacitate civilians in occupied territory without causing harm. The Cabinet's Defence Committee sanctioned more research into nerve gas and other incapacitating agents and a new era of MOD experiments with LSD began at Porton Down.

Prior to 1964, all LSD tests on humans at Porton had been laboratory based. Because the drug was being considered as an aid to interrogation, there had been no need to test it either in groups of people or in the open air. Now the expectations for LSD, as a battlefield incapacitant, were different and new test criteria needed to be developed.

In November 1964, as Britain's nascent hippies were starting their own experiments with LSD, Porton Down began a series of three field trials with the drug. It was hoped these experiments would provide conclusive evidence of LSD's potential as a battlefield incapacitant. The trials were code-named Moneybags, Recount and Small Change, the names being an MOD attempt at wit; LSD also stood for the Latin names for Britain's pre-decimal currency (Libra, Solidus, and Denarius).[17]

Operation Moneybags took place at Porton Down between 27 November and 4 December 1964, with all the volunteers drawn from 41 Royal Marine Commando. The aim of this trial was to test the effect of LSD on the behaviour of troops in field conditions. Psychological tests had now been added to the physical examination and some volunteers were immediately rejected because they failed these new screening procedures. On the first day of the trial, the Marines were not given any LSD and simply carried out a field exercise to acclimatise themselves. On the second day, seventeen Marines took part, sixteen of whom were given 200 μg of LSD in water. One man, for whom 200 μg was thought to be too high, was given 75 μg. They were asked to repeat the exercise. As a film of the trial held at the Imperial War Museum shows, the effect of LSD on the men was dramatic.

Several troops are shown moving through the countryside as the narrator points out that the effects of the LSD were apparent after twenty-five minutes. The broad grins on their faces and the unsteadiness of their gait indicates something is happening, and almost immediately one man has to abandon the exercise. He is shown briefly, sitting in a Land Rover talking to a nurse, his face a mask of concern. Within minutes, the radio operator becomes hopelessly tangled in the wires of his set and the rocket launcher team are unable to aim or focus on their target.

The exercise soon descends into chaos. The troops quickly lose all sense of military discipline, for instance going against standard operational procedures by bunching together as they enter a wood occupied by the "enemy". An attempt at map reading dissolves into confusion and men are seen wandering aimlessly, unsteady on their feet and giggling hysterically. Although some are still capable of sustained physical effort, the soldiers are clearly ineffective as a fighting force and would have been quickly annihilated or captured by an enemy. Some of the soldiers were clearly fighting the drug, trying to maintain their composure so they could continue with the exercise, but it was impossible. Seventy minutes into the exercise, with one man climbing a tree to feed the birds, the troop commander admitted he could no longer control himself or his men, lying on the ground, racked with laughter.[18]

Though the MOD files at the National Archives do not reveal the depth to which the Porton scientists were liaising with their

American counterparts, there was certainly some on-going contact. In late 1965, Bill Ladell, then in charge of human experiments at Porton, invited James Ketchum to visit him there. Ketchum, a psychiatrist working at the Edgewood Arsenal, America's Porton Down, wrote: "Bill thought I would find it useful to observe an LSD field test, which was designed to test the ability of highly trained LSD-dosed commandos to defend their position against un-drugged 'attackers.'" Ketchum arrived too late to observe the trial but was shown the film of the exercise, commenting: "No doubt about it – LSD could disrupt even the most elite troops."[19]

While in England, Ketchum met up with Dr. Maxwell Hollyhock, one of the organisers of the Porton LSD trials, and discussed his article in the *New Scientist*. The article, "Weapons against the Mind", in the September 1965 issue, was a brief but cogent discussion of all aspects of chemical warfare. Although Hollyhock didn't mention his involvement with the experiments at Porton Down he wrote about LSD at length. For Hollyhock, there was no chemical warfare agent to surpass LSD as an incapacitating agent. He placed the drug in a historical context, pointing out how successive eras have argued against, but eventually allowed, the use of certain kinds of weaponry from explosive bullets to mustard gas to aerial bombardments.[20]

Hollyhock's article was illustrated with drawings carried out while he was under the influence of LSD. Snakes, spiders and crocodiles stare from the page, child-like yet disturbing in their simplicity. Another drawing hints at the revelations LSD can bring: Einstein's $E=mc^2$ formula is glimpsed behind curtains. Hollyhock, who was incapacitated by stroke in 2007 and so unavailable for interview for this book, took his governmental duties and the Official Secrets Act very seriously. His daughter commented: "I am unable to help you since my father did not discuss his work with the family."[21]

Despite the success of Moneybags, there was an eighteen-month hiatus before the next LSD field trial. Some staff on Porton's Committee on the Safety of Human Experiments (COSHE) did not share Hollyhock's view that there were no long-term risks from using LSD and the tests were halted. The Applied Biology

Committee recorded they were "unsure of the justification for restarting the LSD trials until, more is known of the persistence of mood effects." Rather mysteriously, the report also notes the tests were stopped because there had been "disconcerting results in one particular case of multiple self-administration and concern over possible addiction". There is nothing more about this supposed catalyst to the tests being halted, but it presumably refers to an individual who had access to LSD and had taken so much they had, in the parlance of the counter culture, "freaked out". As the only people who had access to repeated doses of LSD at Porton were the scientists who conducted the tests, the inference is that it was one of their own men who had taken a liking to the drug![22]

These ethical issues were either ignored or circumvented because in 1966 the success of Operation Moneybags led staff at Porton Down to plan another trial, in which sixteen out of twenty-eight soldiers were given LSD. This exercise, Operation Recount, involved volunteers from the Royal Artillery's 37th Heavy Air Defence Regiment. The men were not told what drug they would be given or what symptoms to expect and, in an attempt to make it difficult for the men to pre-empt what was going to happen, the exercise was spread over three days. Of the eighty volunteers, sixty-one were rejected, twenty-seven because their jobs were not suitable for the type of trial envisaged and thirty-four due to the psychological screening tests.

Operation Recount was poorly organised. Initial plans to give the soldiers 200 µg of LSD, to make the test identical to Moneybags, were scrapped when it was found that the medical officers in attendance had no experience of dealing with high dosage levels. It was recommended to Porton Down's director that the dose be reduced to 50 µg. But such a low dose would have rendered the trials worthless so a compromise was reached; each soldier would receive a dose of 100 µg of LSD. The men were given orange squash each morning, with the LSD being added on the second day.[23]

When Recount took place in September 1966, the results were inconclusive. Those who took LSD displayed the usual erratic and chaotic behaviour but all tasks issued to the group were completed within the allocated timescale. The relatively weak does of LSD, coupled with army discipline and team spirit enabled the unit to continue to function even though over half the unit were drugged. Porton's scientists concluded that Recount's success was limited. If the scientists had understood anything about LSD and the importance of set and setting, they might have taken a different view. Being on LSD in a peace time exercise when you are confident you will not come to harm is completely different from being given LSD in a battle zone with the real possibility of death or serious injury and the sights and sounds of men being torn apart by ordnance.

Some of the LSD used in the three Sixties field trials might have originated with the US military. The US Army supplied Porton with 10 grams of LSD in December 1965 and another 10 grams in June 1966. At the optimum dosage level of 200 µg, this represents 5000 powerful doses of LSD, double that amount if doses of 100 µg were used. As the MOD only tested the drug on a handful of troops after June 1966 and claim to have ceased LSD research on humans entirely by 1969, this raises the question of what happened to the stockpile of LSD Porton must have held at the end of the Sixties.

The final field test of LSD at Porton was code named Operation Small Change. Because staff at Porton believed rumours about the trials had spread among the volunteers, this one was structured in a different way, running over seven days, making it difficult for the men to anticipate on which day they might be drugged.

Twenty-eight soldiers took part in the trial, split into a headquarters unit and three other units, simulating anti-terrorist sweeps on the Porton Down ranges. Half the men received an oral dose of 160 µg of LSD, the other half a placebo. The results of Small Change are somewhat perplexing. Three men were withdrawn from the trial when they exhibited florid symptoms from the drug, and the LSD incapacitated other two men, but the remaining twenty-five carried out the exercise with "little overall reduction in the unit's military efficiency".[24]

Porton's analysis of Small Change concluded those soldiers who did not receive LSD had acted as a stabilising influence on those who had been drugged. Nonetheless, it is highly unusual for anyone to be able to function normally, in any circumstances, when under the influence of 160 μg of LSD. As with the previous tests, there was a fundamental flaw in the Porton scientists' reasoning. LSD is a powerful amplifier of the senses and a "safe" field trial at Porton, while disorientating and bewildering, would have nothing like the effects on LSD-dosed troops in the chaotic horror of the battlefield. Having to contend with simple map reading exercises, guarding prisoners and pretending to capture a wood on a bright, quiet December day is a complete contrast to having to advance on an enemy in battle. This fact was not grasped by those in charge of the tests. If the organisers of the LSD field trials had taken the trouble to read the literature being created by the psychotherapists and the counter culture they would have had a much better understanding of the complexity of LSD and its potential for use in warfare. It is probably a good thing that the Porton scientists didn't understand this or LSD could well have turned out to be a terrifying weapon.

The varied and inconclusive results of the three field trials with LSD led the MOD to abandon LSD tests on service personnel altogether. Whatever its potential, the effects of LSD were not predictable and no two doses would guarantee a consistent result. From a tactical point of view, using LSD as a weapon would be analogous to using a gun that refused to be accurately aimed, worked intermittently, and fired different calibre shells in all directions. A meeting of COSHE on 14 February 1968 concluded that LSD "is of doubtful chemical value" and no further tests were conducted on humans.

In March 1971, Porton began to trace the soldiers who had been involved in their Sixties LSD field trials. By July, sixty-six out of sixty-seven volunteers had been located and interviewed. Unfortunately the report on these follow-ups, if it was written, has never been located. The results of these follow-up interviews might have been useful in later years when the MOD were challenged in the courts about the long-term effects of LSD tests.

Government files documenting the Sixties LSD trials at Porton gloss over the detrimental effects suffered by some volunteers. Other than noting a few men were withdrawn from tests, there is no reference to anyone suffering serious mental health issues. Yet the numbers of those rejected because they were psychologically unsuitable indicates there was considerable potential for severe mental disruption. The fact that the volunteers had no idea what drug they were taking, coupled with the often-high dosages, suggests that at least a few servicemen would require longer-term treatment or hospitalization. Harry Collumbine's unpublished autobiography also indicates there were problems with LSD tests in the Fifties, which he alleges were stopped because of fears for the mental health of the volunteers. There is nothing in any government file to imply this was the case. However, one anecdote suggests that Netley Military Hospital in Southampton might have been used to treat those who didn't recover quickly from the effects of LSD.

Brigadier John McGhie was colonel-commander of Netley during the Fifties and Sixties. He would often take his nephew, Robert Owen, with him when he carried out his daily round of the wards. The young boy was shocked by the sights and sounds he witnessed, at first believing the sufferers to be mentally ill. His uncle told him these unfortunate soldiers were "... victims of chemical experiments such as LSD, from both grenade canisters and artillery shells, 'to see what effect they had on the human mind in a battle situation.'"[25]

No documentary evidence has yet emerged to support this anecdote. If true, it suggests that government agencies were testing LSD in a much wider series of trials than they have admitted. It also seems probable that servicemen were being used as human guinea pigs in LSD experiments at Netley. LSD psychotherapist Ronnie Sandison, though having no involvement with the MOD's use of the drug, has stated, "I believe LSD was used at Netley, but I have no details of who was involved".[26]

Though the British public were largely unaware of the truth about LSD experiments at Porton Down until the early years of the new millennium, strong hints had appeared in the media that the drug was being used there. In May 1964, *The Times*' defence correspondent reported that Porton was testing a wide range of substances including LSD "... the lysergic acid derivative having the property of removing the will to fight or even to offer defence against attack."[27] This reference, however, would have meant little to readers as LSD was virtually unheard of in the British media before 1966.

At that time, no servicemen had yet come forward to relate their personal stories to the media. But they were beginning to reveal their often-harrowing experiences to those they felt able to trust, such as members of the clergy. For instance, in October 1968, the Reverend McNichol publicly criticised the Porton scientists for administering LSD to volunteers without their knowledge, commenting: "This is entirely the wrong thing to do. This attitude is dangerously similar to that of the Japanese in the last war." An MOD spokesperson quickly, if blandly, retorted, claiming experiments had taken place into how troops and civilians would react to the drug if a war took place.[28]

In the summer of 1969, at a week-long series of public, "nothing to hide", open days, Neville Gadsby, Porton's director, was quite open about the LSD experiments that had taken place. Film of the 1964 Operation Moneybags LSD trial was shown to the public for the first time, Gadsby pointing out the problems of administering the drug to troops in the field. Though this was widely covered in the media, the story faded away within a week because there was no accompanying editorial outcry against testing chemicals on troops.

Perhaps because of the authoritarian and secret nature of the armed forces, military personnel have often felt unable to challenge the testing of chemical weapons. This situation changed in 1991, when troops returning from the first Gulf War began to complain of symptoms they believed were brought on by the chemicals they had come into contact with. The media became interested and the effects of chemicals on service personnel became a frequent and hotly debated topic in the newspapers and on television. Some individuals who had been chemical test volunteers at Porton were now starting to review what had happened to them and in July 1999, following a complaint by a former military volunteer, Wiltshire Constabulary began Operation Antler, an investigation into allegations of malfeasance at Porton Down.[29]

Antler was funded by a £900,000 government grant and covered a wide range of allegations from the period 1939 to 1989. The investigation was a huge undertaking, with staff interviewing over 700 of the 20,000 military personnel who had participated in tests at Porton Down. Those involved in LSD tests comprised a small minority of the volunteers, but the Antler staff were very interested in the MI6 LSD tests of the early Fifties and went to considerable lengths to unearth new evidence.

Detectives working on Operation Antler were keen to get to the bottom of whether those who volunteered for the LSD trials in the Fifties had been duped into thinking they would be helping to find a cure for the common cold. Newspapers ran appeals for a copy of the original poster, or the newspaper advertisement. However, although several people came forward to say they remembered seeing the poster, no one could provide a copy and nor could one be found in government archives.

After several years' investigation, the Operation Antler team submitted eight cases to the Crown Prosecution Service (CPS), none of them related to the LSD tests. In July 2003, the hopes of the Porton Veterans Group were dashed when the CPS advised that nobody would face criminal charges arising from the experiments carried out on human volunteers at Porton Down.

In 2005, the UK government were forced to reveal that LSD tests had taken place in the 1950s when Liberal Democrat MP, Matthew Taylor posed a Parliamentary Question. Secretary of State for Defence, Jack Straw responded: "In 1953 and 1954 the Secret Intelligence Service commissioned Porton Down to conduct tests on military service volunteers, and also on Porton scientists themselves, to examine their reactions to LSD. The Government's defence interest in LSD began in the early 1950s because of its perceived potential as an incapacitant and/or interrogation aid. The 1953–54 LSD tests were but a small part of the continuing Porton Down volunteer test programme. The conclusion of the tests was that LSD has no demonstrable value for intelligence purposes."[30]

This was the first official acknowledgement that the SIS tests had taken place in 1953 and 1954 and that LSD was the drug used. Several of the Porton Down veterans who had been involved in the Fifties LSD tests now instructed solicitors to seek compensation for injuries sustained because of the experiments. Eric Gow, chair of the Porton veterans group commented: "What was done to us all was totally unforgiveable. However, recognition of this through the resolution of these claims will go some way towards righting this historic wrong."[31]

When Gow approached the MOD he was told "… much of the information concerning LSD involves research conducted at the behest of the Secret Intelligence Service … We are more than happy to speak to them on your behalf and will pursue the question of downgrading the security classification of certain documents to allow us to disclose them to you."[32]

Gow's solicitor, Alan Care commented: "Clearly these men were duped and subjected to unethical LSD thought control experiments. MI6 should release all its documents about these trials – national secrecy will not be compromised."[33]

Gow's fight to uncover just what had happened to him on that January day in 1954 typified the British government's attitude both to its subjects and to secrecy. Initially Gow was told that there had been no LSD tests in the Fifties, despite evidence to the contrary in Peter Wright's 1985 MI5 memoir. The government were forced to change their mind in January 2002 when Wiltshire detectives working on Operation Antler unearthed fresh evidence. This led Junior Defence Minister, Lewis Moonie to concede that "… there was, in fact, research being carried out at Porton Down involving LSD, as early as 1953."[34]

Eric Gow and his two colleagues' lawsuit against the MOD concluded in February 2006 when they were offered an out of court settlement, thought to be £10,000 between them. However, it seems that this settlement was only agreed because MI6 feared that a court case might have forced them to reveal more of their closely guarded secrets about the chemical and biological warfare experiments they were involved in. In a typically convoluted statement a spokesman for the Foreign Office, acting on behalf of MI6, commented: "The settlement offers were made to the government on behalf of the three claimants which, on legal advice, and in the particular circumstances of these cases, the government thinks it appropriate to accept."[35]

One of the beneficiaries of the compensation, Don Webb, thought

MI6's offer too little, too late: "They stick to the old maxim: never apologise, never explain. But in this case they have decided to pay some money. I think that is as near to an apology or an explanation I'll get."[36]

Not everyone, though, who took part in the government's LSD trials was interested in compensation. George Logan Marr was an RAF radar operator in the Fifties and a volunteer at Porton Down, where he was given three glasses of water containing LSD and asked to record the effects it had on him: "It made me laugh uncontrollably and I had a curious tingling in my joints. I can't say it was particularly unpleasant." Asked if he was going to pursue a claim for compensation Marr said he wasn't because: "I was a volunteer. I signed up for it. No one told me what I was taking and I didn't ask. I wasn't under orders. I did it because I got extra pay and a few days extra leave."[37]

Another serviceman who chose not to claim compensation was Derek Channon, who had taken part in the 1953 trials. Channon remarked of his experience, "Rightly or wrongly, I was a volunteer. I was paid extra money and I was given weekend leave. If you volunteer for something, you take your money and take your chance."[38] These attitudes are admirable support for the armed forces and a testament to how well discipline and professionalism was instilled in service personnel. Nonetheless, even a volunteer has the right to know what they are volunteering for.

Though the government had admitted servicemen had been used as LSD guinea pigs, the culture of secrecy continued even after the court case was over. A request that documents relating to Gow and his colleagues' legal action be placed in the public domain was denied. This means that the out of court settlement effectively meant the intelligence services were off the hook. Had solicitors pursued the case, perhaps the government would have had to reveal the full extent of its files pertaining to LSD and other biological and chemical weapons. As it stands the full extent of experiments sponsored by the intelligence services in the early Fifties remains cloaked in mystery.

Despite the government finally admitting they used LSD on volunteers without their permission, and despite the information that Gow and his colleagues forced out of the government, questions about the intelligence services' involvement with LSD remain. To what degree were the American military and intelligence services involved? Were tests carried out on the public? From where did Porton obtain its LSD in the Fifties? What was Joel Elkes' role? To what extent was Netley Hospital used for casualties of the LSD trials? These and other questions will remain unanswered as long as Britain's archaic secrecy laws are allowed to override public interest.

In the end, the LSD experiments at Porton Down were futile. Fifteen years of on-off tests on human volunteers had proved nothing and had brought the Porton scientists no closer to their goal of harnessing LSD, either as an aid to interrogation or as a battlefield incapacitant. They had been looking for a chemical that would make people tell the truth or would render them incapable of fighting. What they found was a drug whose effects seemed inconsistent and uncontrollable, qualities that did not sit well with the regimented mindset of the intelligence services and the MOD. If the Porton scientists had understood the subtle power of LSD and its potential to affect the delicate mechanism of the brain, rather than desiring to use it as a blunt instrument, the story of LSD as a weapon might have been completely different.

In retrospect, it is perhaps a positive outcome that Porton failed to bend LSD to its will. The idea of any government being able to use a drug to control the minds of its enemies, and by extension its own subjects, is a sinister one. Though the use of LSD in the counter culture might have caused problems for some individuals, they were at least taking the drug from a position of informed choice. For men such as Derek Channon, Eric Gow and the other LSD volunteers, there was no choice. Tricked into taking LSD, they were expected to hallucinate for Queen and country, unwitting guinea pigs in the search for a weapon that could be used in the imposition of one ideology over another. Ironically, this was exactly what the intellectuals of the LSD counter culture wanted to do; but instead of fighting enemies abroad, they were fighting their own society from the inside.

5

THE JOYOUS COSMOLOGY

He not busy being born, is busy dying.
Bob Dylan[1]

Once LSD became available in Britain, outside the military or psychiatric contexts, it was quickly adopted by a generation of young people as their recreational drug of choice. It is clear from accounts of these early British LSD adventurers that the drug arrived already freighted with concepts about its effects and purpose. These concepts informed and shaped the drug's course through British society in the Sixties and still resonate within LSD use to the present day.

Central to these concepts are the insights frequently experienced by LSD users: heightened awareness, experience of the transcendental and the numinous, a reverence for all sentient beings and the vision of a lifestyle antithetical to the rampant consumerism of the twentieth century.

These insights appear not to have been inherent in the drug itself. If they were an automatic consequence of taking LSD, then everyone who used the drug would have them. For instance, we would expect there to be evidence from the MOD's LSD trials at Porton Down that soldiers had undergone religious experiences.

No such experiences were reported and nor did any of the Porton Down veterans later refer to any such effects in their statements to the Operation Antler investigation. Neither is there any indication from the literature of LSD psychotherapy that patients had similar experiences to those typically enjoyed by the emerging counter culture.

Set and setting, the mind set prior to taking LSD and the physical setting in which the experience takes place, seem to be the defining factors in how people interpret the LSD experience. The mind set and philosophy at the root of the first wave of serious LSD users in Britain can be traced to the experiences of a few key figures in the early American LSD movement. This group of people comprised a pair of British philosophers, together with a smattering of Americans, all of whom discovered LSD in the Fifties and early Sixties.

Gerald Heard and Aldous Huxley both emigrated to America in 1937. Prior to their move both were well-known in Britain as writers. But it was America that brought out their genius as philosophers of altered states of consciousness. In California, Heard introduced Huxley to the Hindu philosophy of Vedanta, as well as to meditation. Their perennial theme was how to change man and society, both of them believing that humans could – should – pursue the intentional evolution of consciousness.[2]

Even before LSD was synthesised, there was considerable interest in mind-expanding drugs. Mescaline, found in a variety of cacti including the peyote cactus, was first synthesised in 1919. In its cactus form mescaline already had a history of structured religious usage in America which pre-dated the European invasion. Word of mescaline's effects spread and soon after the end of World War II the drug was used by the US Navy in Project Chatter, an attempt to find a drug to aid interrogation. Shortly afterwards, in 1952, Dr. Humphrey Osmond an English émigré in Canada took an interest in mescaline in his work on schizophrenia.

A few adventurous individuals had also heard of mescaline and wanted to see what all the fuss was about. Captain Alfred M. Hubbard was one of the first individuals to try mescaline outside military or medical experiments. Hubbard worked for the Office of Strategic Services during World War II, conducting barely legal covert operations such as smuggling American weapons to Britain via Canada, before Pearl Harbour officially brought America into the war. His clandestine activities were approved by President Roosevelt and to all intents and purposes he was an establishment figure, albeit somewhat of a maverick.

Hubbard entered the world of mind altering drugs when he appeared unannounced at Humphrey Osmond's hospital, took the doctor out for lunch and asked if he could buy some mescaline. Hubbard took to the mescaline experience like a duck to water and set himself on a course of consciousness exploration which lasted until his death in 1982.

Controversy surrounds Hubbard's role in the history of LSD. It has been suggested he is part of a mysterious and unarticulated government conspiracy to introduce LSD into society. These same conspirators, however, offer no evidence other than Hubbard's links with the intelligence services. It is more likely that Hubbard simply was one of those individuals who took LSD and was instantly converted into an acid evangelist. Yet there are some inconsistencies in the accounts and chronology of how Hubbard first came to take LSD. *Acid Dreams* author Martin A. Lee wrote that Hubbard had been introduced to LSD in 1951 by British psychotherapist Dr. Ronnie Sandison.[3] Yet Sandison, by his own account, did not come across LSD until late 1952 and has no recollection of Hubbard: "I do not think that I ever met him. If I did it must have been briefly in the States, and certainly not in the UK. I certainly never gave him his first, or any other, LSD trip."[4]

That mystery notwithstanding, Hubbard's first trip astonished him. Among other experiences he witnessed his own conception, "... the deepest mystical thing I've ever seen." LSD led him to see that most people were sleepwalking through life, unaware of the larger reality they existed in. Hubbard wanted to enlighten them through the agency of the drug so that they would "... see themselves for what they are."[5] Hubbard felt it was his mission to turn as many people as possible on to LSD. Reputedly, he introduced over 6000 people to LSD, including scientists, politicians, intelligence officials, diplomats and church figures.

Hubbard travelled with a leather case containing pharmaceutically pure LSD, mescaline and psilocybin, earning the sobriquet of the "Johnny Appleseed of LSD".

In January 1953 Aldous Huxley received a letter from his old friend, Dr. Humphrey Osmond. Huxley's reply railed against the herd mentality of most human beings. It seemed to him that: "Under the current dispensation the vast majority of individuals lose, in the course of their education, all the openness to inspiration, all the capacity to be aware of other things than those enumerated in the Sears-Roebuck catalogue which constitutes the 'real' world."[6] Huxley suggested that mescaline, which he had not yet taken, might play a role in opening people's minds to the reality hidden behind the material world. Osmond immediately planned a visit to see Huxley, promising to bring some.

Huxley prised open the "doors of perception" at eleven o'clock on the morning of 4 May 1953 when he swallowed four-tenths of a gram of mescaline. The trip was carefully planned and under Osmond's medical supervision. Huxley's biographer, Nicholas Murray has described this event as "... the most famous literary drug taking since De Quincy." Though Huxley took mescaline and not LSD, this occasion was the genesis of the modern world's fascination with mind-altering drugs.[7]

Huxley was initially disappointed. He had hoped, expected even, to see visions of the kind experienced by the poets, Blake and "A.E". But there was nothing so dramatic. The drug's effects were subtle and imperceptibly crept up him. After an hour and a half, as he observed a glass containing some flowers, his perception of the world changed. He noted: "I was not looking now at an unusual flower arrangement. I was seeing what Adam had seen on the morning of his creation – the miracle, moment by moment, of naked existence." When asked whether the experience was agreeable Huxley could only answer: "It is neither agreeable nor disagreeable. It just *is*."

As his mescaline experience deepened, everything in his field of vision shone with an inner light. Huxley's perception of time altered to the point where he was completely indifferent to it. When Osmond enquired what his views on time were he replied: "There seems to be plenty of it." Indeed, he spent "several centuries" examining furniture in the room, furniture which had lost all utilitarian function; now Huxley was seeing it as "... the sacramental vision of reality ... Infinite in its significance."[8]

Throughout the trip, Huxley repeatedly uttered variations on "This is how one ought to see, how things really are". Nevertheless, even at the height of the altered state, the philosopher questioned what life would be like if everyone viewed the world with mescaline vision all the time. People, he believed, would just spend their time just *looking*, just *being*. Valuable as the psychedelic experience was, Huxley wondered: "How was this cleansed perception to be reconciled with a proper concern for human relations, with the necessary chores and duties, to say nothing of charity and practical compassion?" This was the fundamental problem at the root of the psychedelic lifestyle. Going to work or doing the household chores after a psychedelic experience might seem tame by comparison.

Huxley wrote about his mescaline experience in *The Doors of Perception,* published in 1954. He took the title from William Blake's belief that "if the doors of perception were cleansed, everything will appear to man as it is, infinite". The book became a best seller and one of the crucial texts in the counter culture's attempts to understand the psychedelic experience. The title, from which the rock band the Doors took their name, has been used countless times in books and articles about LSD and related drugs and is a now recognised phrase cognate with mind altering substances.

Despite his enthusiasm for the drug's effects, Huxley did not immediately see psychedelics as being a route to spiritual enlightenment, "I am not so foolish as to equate what happens under the influence of mescaline or of any other drug, prepared or in the future preparable, with the realisation of the end and ultimate purpose of human life: Enlightenment, the Beatific Vision." Though he had doubts about the nature of the mescaline experience, he was certain that anyone who used the drug in controlled circumstances would return "... wiser but less cocksure, happier but less self-satisfied, humbler in acknowledging his ignorance yet better equipped to understand the relationship of words to things, of systematic reasoning to the unfathomable Mystery which it tries, forever vainly, to comprehend."[9]

Huxley had desperately wanted Gerald Heard to join him on his initial mescaline experiment, but it was not possible. Heard eventually took the drug with him in November 1953. On this occasion Al Hubbard joined them, Huxley writing to Osmond afterwards, "Your nice Captain tried a new experiment – group mescalinisation ... Since I was in a group the experience had a human content, which the earlier, solitary experience, with its Other Worldly quality and its intensification of aesthetic experience, did not possess ... it was a transcendental experience within *this* world and with human references."[10] They repeated their mescaline experiments on several occasions, discussing their experiences with friends who were curious about the meaning and purpose of psychedelics. This was the genesis of a movement concerned with the theory and practice of consciousness-altering drugs, and the results of Huxley and Heard's experiments had unknowingly triggered the coming revolution in consciousness.

On 2 September 1955 the British Labour MP, Christopher Mayhew agreed to be filmed taking mescaline for a BBC TV *Panorama* special. This extraordinary state of affairs came about because Mayhew had been contacted by Humphrey Osmond, an old friend, who was looking for ways to spread news of the amazing effects of mescaline. "I took the drug because I am an old school friend of Dr. Humphrey Osmond. ... He said he was coming over to England and could I recommend him for a BBC Third Programme broadcast to describe his research work. I said, 'Don't go on sound radio. No one listens to that. Explain about hallucinogens on television and give me this stuff in front of a film camera.'"

As Mayhew was a well-known politician and TV broadcaster it was thought the most effective way to structure the programme was to have Mayhew take 400 mg of mescaline while being supervised by Osmond. The film was made at Mayhew's home in Surrey. The full programme was never shown, although extracts have appeared on various documentaries dealing with psychedelia. Transcripts of the film reveal Mayhew, the epitome of the English gentleman, slowly loosening his grip on consensus reality as

Osmond asks him a series of mundane questions. Mayhew gets the answers correct but seems rather detached from them. As the trip progresses Mayhew continues to respond to Osmond's questions but is clearly drifting in and out of a reverie.

When Osmond queries Mayhew about his perception of time, asking him if he is experiencing time and space differently, Mayhew replies, "I'm perfectly certain of that! I haven't the slightest doubt. And I'm saying that with my conscious mind now, as well as my unconscious mind." Interesting though the experiment was, it's clear Mayhew thought the questions being asked of him were superficial compared with the actual experience he was undergoing. He was fascinated by time and how its passage was completely different in his altered state. By mid-afternoon Mayhew had reached the point where there was "… no absolute time ... no absolute space ... it is simply what we impose on the outside world ... and, er, the more closely I feel this, the more relaxed I feel ... and, er ... the less I feel inclined to talk …"[11]

Mayhew's televised journey into inner space proved that the psychedelic experience was not amenable to being studied in any objective way. What appeared obvious to the mescaline voyager sounded illogical to the trained observer and vice versa. Osmond, no stranger to Mayhew's altered state of consciousness, concurred, "Now, I know quite well ... *some* of the experiences that you're having but I don't know how one gets them across in words, and I've been trying to puzzle out ways in which we can demonstrate this, and I'm still quite defeated."

Prior to 1956 there was no catch-all term for the effects of mescaline, LSD and similar drugs. Louis Lewin, the German toxicologist, had coined the word Phantastica to refer to drugs that caused visionary states and hallucinations, but the word was too Victorian in tone and failed to enter popular usage. The term hallucinogen was often used but was a prescriptive term suggesting that hallucinations were the main characteristic of this type of drug, which was not always the case. Huxley, perturbed by the lack of a suitable name, wrote to Osmond, "About a name for these drugs – what a problem."[12] After some thought Huxley came up with *phanerothyme,* from the Greek, and meaning to make the soul visible. Huxley was so pleased with the word he suggested it to Osmond with the rhyme: "To make this trivial world sublime; Take half a gramme of phanerothyme."[13] Osmond thought the word was clumsy and quickly responded to Huxley with his own term, *psychedelic*: "To fathom hell, or soar angelic, take a pinch of psychedelic."[14] Psychedelic was also taken from the Greek root words: "psyche" – mind and "delos" – clear or manifest. Psychedelic literally means "manifesting clear mind". It is also sometimes defined as "mind-expanding" or "mind-manifesting".

Huxley's first encounter with LSD was in October 1955 when he took two 200 µg doses separated by an interval of forty minutes. He had read that the drug had helped someone uncover some childhood memories and he hoped it would do the same for him. When the drug took hold memories were soon forgotten as he became imbued with "... the direct, total awareness, from the inside, so to say, of Love as the primary and cosmic fact."[15]

Shortly after this experience Huxley wrote to Osmond: "I found the stuff more potent than mescaline," concluding the effects were a "... transfiguration of the external world, and the understanding, through a realisation involving the whole man, that Love is the One, and that is why Atman is identical with Brahman, and why, in spite of everything, the universe is all right."[16] Huxley's use of the Hindu terms Atman (individual soul) and Brahman (supreme spirit of the universe) reflected his interest in Hindu philosophy. As we will see, eastern philosophies, specifically variants of Hinduism and Buddhism, became very attractive to many people who had taken LSD.

Huxley's identification with love as a primary fact of the universe has echoed through the LSD subculture ever since, being recognised as a characteristic of the well prepared LSD trip and frequently alluded to by commentators on the scene. Perhaps the most public statement of this principle came in the Beatles' classic 1967 LSD song "All You Need Is Love". Of course universal love is a tenet of many religions, but often as an abstract concept. For Huxley, under the influence of LSD, it had been a living reality.

Huxley was keen to repeat the LSD experience and did so two months later with Gerald Heard and Al Hubbard. They listened to music, something millions of recreational LSD users have since found to be a source of amazement. Huxley found Bach's B-minor suite to be "a revelation". He was so impressed he later wrote to Osmond: "Meanwhile, let me advise you, if you ever use mescaline or LSD in therapy, to try the effect of the B-minor suite. More than anything, I believe, it will serve to lead the patient's mind (wordlessly, without any suggestion or covert bullying by doctor or parson) to the central, primordial Fact, the understanding of which is perfect health during the time of the experience, and the memory of the understanding of which may serve as an antidote to mental sickness in the future."[17]

Heard became another instant convert to LSD and wrote and lectured widely on the subject in America. In August 1956 he was instrumental in guiding Bill Wilson, the founder of Alcoholics Anonymous, on an LSD trip. Wilson said the session allowed him to re-experience the spontaneous spiritual experience which had enabled him to overcome his own alcoholism. Wilson's experience would validate later work carried out in Canada and elsewhere in treating the root causes of alcoholism with LSD.[18]

On a visit to London in 1961 Huxley gave an interview to the BBC's John Chandos in which he revealed he had taken mescaline twice and LSD five times. The nation heard that he had found his LSD experiences to be positive, giving him a "gratuitous grace", a term borrowed from Catholic theology meaning a gift conferred on particular persons for the salvation of others. Huxley told the nation that his experiments with psychedelic drugs had given him the experience of knowing "the Universe is All Right. Capital A, Capital R."[19]

Toward the end of his life, Huxley encoded his philosophies, including his beliefs about psychedelic drugs, in his final book, *Island.* The novel describes a fictional utopia, the island of Pala, where people live in harmony with nature and each other. The islanders' central philosophy is Buddhist in nature, the first principle of their core beliefs being: "Nobody needs to go anywhere else. We are all, if we only knew it, already there". The Palanese philosophy teaches that everything should be done with "... the minimum of strain and maximum of awareness." Paying attention to every act is fundamental to the islanders' day-to-day existence and through this total awareness the Palanese turned the act of living into a yogic art.[20]

Central to the story is the Palanese use of Moksha, a psychedelic drug given to children as a rite of passage and used to guide the dying as they pass from life. Clearly based on Huxley's own drug experiences and his vision of the perfect society, *Island* was an immediate success, becoming a counter culture classic, a status which it enjoys to the present day.

Huxley's writings, in particular *The Doors of Perception* and *Island,* had a major influence on the developing LSD philosophy in Britain. The psychedelic drug states described by Huxley were fiercely sought by the first wave of LSD users and the model community described in *Island* became the vision and goal of personal and communal living. After his first LSD trip in early 1966 underground DJ Jeff Dexter, like many of his contemporaries, saw himself as being on a spiritual journey, drawing inspiration from the available psychedelic literature. "This was the beauty of people that we read, like Huxley – 'here and now boys, here and now.'" This is the phrase intoned by the parrot in Huxley's *Island* and the message which runs throughout the book. For Dexter, Huxley's writing informed his psychedelic experiences, giving him the sure and certain knowledge that "the fact is you're on a journey but you're already there."[21]

On Friday 22 November 1963, Huxley's cancer, diagnosed in 1960, worsened and he believed he was close to death. In a bold act of self determination, he asked his wife Laura for paper and wrote: "Try LSD 100 mmg intramuscular". The doctor in attendance was unhappy about giving LSD to a dying man but Laura overruled his concerns, administering the injection herself. Later she gave Huxley another 100 µg and sat with him, repeating the words, spoken by Maria in *Island* as Lakshmi lies dying, about moving toward the light. Huxley acknowledged Laura's presence by squeezing her hand and he died peacefully under the influence of LSD.[22]

Huxley's ideas about the use of LSD and other psychedelics were hugely influential on the burgeoning counter culture. It was

Timothy Leary, though, who made the most significant contribution to how LSD was perceived by the British public and who was responsible for the worldwide explosion in the drug's use.

However, were it not for a mysterious Englishman, it is possible that Leary might not have taken LSD until much later in the Sixties, or taken it in a much weaker form. American histories of LSD often omit or minimise the role of Leary's British mentor. This is partly out of ignorance and partly because recreational LSD use is often thought to have its origins solely with Americans. Just as the first LSD philosophers were British émigrés to America, the person responsible for turning America on was also British.

Very little is known about Michael Hollingshead, yet he is a crucial figure in the history of LSD. Had he not come into Leary's orbit the course of psychedelic history would have taken a completely different trajectory. Hollingshead is the archetypal trickster figure, eclipsing Leary for spontaneity and intellect but without Leary's public flair or need for massive public approbation. Indeed, Leary referred to him as a "divine rascal". Others have been much less complimentary.

Known to the psychedelic community as Michael Hollingshead, his birth certificate reveals his real name is Michael John Shinkfield. He was born on 30 September 1931 in Darlington in the north-east of England, the son of a colliery clerk with the National Coal Board. He had a tumultuous relationship with his father and in his mid-teens was sent to a school in London that dealt with "bright but troubled boys". Hollingshead later claimed he had been under psychoanalysis in London with Anna Freud, but this could have been one of the many yarns he spun to reinvent his past and to impress the gullible.

After serving his National Service in the Royal Air Force, Hollingshead worked in London for Thomas Cook, the travel agents. During this time, he met and shared a flat with Dr. John Beresford, a paediatrician, who was also to prove crucial in the story of LSD's early years. At some point in the late Fifties Shinkfield changed his name to Hollingshead. No one is certain why he did this. Hollingshead himself has said it was to sound more "English" when he was in America. Later he said it was a play on words of hole in his head, a reference to the psychedelic effects claimed from trepanation.[23]

His daughter Vanessa (now one of America's leading comediennes) also had a difficult relationship with her father, having witnessed both sides of his personality. It is these dichotomies in his psychological make up that both attracted and repelled those who he came into contact with. As Vanessa Hollingshead says, "Stripped bare of all his quirks and darkness, he just wanted to be loved, accepted ..." But he could be as ruthless as he was charming, once telling Vanessa "... you must learn to manipulate people, that's the name of the game".[24]

It was this character who travelled to New York in the late Fifties to take up a post with the British-American Institute for Cultural Exchange, an organization promoting friendship between the two nations. Those who believe there is some dark conspiracy at the heart of LSD culture have claimed that the Exchange was a cover for a nebulous intelligence operation. It appears in LSD history that anything which cannot be immediately explained, or has some connection to the intelligence services, must form part of a conspiracy. Other than the anecdotal, join-the-dots attempt to link names with organizations there is no available evidence to suggest Hollingshead was an asset of the British intelligence services.

In New York, Hollingshead once again moved in with his friend Dr. John Beresford. By now the doctor was mingling with a small group of consciousness explorers centred on a shop in Greenwich Village that sold a variety of legal, organic, psychedelic substances. Hollingshead was aware of Huxley's experiments with mescaline and phoned him to enquire how to obtain some of the drug for his circle of friends. During the conversation Huxley mentioned LSD but cautioned, "It is much more potent than mescaline, though Gerald [Heard] and I have used it with some astonishing results really."[25]

LSD sounded promising, so in late 1960 Hollingshead asked Beresford to order a gram of LSD direct from Sandoz in Switzerland. Beresford did so, using his hospital's letterheaded notepaper, claiming he needed the drug as a control for a series of bone marrow experiments. Beresford soon received a package containing a bill for $285 and a gram of pure LSD, enough for at least 5000 powerful doses.

Lot Number H-00047 arrived contained in a small, dark jar. The magic gram was in powder form and Hollingshead was now faced with the problem of how to divide it into equal doses. By mixing the powder with distilled water and confectioner's sugar he made a glutinous paste divided and sub divided until he had exactly 5000 x 200 µg doses which he transferred to a 16 ounce mayonnaise jar. During the mixing process Hollingshead had licked his fingers several times, taking in the equivalent of at least five substantial doses. As the drug hit he moved to the rooftop and spent the next fifteen hours totally absorbed by its effects, experiencing the death of his body and stepping into, "… some other strange land of unlikeliness, which can only be grasped in terms of astonishment and mystery, as an *etat de l'absurde*, ecstatic nirvana."[26]

Hollingshead, like Huxley, was amazed with the drug. He now understood why people might believe the LSD experience was the "Real Thing", the "ultimate illumination, Nirvana!" but was cautious not to ascribe this potential to it. In fact he speculated that LSD could be the exact opposite of spiritual illumination, the ultimate distraction. Nevertheless, after just one session Hollingshead concluded the drug, "… does allow one to live at least for a moment of time in a window into eternity, that the absolute is manifest in every appearance and relationship, and that Love is Wisdom in daily practice … It is the development of another state of consciousness within one's own self. One that leads to a vision of existence in which only the sense of wonder remains and all fear is gone. It is also the impetus that makes a few travellers in each generation set off in search of the grail, the genii in the bottle, the magic ring …"[27]

Dr. John Beresford was with Hollingshead and had also taken some of the pure LSD. When he returned to some semblance of normality he was just as impressed as his partner. Beresford would continue to champion psychedelics for the rest of his life, believing LSD to be a portent of evolutionary change and relating it to the first self sustaining nuclear chain reaction in the development of the nuclear bomb. "The reckless act of science in Chicago in December, 1942, was remedied in Basel four months later, with Albert Hofmann chosen as the instrument to perform the cure."[28]

The LSD experience both baffled and excited Hollingshead. It was, he thought, "… a bundle of solutions looking for a problem". He phoned Huxley to discuss his findings, now speaking with the authority and perspective of one of the inner circle of LSD initiates. It seemed to Hollingshead that modern man had lost his way and was caught in a world of external illusion, a stranger to himself. Perhaps, he suggested to Huxley, LSD was the antidote to this existential malaise. Moreover the drug could even be "… a therapy for the widespread sickness of insensitiveness and ignorance which psychologists call 'normality' or 'mental health.'"

Huxley was sympathetic to Hollingshead's predicament but advised him that little was known about LSD. They spoke again a couple of days later, Huxley suggesting Hollingshead should meet a Harvard professor by the name of Dr. Timothy Leary. "If there is any one single investigator in America worth seeing," Huxley assured Hollingshead. "It is Dr. Leary."

There are numerous histories of Leary's life that cover in minute detail his journey from trainee priest to LSD evangelist. In 1957, when he was a lecturer in psychology at Harvard University, he tried psilocybin mushrooms on a field trip to Mexico. The psychedelic experience, as it had done with so many others, profoundly changed Leary and he commented that he had "learned more about ... (his) brain and its possibilities ... (and) more about psychology in the five hours after taking these mushrooms than ... (he) had in the preceding fifteen years of studying doing [sic] research in psychology."[29]

On his return from Mexico, Leary set up the Harvard Psilocybin Project with colleagues Ralph Metzner and Richard Alpert, using a synthesised version of the drug. Leary's interest in behaviour change, in which he was an expert, led him to believe that psychedelics, in the correct dosage and set and setting, could radically alter behaviour. It was at this stage in Leary's exploration of psychedelic drugs that he came into contact with Hollingshead. Leary had been warned off Hollingshead by someone he knew, a millionaire by the name of Winston London. A "no-good, two-bit English con-man" was London's bodyguard's view of Hollingshead and he advised Leary to have nothing to do with him. But Leary was intrigued by the persuasive, roguish Englishman and within weeks Hollinsghead had moved in with the Leary family as their lodger.[30]

At first Leary was wary of LSD. He was a veteran of many psilocybin and peyote trips but believed these drugs were acceptable because they were organic and had long traditions of structured use among the world's indigenous peoples. LSD, in contrast, was only partly organic, had been created in a sterile laboratory and was primarily used by the military and the secular psychiatric establishment. Psilocybin and peyote, Leary rationalised, were familiar to him. He knew their moods and how to navigate their twists and turns. This rationalization only partly concealed Leary's underlying fear that, "… the more powerful LSD swept you far beyond the tender wisdom of psilocybin."[31]

Leary initially evaded Hollingshead's invitations to take LSD. Then, in December 1961, the jazz trumpeter Maynard Ferguson and his wife Flo stayed with the Learys after a performance in Boston. The Fergusons were considered to be an urbane, hip couple who liked to smoke marijuana and so naturally, over dinner, LSD came up as a topic of conversation and Hollingshead soon realised that the couple had never taken the drug. When they found Hollingshead had more than enough LSD they suggested he ran a session for them and Leary. Leary excused himself, claiming he had work to do, while the Fergusons and Hollingshead each took a spoonful from the mayonnaise jar and settled down in front of the roaring log fire.

Hollingshead described their reaction: "After about thirty minutes, Flo, who until that moment had been lying fully reclined on the sofa, sat up, suddenly her face one huge smile, and started waving her arms at Tim. 'You gotta try this Tim, baby. It's f-a-n-t-a-s-t-i-c.' Her husband was equally enthusiastic, 'Yeah, really Tim', confirmed Maynard, his face glowing like an electric toaster. 'It really gets you there – wow – it's really happening, man …'"

Leary was curious, noticing that when Flo laughed, "It was not a nervous or a funny laugh. It was the chuckle of someone who was dead and gone and sitting on some heavenly mountain top and looking down at the two billion years of evolution the way you'd look at a transient episode in a children's playground." And with that, Leary's curiosity finally got the better of him. He swallowed a spoonful of the sweet LSD mixture from Hollingshead's jar and with it the cultural landscape of the developed world changed forever.

As his mind spun outside of time and space, no longer linked to mundane reality, Leary literally saw the light. "But not just light. It was the centre of life. A burning, dazzling, throbbing, radiant core, pure pulsing, exulting light. An endless flame that contained everything – sound, touch, cell, seed, sense, soul, sleep, glory, glorifying, God, the 'hard eye of God'. Merged with this pulsating flame it was possible to look out and see and participate in the entire cosmic drama. Past and future. All forms, all structures, all organisms, all events were illusory, television productions pulsing out from the central eye."[32]

Perhaps because he was already an experienced psilocybin user Leary was able to tap into the religious aspect of LSD. Or he could have just been very lucky that his first trip was a journey into the heart of light rather than the torments of hell. But Leary's trip consisted of more than just the fantastical visual hallucinations. The drug allowed him to see through all social roles and games, realizing they were just masks to wear for a time. LSD had "... flipped consciousness out beyond life into the whirling dance of pure energy, where nothing existed except whirring vibrations, and each illusory form was simply a different frequency."[33]

Leary returned from his trip a convert to the power of LSD. The drug had shown him that "... everything is a message from the impersonal, relentless, infinite, divine intelligence, weaving a new web of life each second, bombarding us with a message. Don't you see! You're nothing! Wake up! Glorify me! Join me!" Leary became an immediate acid evangelist.[34]

Leary's overnight conversion presented problems for Alpert, Metzner and the others who were already involved in a programme of psilocybin experimentation. In his penetrating study of LSD in

America, *Storming Heaven,* Jay Stevens comments how this cosy world of psilocybin exploration was shattered by the advent of LSD. Psilocybin had become just about manageable but LSD threw the user back into mental chaos and Alpert in particular feared they would never understand how to use the drug. Leary had different ideas and exhorted his colleagues to persevere with LSD.

Hollingshead quickly became a central figure in Leary's circle of serious scientific psychedelic explorers. But Hollingshead was not bound by any scientific ethics, or by any ethics at all. He was disruptive on group LSD trips, often trying to manipulate or dominate the proceedings. Yet when confronted he denied everything and turned on the charm. Despite his obvious shortcomings Leary fully supported him; everyone had a sneaking respect for him and the path he had now set them on.

Leary's books and magazine interviews were widely read in Britain. His translation of *The Tibetan Book of the Dead – The Psychedelic Experience* – was highly regarded as a tool for guiding LSD users through their early trips. His other later writings, however, such as *The Politics of Ecstasy,* though they sold well, were less influential on the counter culture in Britain. London DJ and psychedelic adventurer Jeff Dexter, for instance found "Leary hard going ... too falsified in some ways, whereas reading Huxley there was a certain clarity to it."[35] Leary was effective at being a self-promoting figurehead for the worldwide psychedelic movement and he had a huge impact on the public's perception of LSD. Hollingshead might have known how to manipulate individuals, but Leary was equally adept at manipulating the media. His perma-grinning visage and portentous announcements about a new religion based on LSD use, or how a woman could have thousands of orgasms during an LSD session, were guaranteed headline grabbers.

The relationship between Leary and Hollingshead ran hot and cold for a number of years in the early Sixties. It culminated in their abortive plans for the American psychedelic vision to be transposed to Britain. Leary's activities in America after he had been turned on to LSD by Hollingshead have little direct relevance to the social history of LSD in Britain. For the time being we must leave Leary on the cusp of his adventures in consciousness and his love/hate relationship with mainstream America.

The last key individual who influenced the mind set of the British psychedelic generation was American writer David Solomon. Solomon is another advocate of LSD with his roots in military intelligence, in which he served during World War II after being reassigned from a combat unit when his two brothers were killed in action. It is not known when Solomon first took LSD but in the early Sixties he was literary editor for *Playboy* magazine and published Timothy Leary, Ram Das (Richard Alpert), Alan Watts and Humphrey Osmond.

LSD: the consciousness expanding drug edited by Solomon, with an introduction by Leary, featured essays by Huxley, Watts and Osmond, among other luminaries of the psychedelic scene. The book's dedication was, "For Aldous Huxley, *guru extraordinaire*, whose words first beckoned me through the doors of perception."[36]

In the preface, Solomon clearly states his views on the purpose of LSD. He believed psychedelic drugs "... frequently enable one to see through the myriad pretensions and deceits that make up the mythology of the Social Lie. Thus, to the extent that power structures rely on the controlled popular acceptance of the Lie to shore up and stabilise their hegemonies, psychedelic substances do indeed represent a kind of political threat." Solomon saw the spiritual uses for psychedelic drugs but tempered this view with his belief they could be used to change socio-economic patterns to bring about a new society based on their insights. For him the psychedelic experience was "no evasive flight *from,* but a deep probe *into* reality". It was Solomon's fundamental tenet that the human brain was man's most inalienable possession and individuals should have complete autonomy over their own consciousness. "No person or institution has the moral right to muffle or inhibit its development. No social authority can successfully arrogate unto itself the rights to dictate and fix the levels of consciousness to which men may aspire, whether these states are induced pharmacologically or otherwise. *Die Gedanken sind frei.*"[37]

Though Solomon provided only the preface for his book,

his selection of essayists was carefully chosen to give the most positive view of LSD, providing the reader with some of the history, rationale, subjective accounts, and mystique that launched the drug movement. Of all the early psychedelic pioneers and philosophers, only Solomon would go on to be an active, physical presence in Britain's LSD culture.

The philosophies and writings of Heard, Huxley, Watts, Solomon and Leary spread rapidly through the burgeoning psychedelic movement in Britain. Between them a template had been forged for the expectations and parameters of the LSD experience. Anyone who used LSD need pay no heed to the dire warnings issued by the media because they had their own textbooks written by the forerunners and philosophers of the counter culture. These books were important because they were written by those who had been there and had experience of the transcendent through the agency of LSD, a religious experience unmediated by priest or parson.

Huxley and Leary's books in particular became sacred texts for the LSD counter culture just as much as the Bible and Koran were to Christians and Muslims. They were treasured by British LSD users, discussed intensely and pored over for clues as how best to interpret an LSD trip, or how to successfully navigate one. All the influential authors described here were optimistic for the future of LSD use. That optimism would soon be taken up by the tens of thousands of young people in Britain who were soon to be offered their own key to the doors of perception.

6

THE FOGGY RUINS OF TIME

> There is some possibility that my friends and I have illuminated more people than anyone else in history.
>
> Michael Hollingshead[1]

It's impossible to be certain who took the first recreational dose of LSD in Britain. Though some who took LSD as part of the military and medical experiments carried out in the 1950s and 1960s may have enjoyed their experience, this could hardly be classed as recreational use. By the mid-Fifties, word of the drug's powerful, often enjoyable, effects had reached Britain through American magazine articles, books and traveller's tales and there was a ready market for chemical thrills. Poet Dave Cunliffe cogently sums up the scene at the turn of the decade:

"Late 1950s' British urban Bohemia included a varied mixture of dedicated individualists and loosely affiliated sub-cultural group devotees. Traditional European middle-class artistic life-styles were gradually being swamped by a younger, less identifiable manifestation. Forties hipsters, newly emergent beats, extrovert beaus, traditional jazz ravers, modern jazz cool, opiate junkies, speed freaks, pot-smokers, out of the closet sexual trail-blazers, creative innovators, anarchists, eccentrics, deviants, dissidents, outlaw bikers, student dropouts, religious cultists, dedicated Utopians, born-again Luddite and all kind of known and unknown orientations and tendencies. A rich counter-cultural soil in which the unifying hippie flower was about to explode."[2]

At the tail end of the 1950s, the teenage Cunliffe was a courier for a firm of London drug dealers. He delivered packages, no questions asked, in response to orders placed by phone. Cunliffe had no idea what was in the packages unless they were unwrapped in his presence. When they were, it was invariably marijuana, amphetamine or heroin. These substances had been staples of the jazz scene and those within its orbit since the 1920s, jazz musicians traditionally being the first social group to seek out and make recreational use of any new drug. Now, in the "you've never had it so good" decade they were reaching a wiser audience.

Far from 1950s Britain being a psychedelic wasteland, a variety of mind-expanding drugs was available if you knew the right people.

Cunliffe had been aware of LSD use in London for some years but was under the impression that the drug was fake or exceptionally weak. Rather than LSD, mescaline with its longer pedigree and body of literature was the holy grail of mind-expanding drugs at the time. Nevertheless, LSD was accessible, science fantasy author Michael Moorcock recalling that it was available as early as 1956, with a doctor's script, from London pharmacists John Bell & Croyden. Liberty cap mushroom, *Psilocybe semilanceata,* was also widely used, ingested as a tea or in the form of a chewy sweet. Unlike LSD and mescaline, psilocybin was freely available in the countryside during early autumn. Cunliffe writes, "After a time, those in the know went on weekend nature walks and parts of idyllic pastoral Fifties Britain often resembled Seventies hippie festival sites." This, anecdotally at least, locates the genesis of recreational use of LSD and other psychedelics in Britain in the period 1956–59.[3]

There was little media or public sensationalism surrounding illegal drug use in this era. What interest there was from the fourth estate revolved around the barely concealed racist notion that West Indians and other non-whites were corrupting Britain's youth with cannabis or heroin. The possibility that young white people were, of their own volition, seeking the intense, psychedelic, experience offered by mushrooms, mescaline or LSD had not yet been dreamed of in Fleet Street's tobacco and alcohol suffused editorial meetings.

On a winter's day in late 1959, shortly after his eighteenth birthday, Cunliffe made a delivery to Samuel Thomas, a jazz trumpeter living in London's Notting Hill district. Thomas opened the package in front of Cunliffe, revealing small squares of blotting paper. "Grade A acid," he purred, suggesting Cunliffe try one. Wary at first and mindful of Thomas' reputation as a notorious conman Cunliffe hesitated briefly but, '… the mind manifesting lure was too great, and I greedily swallowed the diminutive blotter. It was truly a cosmic eruption … This was the real thing. Conversion and evangelism would soon follow."[4]

Although Cunliffe and others had limited access to LSD at this point in the late 1950s, the drug was of variable quality and its usage was largely confined to the jazz and beatnik scenes. A distinct LSD subculture was yet to form and for this to take shape a central figure was necessary. This catalyst appeared in the form of a drug user who, perversely, preferred the dreamy certainties of opiate-based drugs to the mind-expanding possibilities of psychedelics.

Several people have described Alex Trocchi as a monster. Indeed, Andrew Murray Scot's biography of Trocchi is subtitled *The Making of the Monster,* and few have anything good to say about him. One memory of Trocchi from the 1950s paints him as being, "… extraordinarily magnetic, some would say manipulative – able to get what he wanted out of people. He was very charming, but with a hint of danger."[5] Trocchi's early promise as a poet had ebbed in the wake of a failed relationship and the end of the 1950s saw him addicted to heroin, often injecting in public, eventually fleeing America as a wanted man for supplying the drug to a minor. In 1959, during his American sojourn, Trocchi encountered LSD in Los Angeles, where he took it under the guidance of Dr. Oscar Janiger, one of the early American psychedelic pioneers.

In 1962, after several years in Paris, America and Scotland, Trocchi settled in London's Notting Hill Gate. There he held court to a shifting population of counter culture heroes such as William

Burroughs and many of those who would become influential in the British hippie underground. One such visitor to Trocchi's flat was Brian Barritt, a young artist and heroin user. Barritt was no stranger to opiates, amphetamines and cannabis and equally experienced with the effects of the psychedelic compounds present in Mexican cacti and morning glory seeds. He was keen to try any drug he believed would expand his mind. But for all his experience, Barritt admits he had "no precedent for acid". His opportunity to try the drug came when Trocchi gave him twelve 250 µg doses of LSD in exchange for some ink drawings. The LSD had been sent by Michael Hollingshead from the USA and was in liquid form. Just one 250 µg dose would have provided a mind shattering psychedelic experience but Barritt decided to split the entire twelve doses between him and his girlfriend Paula; 1500 µg each. Rather than take the drug orally Barritt opted to inject the LSD.

The effect was instantaneous. "We leaned back, pressed the plungers and were out of our heads, out of north London, out of the known universe, almost before the needles were out of our arms."[6]

It's impossible to adequately describe the effects of such a powerful dose of LSD and Barritt's eloquent account in his aptly named autobiography *The Road of Excess,* only hints at what went through his mind for the next twelve hours: "... the Devil (Pan) is projected onto the bedroom wall. A huge, hair covered man-face with the corners of its mouth turned up in a lecherous satyr smile. On each side of his head, where his horns should have been, are his hind legs, all glossy with fur, as his hooves kick they draw up the corners of his mouth with each shudder so that the whole face spasms in continuous orgasm. His eyes are glowing and terrible with wisdom, but what sends my spirit soaring is not only his tremendous lust and vitality, but the gigantic humour that seethes about him. The universe was literally shaking with mirth, the earth was part of a vast Cosmic Joke – and all I had to do was to see the funny side of it! The terror of the vision suddenly shooting out at me as I opened the bedroom door had startled me nearly into panic but now I could see that it was just the joy of existence to which he was dancing, his fear inspiring mien was just the knowledge and acceptance of the mixture of awfulness and wonder that is the human condition."[7]

Fortunately Barritt's mind set was untainted by later media propaganda about the possible dangers of LSD and he clung to the belief that whatever was happening he had taken a drug the effects of which would eventually wear off. But LSD was radically different to the other drugs Barritt was acquainted with. LSD could effect permanent change in the personalities of those who took it and as he began to descend down from the peak of the experience he realised: "This LSD was serious stuff, it could change the world, and it was the key to the inner self."

If his words sound like those of a religious convert that is the closest analogy to the experience he had undergone. Barritt amplified the numinousity of his experience when he wrote, "The Psychedelic Goddess had chosen to manifest Her divine presence on this planet and I was one of the channels She had chosen."

Like Cunliffe, Barritt became an evangelist for LSD and set about spreading the word, seeing "… acid trickling through the veins of all London, changing those who wanted change …" He distributed hundreds of doses and his customers came back for more, amazed at LSD's effects and the experiences and insights it gave them. Barritt had become an LSD dealer and was buying large quantities of liquid LSD from Trocchi, who was obtaining his supplies by post from Michael Hollingshead. The LSD had to be broken down into manageable doses and Barritt found the easiest method of preparing it for distribution was to drop it onto sugar cubes. He soon discovered that LSD could be absorbed through the skin when the Tate & Lyle logo, a figure with a sugar cube for its body, leapt out at him from the box and started to dance! As with so many others who took strong doses of LSD, Barritt found that the drug raised questions about the nature of personal identity and consensus reality. This interest led him to explore other techniques of consciousness expansion, such as yoga, and he also immersed himself in magic and mysticism focusing on the works of English magician Aleister Crowley, a keen user of mescaline in the 1920s.

Barritt believes that Trocchi was crucial to the early LSD subculture in Britain. Although not a frequent user of the drug,

Trocchi was one of the first major importers and his flat became a focus for those wanting to buy, use or discuss the amazing new substance. Through this psychedelic salon Trocchi provided a fertile breeding ground for LSD users and the genesis of a London LSD scene.

While the beatniks and embryonic hippies were revelling in the wonders of the universe viewed through a psychedelic lens, others were also coming into contact with the drug, albeit sometimes unintentionally. A 1962 dinner party attended by Conservative peer Lady Lane-Fox turned out to be an unusual experience when she unwittingly ate food that had been spiked with LSD. Twenty-one years later, in 1983, she called on the Government during parliamentary Question Time to warn the public of the dangers of the drug. Yet the account she gave of her LSD experience wasn't entirely negative: "The trip I went on was quite amazing, an incredible sensation. I felt I could do anything in the world and of course that is the danger because you want to repeat the experience … I had been invited to dinner but unbeknown to me the drugs had been put in mandarin oranges. I ate them and immediately felt a million dollars."[8]

Because LSD was still legal, the medical profession could obtain it without question. This ease of access led to an interesting statement at an inquest in February 1963 during which the Coroner revealed that Willesden's Medical Officer for Health, Dr. Samuel Leff listed "… swimming and intermittently to take LSD" as being among his hobbies. Leff's friend, Dr. Leonard Henry, told the inquest, "Three years ago he asked me to supervise him having LSD, and hypnotise him so that we could study the effects, which I did." Leff had drowned and the Coroner strongly suspected this was because he was under the influence of LSD at the time, having also mistakenly injected himself with his wife's insulin. The Coroner returned an open verdict. Clearly the LSD cat was well and truly out of the bag and the substance was spreading slowly through London, permeating society at all levels.[9]

Trocchi's influence in kick-starting the British LSD subculture of the 1960s was immense. But the influential driving force behind him, and the link to the evolved psychedelic philosophies of

Leary, Metzner and Alpert was Michael Hollingshead, still with Leary in the USA. Hollingshead's relationship with Timothy Leary had soured over a variety of issues; Hollingshead's propensity for control and allegations that he had tried to blackmail Richard Alpert were among them. Leary and a hard core of psychedelic idealists had flown to Mexico to start a utopian community based on the model outlined in Aldous Huxley's novel *Island*. Hollingshead and his girlfriend Karen decanted to Jamaica where they spent several months living another kind of island life in a beach house in the grounds of Kingston's Copacabana Club. There they swam, walked and communed with nature. But true to his nature, Hollingshead wasn't satisfied and was soon yearning for London again. Tapping into his list of wealthy contacts he wrote to the world famous psychic Eileen Garret who immediately sent him a first class plane ticket to France where he spent several days as her guest. Hollingshead must have impressed the psychic because she then gave him a cheque for $3000, a considerable sum in 1962, on the proviso he wrote her a report on the Harvard-Concord prison project.

By early November 1962 Hollingshead, once again in possession of funds, was back in London, staying briefly at a flat in Brompton Square. Towards the end of November he moved to Pinefield near Battle in Sussex where he rented an old, rambling house. His description of his new home to Leary could have come straight from the pages of a H.E. Bates novel: "My dear Timothy, there is a village in South England remote from civilisation; an unvisited oasis, a symbol of what some say is reserved for the soul – a group of elms, a little turn of the parson's wall, a small paddock beyond the graveyard close, tended by one man, with a low wall of very old stone guarding it all round, a pub, a cricket green where the scent of grass in summer is breathed only by those who are native to this unvisited land."

Perhaps Hollingshead was hoping this sentimental amplification of the English archetype which he had already foisted on Leary's circle would soften their feelings towards him. From his rural idyll Hollingshead wrote Leary a series of letters in which he essentially tried to lull him into taking him back into his confidence. Of their breakdown in communication and trust Hollingshead wrote, with typical spin: "May we not now look upon all of this as a spiritual exercise – I know that I would personally prefer to forget all about it and return to the friendlier, more colourful and positive status anti-quo."[10]

The purpose of Hollingshead's return to England remains unclear. But he did everything for a reason and one odd incident which took place in 1963 has his fingerprints on it.

Maverick psychoanalyst Ronnie Laing first took LSD in 1960 becoming, by 1967, a key figure in Britain's LSD subculture. In the spring of 1963 however both he and his interest in psychedelic drugs were barely known. Laing had visited America in 1962, but had not yet encountered Timothy Leary or his circle of psychedelic initiates. His stance on LSD was diametrically opposed to Leary's, and unlike the former Harvard professor Laing did not believe LSD should be available for everyone. Yet someone desperately wanted to link Laing and Leary, as this extract from Laing's unpublished autobiography indicates. Referring to the aftermath of his trip to America Laing writes of a mysterious visitor to his Granville Road flat: "A few months later one of the self-appointed generalissimo-guru-high-priests of the acid revolution came over to see me. They were thinking of doing a similar experiment in London, but since this was my territory, if I said 'No', that would be the end of it no argument without question and if I said yes then it would be on. What would be on was this. A number of people had arranged to distribute 300,000 x 304 μg units of acid (one serious trip) in the form of pills to the 17–20 year olds especially in chosen sections of the Berkley-Bay area. Could such a collective clarification of consciousness all at once all in the same territory possibly be a spark which might spread like wildfire once lit? ... it was really changing America – how about it here? I said 'No' and that was the end of it."[11]

Though neither Leary, Metzner nor Alpert were known to have been in Britain during 1963, "one of the self-appointed generalissimo-guru-high-priests of the acid revolution" implies it must have been Leary or one of his close associates. In 1992, Laing's son Adrian asked Leary if he had been the trans-Atlantic acid evangelist only to have the notion rebuffed as "ludicrously false". In fact Laing and Leary didn't meet until October 1964. Perhaps Hollingshead, up to his old tricks again, was trying to gain Laing's cooperation in an attempt to curry favour with Leary.

Although an enthusiastic advocate of LSD use in both therapeutic and recreational circumstances, something about the visit pricked Laing's social conscience. He was only too aware of LSD's potency and potential for serious psychological disturbance and, sensing something wasn't right, he tried to report the encounter to the Home Secretary. After being told this wasn't possible he was eventually referred to "Chief Superintendent Jeffries and his colleague Sergeant Bing, of Scotland Yard".

Jeffries may have been from Scotland Yard but "Sergeant Bing" was in fact Henry "Bing" Spear from the Home Office Drugs Inspectorate. A meeting took place in which Laing disclosed details of his mysterious visitor, privately assuaging his worries about the possible indiscriminate spread of LSD.

Whether or not Hollingshead was involved in this incident, his entreaties paid off, and by the autumn of 1964 he was once again back with Leary in America. Leary had returned from Mexico, and was in the process of setting up an LSD research centre in upstate New York at Millbrook, a huge mansion rented from psychedelically inclined millionaire Billy Hitchcock. All manner of psychedelic experimentation took place at Millbrook, with Hollingshead working hard on ways of understanding, enhancing and expressing the psychedelic experience.

Leary and his coterie of psychonauts may, initially at least, have been happy to have Hollingshead back in the fold, but others were not so sure. Millbrook resident Art Kleps' first encounter with Hollingshead was "bizarre and vaguely unpleasant":

"I was in the kitchen during the first evening of my visit, talking to Ralph [Metzner] and Susan [Leary], when a tall man with unreadable features, dressed in slacks, a sport coat and a fedora with a ribbon of photographs around the brim, came twirling into the room … As this apparition spun around the table muttering to himself, Ralph's eyes narrowed and Susan took a deep breath and held it. He acted as though he wanted to sit down on one of the empty chairs but couldn't figure out how to do it. I pulled one out for him, which seemed to piss him off. He moved his arms angrily and sputtered. Still twirling, he moved out of the room.

"Susan exhaled.

"'What the fuck?' I asked.

"'Michael Hollingshead,' Ralph said, poker faced as usual."[12]

Everyone who came into contact with Hollingshead was struck by his personality and charisma, yet few seemed to like the man. It appeared that Hollingshead, while being a consummate psychedelic explorer, was a control freak. This perception was picked up even by casual visitors to Millbrook, including a journalist from the *Charlotte Observer,* who opened his article about Millbrook with: "'I am Michael Hollingshead,' says the man in the doorway, half an hour later. He is tall, thirty-ish, baldish, with cold, cruel grey eyes. 'I am your guide for the weekend. Will you follow me?' He has an English accent and a soft voice of sinister authority."[13]

Hollingshead's presence at Millbrook had an important effect on the LSD experiments there. As a confident and experienced LSD user he was good to have around, especially when the going got psychically rough. Off LSD Hollingshead was at best a difficult personality, at worst downright dangerous. But when high on psychedelics he became something else; a natural guide, a benevolent presence, someone who exuded a sense of safety. Hollingshead, for all his failings, understood LSD and, like Leary, recognised the drug's tendency to engender a desire for spiritual knowledge in those who took it.

Leary also understood the cosmic joker in Hollingshead's psychological make up, referring to the times at Millbrook when, "he would have everyone holding burning candles. With dilated eyes and spinning heads, people would follow him down ... You'd crawl through various passageways, then suddenly come around a corner where the mischievous prankster Michael Hollingshead had put a mirror! That was the ultimate confrontation with the wisest person in the world!"[14]

During this period with Leary at Millbrook, Hollingshead was still sending LSD back to various friends in London. The majority of those using the still legal drug were having the time of their lives with no adverse psychological reactions. Bad trips were few and far between and when they took place were recognised as just another part of a rich and varied experience. People began to realise they could affect the mood of an LSD trip by changing the lighting, the music or other environmental variables. Bad trips could be prevented and good trips enhanced.

Inevitably though, LSD, as with any drug which affects consciousness, was causing serious problems in some individuals. Such cases were rare, but the damage could be permanent, often resulting in admission to psychiatric wards and occasionally in suicide. Others had their mental equilibrium so disturbed that they could never again regain the quality of life they enjoyed prior to the LSD experience. LSD proselytisers dealt with these very real dangers of LSD in different ways. Some ignored them altogether. Others accepted that there were bound to be casualties with any mind expanding drug as powerful as LSD. The general consensus among the LSD subculture was that the benefits of the drug far outweighed the disadvantages and, as we will see, considerable time and effort was put into harnessing the LSD experience to prevent unpleasant experiences. But for those who reacted badly to LSD and lost everything this was little comfort.

One of Britain's earliest rockers, Vince Taylor described by Joe Strummer of The Clash as, "... the beginning of British rock'n'roll. Before him there was nothing. He was a miracle" had his career and life destroyed by a single LSD experience. The result of Taylor's encounter with LSD, and that of others who have suffered long term psychological reactions to the drug, begs the question whether these individuals had a predisposition to mental illness. In Taylor's case there is some evidence for this; his reaction to smoking cannabis on one occasion in 1962, when he believed he was in a giant coffin and couldn't recall doing his show that night, suggests undiagnosed mental problems, while on another occasion he told friends he was an aeroplane.

On 22 May 1964 he turned up late for a gig in Paris looking dishevelled and clutching a bottle of Mateus wine. In response to his band mate's concerns Taylor said, "You think I'm Vince Taylor don't you? Well I'm not, my name is Mateus, I'm the new Jesus, the son of God."[15]

The night before, in London, Taylor had taken his first LSD trip at a party thrown for Bob Dylan (who allegedly thought the quality of the drug that night to be so good he bought £200 of LSD to take back to the US).

For the next few years Taylor lived a street existence, taking more LSD and whatever other drugs he could get hold of, preaching he was Jesus Christ and wallowing in paranoid fantasies. In 1966 Taylor met David Bowie in a coffee bar, monopolizing the conversation with stories from the other side of madness. Bowie couldn't "… remember if he said he was an alien or the Son of God, but he might have been a bit of both."

Later that night Taylor showed Bowie a map of the world marked with alien bases and treasure locations. Taylor was a rock star who had lost the plot and had nowhere to go but further into his own delusions. Bowie remembered that meeting and later based his Ziggy Stardust persona on Taylor's fractured rock life.

A similar psychological fate would later befall Pink Floyd's Syd Barrett who first took LSD when it took a firm foothold in the university town of Cambridge during 1965. A small LSD scene developed there around a group of creative people, many of whom went on to become movers and shakers in the art and music world. This set included many of the future members of Pink Floyd and their immediate circle, including novelist and playwright David Gale, who remembers, "LSD came to Cambridge, and it was absolutely imperative that you take it; you had to whether you wanted to or not."[16]

LSD was introduced to Cambridge by Nigel Lesmoir-Gordon; he and his friends were already enthusiastic cannabis smokers. They also occasionally dabbled with the psychedelic compound extracted from morning glory seeds. However, morning glory seeds are much less potent than LSD and have to be chewed in bulk or made into a distasteful brew to release the active chemical. This process resulted in variable effects, often making the user so ill they couldn't enjoy the experience. Needless to say, Lesmoir-Gordon and his circle were looking for something stronger and more focused.

In early 1965 Lesmoir-Gordon moved to London to take up a place at the London School of Film Technique, moving into a flat at 101 Cromwell Road in West London. The flat was sub-let from Bill Barlow, Lesmoir-Gordon's Cambridge landlord, and through Barlow, Lesmoir-Gordon met New Zealand expatriate poet John Esam. Esam had a ready supply of LSD – obtained from Trocchi – and soon Lesmoir-Gordon had undergone his psychedelic initiation. His first LSD experience was terrifying because, he believes, he made the mistake of trying to hang on to his ego, refusing to let his consciousness blend into the experience. Nonetheless he recognised LSD's potential for psychological and spiritual change and continued to take the drug. On his second experience a friend, Mike Raggett, who had experimented with mescaline in Saudi Arabia, acted as his guide. Now, with Raggett watching over him, making positive statements such as, "you are the creator, you are god, you are everything, this is all yours,"[17] Lesmoir-Gordon was able to let go into the experience. He stared into a crumpled up tissue for up to two hours, "seeing whole universes being born and dying", listening to Bach's fugues and hearing them "as music of the spheres". He believed LSD "opened the doors of perception and thought everyone should take it." This was a feeling shared by many once they had taken LSD a few times, an evangelical urge to share this awesome, life-changing experience with others … "this is something we should all have, because this is the truth, a really powerful way of seeing the world and this amazing dance we are part of. It put me in touch with the universe. There were times when I just became the whole universe, when I thought I was infinite and eternal and utterly blessed."[18] Lesmoir-Gordon's experiences with LSD led him to conclude that the key to the secret of life was love, and that God was a creative energy called love. Accounts of people's LSD experiences may appear self-indulgent, but the insights and experiences were often indistinguishable from those gained from religious and spiritual practice and were often catalysts to major personal and life changes.

Lesmoir-Gordon was soon joined in Cromwell Road by others from Cambridge and by the end of 1965 Pink Floyd's Syd Barrett had taken up residence on the top floor where he began his descent into LSD fuelled psychoses. Esam sold Lesmoir-Gordon a bottle of liquid LSD and "I took this bottle of LSD and dropped it into sugar cubes and wrapped it in silver paper and told everyone they should take it!" He sold the psychedelic sugar for one pound per trip. Most of the other residents occupying the flats in the three floors at 101 Cromwell Road were enthusiastic LSD takers and word soon spread that it could be bought there. People visited the building every day of the week to buy LSD, many staying to have their first trip there or to repeat the experience with others in the burgeoning hippie subculture. Lesmoir-Gordon and his friends prided themselves in providing a safe place in which people could trip on LSD and they took great pains to ensure a sensuous environment was available where the music, décor and lighting was oriented specifically towards the LSD experience. This type of interior design was the forerunner of the archetypal hippie acidhead pad. Many first time LSD trippers were guided safely through their experience at 101 Cromwell Road making it what Lesmoir-Gordon called "an LSD ashram", which continued for several years.

On weekends throughout 1965 Lesmoir-Gordon would return to Cambridge, taking LSD with him to turn on friends such as Syd Barrett, and becoming known, only half jokingly, as the "acid king". When David Gale's parents left him to house-sit while they went to Australia, his friends moved in and psychedelic experimentation took over.

"Earlier in the day Syd and Paul had each taken a heroic dose, as was the custom, of LSD, on a sugar-lump. Syd had giggled for a while then become contemplative. He had found, in my mother's kitchen, a plum, an orange and a matchbox. He was sitting cross-legged on the manicured lawn, gently cradling the items in his hands, studying them intently. From time to time he would smile at them in a friendly way."[19]

On another psychedelic weekend expedition to Cambridge Lesmoir-Gordon, Syd Barrett and others took LSD and went out to a disused quarry. Lesmoir-Gordon filmed Syd looning about on LSD, the film being later erroneously marketed as *Syd's First Trip*.

Several other well-known musicians passed through 101

Cromwell Road's portals in its years as an acid ashram, Paul McCartney, Mick Jagger, P.J. Proby and Donovan among many others. All were keen to learn how to take LSD in a safe environment. Donovan was a regular visitor to Cromwell Road during his years as a psychedelic troubadour and Lesmoir-Gordon later made films with him. He enshrined the psychedelic ashram in his 1965 song, "Sunny South Kensington".

> So come loon soon down Cromwell Road, man,
> You got to spread your wings.
> A-flip out, skip out, trip-out and a-make your stand, folks.[20]

As 1965 progressed, LSD became more widely available in London. Though no more than a few hundred people at most had experienced the drug's effects, a definite subculture of post-beatniks and psychedelic mods was springing up, forming the nucleus of the hippie movement. The cultural explosion often referred to as the Swinging Sixties was happening all over London, with vibrant fashion boutiques and art exhibitions springing up on a weekly basis. "Happenings" – improvised, often spontaneous art and music events – were taking place and bright colours and abstract design were to be seen in the dress of those young people sensitive to the changing times. It is arguable how much influence LSD exerted on the fashion, art and music of the Sixties. Certainly in the latter part of the decade "psychedelic" was attached to just about everything. But this was largely a commercial response, entrepreneurs selling an ersatz, facsimile fashion trend back to people who hadn't had the core experience but who wished to identify with it. However, in 1965 this had not yet taken place, but the movers and shakers of the art, fashion and music worlds were dabbling to one degree or another with LSD and so it's a reasonable assumption that LSD use was indirectly informing hip culture, art and fashion at that time.

The Beatles were a band on whom the influence of LSD was significant and incontrovertible. They became some of the drug's most famous advocates and for many people represent an aural distillation of the psychedelic Sixties. The band had been introduced to marijuana by Bob Dylan while on an American tour in 1964 and found they liked the drug and its effects on the music they were creating. John Lennon, George Harrison and their wives were unknowingly dosed with LSD by their dentist, John Riley, in April 1965. Unaware of what they had taken and believing they had been drugged so he could inveigle them into an orgy, they fled. The realization they had taken a psychedelic drug hit them once they were in the Powick Club, after driving there in Harrison's mini, a journey which took them several centuries in LSD time. It's possible to read details of this LSD experience into the single "Help!", released in September that year. Huxley's *Doors of Perception* may have influenced "Now I find I've changed my mind and opened up the doors" and the sense of ego loss LSD brought on may have led to the line "My independence seems to vanish in the haze".

Although LSD use was on the rise, with small scenes appearing all over London, there had not as yet been a large event that brought the new underground movement together. This would take place in the summer of 1965 prompted by American beat poet Allen Ginsberg. Ginsberg was hugely popular among this burgeoning subculture. When he gave an impromptu reading at Better Books, the capital's main hip bookstore the owner, Bob Cobbing, along with poet John Esam and others decided the time was right to organise a large gathering to promote underground poetry and see who rallied to the call.

The organisers, who included the omnipresent Alex Trocchi, were bold enough to book the Royal Albert Hall for the event, billing it as the International Poetry Incarnation, to be held on 11 June. The press release made it obvious what sort of event it was, sending out subliminal messages to those in the know.

World declaration hot peace shower!
Earth's grass is free!
Cosmic poetry Visitation accidentally happening carnally!
Spontaneous planet-chant Carnival!
Mental Cosmonaut poet epiphany, immaculate
supranational Poesy insemination!

The risk that few would turn up, never mind enough to fill the Albert Hall, melted away on the day of the event. From all over London, Britain, Europe, the growing underground scene put on its finery and turned out in droves. Several thousand people turned up for the event, filling the Albert Hall, with many being turned away. Cannabis was openly smoked and it was obvious to all in attendance that they weren't alone; others who shared their interests in alternate modes of intoxication and social expression existed.

London poet Harry Fainlight was one of the readers and declaimed his LSD inspired epic "The Spider". As he did so Dutch poet Simon Vinkenoog, high on mescaline, repeatedly interrupted him and Spike Hawkins remembers "Harry dropped a grenade into the audience by saying he'd written his piece under the influence of LSD, which was considered extremely risqué at the time – especially at the Albert Hall."[21]

The event, captured on film by Peter Whitehead as *Wholly Communion* was a complete success. Friendships were forged and underground tribes came together. At the end of the day, poets and audience alike returned home encouraged by the huge attendance. The first major happening of the London underground had taken place.

Across London and in other parts of Britain hundreds, perhaps thousands, of people had now taken LSD and had experienced the permanent change in consciousness it was capable of. A few LSD experiments went badly wrong, leaving the unfortunate drug user a psychological wreck. Often those who had experienced bad trips never took LSD again. Others worked at altering set and setting to ensure there was no repetition of the experience or, should it happen, to have a way of navigating out of it.

For Dave Tomlin, one of the unsung foot soldiers of the psychedelic era, taking LSD was a cataclysmic event which severed his ties to normality and the "straight" world, plunging him into a new way of living. In 1965, Tomlin was living in Notting Dale, married and an up and coming musician, playing with one of the emergent bands on Britain's jazz circuit:

"I took my first trip in the winter of 1965 given to me by Steve

Stollman, an American jazz record producer. At that time I was playing soprano sax with the Mike Taylor modern jazz quartet and we had just recorded an LP for Decca entitled *Pendulum*. Steve gave us the acid on a sugar cube wrapped in silver foil and after taking it we went to a happening in a flat in the Cromwell Rd. From that point on the group fell apart with paranoia etc. Mike Taylor went on to write material for the rock band Cream, before walking into the sea to commit suicide."[22]

The experience had a profound and lasting effect on Tomlin: "It was like the feeling that everything you'd ever based and founded your life on was suddenly gone."

With his jazz career over and his personality in tatters it would have been logical for Tomlin to fight to regain his pre-LSD state or to seek medical help. Instead, he walked out of his house, his marriage and into the burgeoning underground where he became a key figure, becoming immersed in the London Free School, the happenings at the UFO club, and playing violin on the Third Ear Band's album, *Alchemy*.

During the summer of 1965 Michael Hollingshead started to think seriously about returning to Britain. This time his purpose was crystal clear, he wanted to spread the psychedelic gospel. In August he wrote to Alex Trocchi, outlining his plans to raise awareness of LSD in all the major European countries. This would include organizing major rallies in London, Amsterdam, Copenhagen, Stockholm and Frankfurt at which Leary, Metzner and Alpert would speak. His letter was full of enthusiasm and hope for the future and Hollingshead clearly saw himself as a missionary.

"As a European I felt the time had come for us to share with Europe some of the things we had discovered about the methodology of taking LSD in positive settings. I wanted to rid people of their inhibitions about mystical writings and demonstrate to them that *The Tibetan Book of the Dead, the Tao Te Ching,* and the *I Ching* were really basic manuals with fundamental instructions about taking LSD sessions ... From what I had heard in letters and conversations, the psychedelic movement was small and badly informed. It appeared that those who took LSD did so as a consciously defiant anti-authoritarian gesture. The spiritual content of the psychedelic experience was being overlooked."[23]

A meeting took place at Millbrook to discuss how the lessons learned there could be spread to Europe and it was agreed that Hollingshead should return to London. He was to take with him Leary's versions of the eastern spiritual classics *The Tibetan Book of the Dead* and the *Tao Te Ching* as well as copies of the new magazine devoted to mind expansion, the *Psychedelic Review*. Detailed plans were drawn up and October 1965 was chosen as the time for Hollingshead to take Leary's brand of psychedelic religion to the UK.

Although Leary appeared publicly enthusiastic about Hollingshead's planned psychedelic beachhead in Europe, privately he expressed serious doubts about Hollingshead's motivations and capabilities. Author and Sixties luminary Barry Miles recalls Leary telling him, "When Dick [Alpert] and I stood on the dock in New York waving goodbye, I said to Dick, 'Well, that writes off the psychedelic revolution in England for at least ten years.'" Hardly the sort of thing Leary would say if Hollingshead was really capable of acting as his psychedelic apostle for the planned European psychedelic revolution.

Hollingshead arrived in Britain on 5 October 1965, being picked up from Southampton docks and driven to a London hotel by his old Etonian friend Desmond O'Brien. It was decided to set up a mini-version of Leary's Millbrook and, after discussions with O'Brien, a lease was taken out on Flat 2, 25 Pont Street in London's ever fashionable Chelsea district. The World Psychedelic Centre was created with O'Brien, who had funded the expensive flat, as President of the WPC. O'Brien's financial backing came from money he had made as a Lloyd's underwriter. Like Hollingshead, O'Brien also shared a taste for opiates and amphetamines and he too soon became an addict. For some the psychedelic experience wasn't enough to transcend the desire for other, brain-deadening drugs and O'Brien could never free himself from their grip. In 1969 he was discovered in the grounds of his Cheshire estate at the side of his secret drug stash which, among other drugs, was comprised of thousands of heroin, morphine and amphetamine capsules.

London's LSD scene now consisted of several locations to which psychedelic pioneers gravitated. Trocchi's flat, the house at 101 Cromwell Road, antique dealer Christopher Gibb's luxurious Cheyne Walk residence, and now Pont Street were the major centres, each of these scenes having their own philosophy and view on how LSD should be used. Some experienced LSD users advocated doing whatever you wanted whilst tripping, as long as you were safe, having as much fun as possible and letting the insights arise spontaneously. Hollingshead held Leary's view that there should be structure to the experience which should have a guide skilled in the use and meaning of eastern sacred texts coupled with light-shows and readings. Others, such as Joey Mellen, evolved their own ideas on how the LSD experience could be made safe.

Undergraduate Mellen dropped out of Oxford before taking his finals, which would have led to a promising career as a chartered accountant in the City. His 1964 mescaline experience was, "... so wonderful that I am determined to regain that state of mind." He did, a year later, in Ibiza, courtesy of an LSD laced sugar cube given to him by Dutch medical student Bart Huges. Mellen eloquently described his experience: "I felt brilliant, god-like, able to understand everything. At the same time as being fascinated by the way I could see things as though through a magnifying glass, I could hear all the sounds of the town outside the house as well as those inside, and each perception registered quite clearly, distinct from all the others though related to them, like the various instruments in an orchestra. Now I knew what eternity meant. Time seemed to stop and still everything was moving. I was ecstatic. I kept eating sugar lumps. I could feel that this was the energy I needed to get round this universe in my brain."[24]

Through Michael Rainey, who had just started Hung On You, one of London's first psychedelic boutiques, Mellen became aware of a budding hippie scene in a flat on Cadogan Lane. He moved in, acquiring a plentiful supply of LSD from John Doyle and "Cadogan Lane became one of the happiest turn-on centres there's ever been ... I don't think anyone had a bad trip". Mellen attributed this success to another potentially dangerous compound, sugar.

He insisted that bad trips were caused by a deficit of sugar in the system of the LSD user and that if sugar lumps or confectionery were eaten throughout the trip, bad experiences would be minimised. "Sugarlack" was the term he gave to the problems he believed LSD users were encountering, and he worked hard at spreading his particular version of the LSD gospel. Sweets and sugar were always available at LSD sessions run by Mellen and he enshrined the principles of Sugarlack on a wall scroll which he gave out freely to those experimenting with LSD.

Michael Hollingshead visited the Cadogan Lane flat and was "... very impressed by the happy scene he found there. Lots of young people on acid, eating sugar, with no one putting over a big mystery scene." The emphasis was on unrestrained fun, nothing was planned and according to Mellen, "...it was just one long happening."[25]

Mellen's approach to taking LSD was very different from Hollingshead's, which was very much focused on the symbols and texts of Eastern religious systems such as Buddhism and Hinduism. Mandalas, mantras and *The Tibetan Book of the Dead* were staple fare at the World Psychedelic Centre. Although Mellen was serious about LSD as a tool for personal transformation, Hollingshead's approach to LSD sessions disquietened him, being, "... always in a darkened room, smelling of incense, with a commentary by the guru. That was the way the Americans had devised to keep people on sugarlacks in control."[26]

Whatever the differences between the two, LSD became a levelling factor and an alliance was formed, with Hollingshead supplying Mellen with as much LSD as he required. When the owner of the Cadogan Lane flat became aware of what was taking place in his property the LSD scene there came to an abrupt end and the occupants were thrown out. Mellen immediately moved into Hollingshead's Pont Street flat and observed the parade of hip young (and old) things that passed through the World Psychedelic Centre, either as observers or participants. Everyone who was anyone in swinging London wanted to be part of the growing psychedelic revolution. Among them were film maker Roman Polanski, future *Oz* magazine editor Felix Topolski and Paul McCartney.

When not hosting LSD sessions for the elite, Hollingshead kept up his friendship with Alex Trocchi and in doing so revealed yet again the dark side of his personality. On 6 December a meeting took place at which there was a breakdown of relations between the two. Trocchi wrote a heartfelt letter to Hollingshead accusing him of driving a rift between him and Desmond O'Brien. While there is no evidence the disagreement was related to LSD, Hollingshead's response is indicative that he might, once again, have been playing mind games with people. Hollingshead simply returned Trocchi's letter with the words, "What a load of balls. Don't try this kind of con again – last warning" scrawled across the top of it.[27]

At the end of 1965 Hollingshead, in festive mood, sent out a selection of hand-made psychedelic Christmas cards. A typical card was a collage made from a bizarre, detailed drawing of a man's head, imagery cut and pasted from a magazine over an abstract backdrop of paint that hinted at a face and a penis. Affixed to this mélange were a Viva Sativa cannabis badge and a provocative quote clipped from a magazine: "Bizarre reactions become normal under the influence of the controversial drug, LSD, which medical science continues to study to determine whether it is good – or evil."[28]

The first six years of the 1960s had seen recreational use of LSD in Britain develop and spread. What had once been an obscure and hard to find drug, the province of a few thrill seeking jazz musicians and beatniks, was now available to anyone with the will to look. People were still taking it for the thrills but a growing number considered it a holy sacrament and a catalyst for consciousness expansion. The drug was still legal and there had been relatively few problems with those who used it, and LSD's profile had been raised. Influential musicians such as Donovan and the Beatles had sampled LSD and were cryptically singing its praises. Word had reached the authorities that a number of psychedelic evangelists were plying their trade in London and more and more people were turning to LSD as their drug of choice. Big fun was clearly being had, minds were being blown and new ways of thinking and living were coming into being. Behind the scenes the authorities took a dim view of the untouchable goings on in flats across London.

It just wasn't the British way and it wouldn't be long before the media and the establishment took a greater interest in what was going on in sleepy London town and elsewhere in Britain. The times, to quote Bob Dylan, were very definitely changing.

7
STRANGELY STRANGE, BUT ODDLY NORMAL

Things are not what they appear.
Dr. Strangely Strange[1]

LSD took London's bohemian community by storm during 1965, leaving those who had taken it shaken and awed at the drug's effects. Under the influence of LSD many users had a numinous, often religious, experience that changed their lives irrevocably. New ways of thinking and living were being discovered as users threw off their old lives and entered the world of LSD. The new way of living embraced a kaleidoscope of elements: music, food, spiritual beliefs, anti-authoritarianism, interest in ecology and much more. The notion of the "acidhead" – someone whose life was structured around the LSD experience and vision – came into being. The effects of LSD were so powerful that some believed it couldn't have been discovered entirely by chance, investing the substance with an ill-defined supernatural origin.

Albert Hofmann took his famous LSD trip in 1943, the same year the atomic bomb was developed. For those in the LSD subculture who grew up in the Cold War with the shadow of nuclear annihilation still hanging over them, LSD represented the possibility of a worldwide shift in thought. Poet George Andrews, an enthusiastic advocate of psychedelic drugs, went so far as to claim "LSD is the only answer to the atom bomb".[2]

To the early LSD users the new drug signified unconditional love for other human beings and for planet Earth. It was this possibility of personal and planetary salvation that initially drove the LSD culture and which led eventually to its users becoming involved in a wide variety of transpersonal and ecological belief systems.

Hippie author John Michell summed up the hopes and aspirations surrounding the early use of psychedelics: "Occurring at a time when no further progress seems possible within the present system, their appearance as '*deus ex-machina*' to expand the limits of experience is remarkably opportune. It is hardly likely that their development and use at this very time can be a matter of pure chance … there is no doubt that the appearance of increasing use of mind-expanding drugs has already influenced the development of our philosophy, opening the way to what may be an entirely new series of concepts."[3]

Through the World Psychedelic Centre Michael Hollingshead sought to formalise LSD use, hoping that Timothy Leary's approach was transferable to the British LSD subculture. But by the time of Hollingshead's arrival in October 1965, the blossoming London hippie scene had begun to develop its own ways of using LSD. Some people were accepting of Hollingshead's ways; others tolerated his views on the drug because he was a source for good quality LSD and provided comfortable surroundings in which to take it. But for some his overpowering personality was too much. LSD users didn't want to be told how to take LSD, they wanted to explore the psychedelic universe themselves, and although many were in broad sympathy with Leary's thoughts about LSD, they did not want his system imposed on them by an outsider.

January 1966 found Hollingshead's hopes for a British psychedelic revolution in disarray. Though the WPC was still initiating cultural movers and shakers into the psychedelic mysteries, there were problems. The original plan, formulated with Leary at Millbrook, was that Hollingshead would act as a vanguard for Leary's brand of psychedelia. Hollingshead would use the WPC to turn key people on to LSD and Leary and Ralph Metzner would join him in Britain before Easter. They would then stage a psychedelic rally at the Albert Hall, fronted by Leary and featuring key figures from the

British underground. This, they theorised, would establish Leary and Hollingshead as leaders of the British psychedelic scene and promote Leary's pseudo-religious ideas about LSD use. But in January 1966 Leary was on bail for possession of marijuana, unable to leave America and his impending trial in February cast a long shadow over Hollingshead's plans.

The vast majority of London's LSD users neither knew nor cared about Hollingshead's problems and continued to make merry with the new chemical discovery. The parties and LSD initiations at the WPC and elsewhere in London continued unchecked. But the police and press had heard enough rumours about the new mind-altering drug and were slowly and methodically marshalling their forces against the lysergic lotus eaters.

In mid-January, Hollingshead received some unwelcome visitors at his Chelsea flat. The World Psychedelic Centre in Pont Street had been under police surveillance for much of the winter, infiltrated by undercover police officers. The scene there had become wild, the parties growing larger and noisier and with less control on who was attending. This made it easy for police disguised as hippies to mingle unnoticed among the spaced-out WPC crowd. At one party the undercover police were accidentally dosed with LSD when they sampled the fruit punch, which had been liberally spiked. Even without this, the constant stream of visitors, loud music and parties would certainly have attracted police attention. At the back of his mind Hollingshead was aware of the inevitable consequences but was "unable or unwilling to do very much about it", believing, somewhat naïvely, that the situation wouldn't get too serious.

Perhaps because of the problems with Leary or because of his unshakeable inner demons Hollingshead was also acting strangely. He had become dependent on methedrine and heroin, mixing them with LSD and rarely sleeping. Worse, he was surreptitiously giving large doses of LSD to women to whom he had taken a fancy. Spiking (giving people LSD unbeknown to them) was anathema to the LSD subculture and stories about Hollingshead's indiscretions were soon a talking point among London's drug cognoscenti. Yet again Hollingshead, the man who introduced Timothy Leary to LSD and so changed the course of history, had proved he was deeply flawed. As Amanda Fielding, Joey Mellen's partner and an early acquaintance of Hollingshead noted, "he was an extremely clever man, but a black magician at heart".[4] But Hollingshead's mind games only worked on those within his circle and not the Metropolitan Police Force. At the distinctive knock on the door the inhabitants of the WPC went into a well-rehearsed routine to hide or destroy any incriminating evidence. The ensuing search failed to turn up any LSD, but the police did find cannabis and Hollingshead, along with five others, was charged with possession. Hollingshead was also charged with allowing the flat to be used for smoking cannabis and with possession of heroin and morphine.

Though the police had failed to find LSD, the arrest of Hollingshead and friends sent shockwaves through London's psychedelic community. LSD users now had proof that the police had them under close scrutiny and the police knew exactly who the main players on the LSD scene were but were frustrated by the lack of a successful arrest. With typical disregard, Hollingshead's reaction to this worsening situation was to leave London for a skiing holiday in Switzerland. The LSD guru took adequate mind food with him, writing from Gstaad to Alex Trocchi that he hadn't had a broken leg yet because he was "too high to ski".[5]

The World Psychedelic Centre had lasted barely four months, and though it struggled on until April, it was a spent force in the development of Britain's LSD subculture. Its effect within that four month period however had been incalculable. Countless people had their first LSD experience within that Chelsea flat and the vast majority of those who had been initiated went on to spread the LSD gospel, helping the drug permeate all levels of society.

With the rise in LSD use some professionals on the fringes of the LSD scene began to speak publicly about their belief in the drug. Psychiatrist R.D. Laing, who first took LSD in 1960, was one of those who became more outspoken. At the end of January, Laing gave a paper on the "Phenomenology of Hashish, Mescaline and LSD" to psychiatrists at London Hospital. Laing had taken LSD over thirty times by the end of 1965 and was now utterly convinced of its efficacy as a therapeutic tool. His support of LSD and brand of anti-psychiatry made him popular among the underground and he became an active participant at many counter culture events. At the annual conference of the National Association for Mental Health, in the last week of February, Laing shocked the delegates with a twenty-minute speech on the therapeutic benefits of LSD. He summed up his thoughts on LSD and its place in therapy with: "An LSD or mescaline session in one person, with one set in one setting may occasion a psychotic experience. Another person, with a different set and different setting, may experience a period of super-sanity … The aim of therapy will be to enhance consciousness rather than to diminish it. Drugs of choice, if any are to be used, will be predominantly consciousness expanding drugs, rather than consciousness constrictors – the psychic energisers, not the tranquillisers."[6]

While some LSD users preferred to take the drug in the controlled and safe setting of their home, others wanted somewhere to go where they could meet others who shared their interests. Of course it was possible, if you could navigate LSD's powerful effects, to go to pubs and clubs while under the influence, but this meant mixing with the unpredictable "straight" world. Since 1965 small scale events for LSD users had been given by the LSD collective living at 101 Cromwell Road. These events featured musicians and poets sympathetic to the LSD experience, including Alex Trocchi and Harry Fainlight, as well as singer Donovan. A variety of art forms sprang from within the LSD subculture and throughout 1966 music, poetry and art was being created by LSD users for LSD users. There was still a need for regular places to perform, and so a new breed of acid entrepreneur arose to cater for the demand.

In the first few months of 1966, John "Hoppy" Hopkins put on the Spontaneous Underground at London's Marquee Club in Wardour Street. The first event on 30 January featured Donovan and by all accounts LSD was freely available. Subsequent Spontaneous Underground bands included the LSD users' favourite, Pink Floyd. The poster for their 13 March gig may have baffled the straight world but its encoded message to the acidheads was clear: "TRIP bring furniture toy prop paper rug paint balloon jumble costume mask robot candle incense ladder wheel light self all others March 13th 5pm."

Later in the year, Notting Hill Gate's All Saint's Hall hosted Dave Tomlin's ambient event the Fantasy Workshop, soon followed by a Pink Floyd gig billed as "London's farthest out group in interstellar overdrive stoned alone astronomy domine – an astral chant and other numbers from their space-age book." Syd Barrett wrote the psychedelic classic "See Emily Play" at All Saints Hall, the song a lament for his sometime muse Emily Young (now a respected sculptor).

LSD users, who preferred the term "freak" or "head" to hippie, now had a multiplicity of places to socialise and to soak up the new art forms on offer. Where once audience and performer were separate entities, the new psychedelic dance halls offered the chance to be part of the experience. The limited size of the events and the bond of psychedelic drugs meant that often the audience had some social connection with the bands performing. Psychedelic light shows, a new idea from America, often projected on several walls at the same time, depicted amoeba-like blobs one minute and distant galaxies the next. Combined with the insistent pulse of bands like Pink Floyd these events formed the perfect incubators for the burgeoning psychedelic culture.

The influence of the acid-drenched Spontaneous Underground and All Saint's Hall gigs on the development of avant garde rock music in Britain is rarely acknowledged, yet those two venues were responsible for launching the sound of a generation and a soundtrack to the LSD subculture.

After their failure to successfully arrest Hollingshead for LSD, the police stepped up their efforts, and the first LSD arrest in Britain took place in February 1966. The police had received information that John Esam was dealing LSD and though possession of the drug wasn't yet illegal, they believed selling it was. Esam's South Kensington flat was placed under surveillance and after a steady stream of visitors had been observed, a raid by the Flying Squad took place on 21 February. This time the police did find LSD in quantities that suggested Esam was selling the drug. They also discovered a syringe used by Esam to inject the sugar cubes with the correct dosage of LSD. Detective-Inspector Lynch, in charge of the raid, told Esam he shouldn't be selling

LSD because he wasn't a chemist. Esam replied, "I am quite aware of that," adding, "but until you have used this stuff [LSD] properly you do not know how exhilarating it can be."[7]

This was hardly the sort of comment likely to endear Esam to the authorities, but it demonstrated the strength of belief held by the early LSD users. They believed they had found the keys to heaven and hell. Why would they take any notice of a legal, political and social system that couldn't understand their psychedelic experimentation?

Undercover police officers visited many of London's psychedelic hot spots during early 1966 and through a combination of surveillance and infiltration they compiled a comprehensive dossier on who was using and distributing LSD. Although no official study or investigation into the use of LSD had been carried out by the government, a large amount of taxpayers' money was being spent in gathering information about the use of a legal drug. This suggests a decision had already been made that LSD was going to be outlawed and the police were now looking for some high profile arrests as justification. The media had also been very active, sending reporters to many of the same places the police had under observation.

The intense press interest came to fruition in mid-March when *London Life* heavily trailed its forthcoming LSD exposé. *London Life* was the quintessentially Swinging Sixties magazine, featuring hip society gossip, fashion, nightclubs, boutiques and music. The editor had been offered an exclusive interview with Desmond O'Brien, co-founder with Michael Hollingshead of the World Psychedelic Centre. This was O'Brien and Hollingshead's big chance to expound their LSD philosophy to a wider audience. But Hollingshead knew nothing about the interview until he saw the lurid TV advertisement. It was shown during breaks on peak time TV; cheap psychedelic visual effects with a voice-over intoning: "LSD – the drug that could turn on London. Read the exclusive story in next week's *London Life.*"

Hollingshead was appalled, but it was too late to prevent publication. Perhaps O'Brien had been caught off guard by the fact that Hugh Blackwell, one of the reporters, was a friend of

Hollingshead's and regular visitor to the WPC. Or he may have been unaware that Blackwell intended to sell his story to *London Life*. When questioned by Hollingshead, all Blackwell could offer by way of an excuse was that he was so stoned he didn't realise what he was doing.

The *London Life* interview was published on March 19, the day after Hollingshead's first court appearance following the January arrests at the WPC. Luckily the case was adjourned until May, giving Hollingshead the opportunity to read what the "straight" world thought of his psychedelic antics. Headed "The Drug That Could Become A Social Peril", the article opened with O'Brien rather unwisely introducing himself as "Mr. LSD" and claiming that anyone could take control of London in under eight hours by putting LSD in the water system.[8]

Yet if the reader ignored these unlikely tales of psychedelic terrorism and read carefully what O'Brien was saying, a clear picture of the new LSD philosophy could be discerned. O'Brien explained how carefully his LSD sessions were run and what motives lay behind the WPC: "The plan was to disseminate knowledge about LSD to responsible, intelligent people who could appreciate and benefit from its properties. It was introduced to intellectuals, writers, artists and other creative people in London as well as minor people in the lower realms of politics." This was the philosophy Aldous Huxley advocated for LSD but it wasn't exactly what had happened.

O'Brien also acknowledged that the drug could have negative effects: "It must be remembered that while normally agreeable or even beautiful sensations predominate, they are not guaranteed. Their very depth and intensity must give rise to occasional feelings of non-comprehension and disquiet."

Unfortunately these balanced considerations of the drug's use were subsumed by *London Life*'s garish accounts of people imagining themselves to be Robin Hood in Sherwood Forest. The editorial message was summed up with the portentous statement: "In these days of instant trends there is a very real danger of this dangerous drug spreading, as purple hearts did, among wider sections of the population. Who knows what moral lethargy could result?"[9]

If the *London Life* piece were not enough to worry London's psychedelic pioneers, the following day saw both the *News of the World* and the *People* enter the debate. The *People* had infiltrated the WPC so successfully they had been able to take photographs inside the flat, showing bags of sugar and psychedelic posters. The sugar was presumably there in connection with Joey Mellen's theory that it kept people calm while they were under the influence of LSD. The *People* captured the depths to which the WPC had fallen: "The Centre was deserted and in a state of considerable chaos when our investigator gained entry on Thursday. There were used hypodermic syringes, empty drug ampoules and a variety of pills. Among the litter of paper were dozens of phone numbers, some of them well-known show business stars and personalities."[10]

O'Brien was traced to his Cheshire home where he told the *People*: "You could call me Mr. LSD, but I'm not a pusher of the stuff ... Such drugs enlarge the mind, the perception and understanding of life." Among the usual uninformed dire warnings from the police and medical experts the *People* featured a lengthy story about Stewart Gunther-Rains who, they claimed, had been driven insane by his addiction to LSD. The fact that LSD is neither physically or psychologically addictive had been conveniently ignored in the paper's rush to be a player in the moral panic being stoked by the press. At another LSD centre, a flat at Emperor's Gate, West Kensington, LSD dealer Kevin Bayliss gave the *People* just what it was looking for. Bayliss cheerfully sold the undercover reporters LSD on blotting paper saying, "Just chew it and you'll have a nice scene."

News of the World reporter Charles Sandell weighed in with a piece headed "Menace of the 'Vision of Hell'". Sandell discovered he could easily purchase LSD in Chelsea for around £1 and he too stressed the possible psychiatric problems LSD could cause. A detective was quoted as saying, "It presents a much bigger threat than marijuana and purple hearts." Just why it presented such a threat was not explained. The statement, one of many such warnings about LSD issued during 1966, suggests there was concern in the corridors of power about the drug's potential for personal and social change.[11]

The media's ruthless investigation of London's LSD scene had exposed a naïvety among the psychedelic pioneers. No matter how educated and socially sophisticated the leaders of the psychedelic revolution were, they had no idea how to deal with the press. Although LSD was still legal, by allowing reporters into the WPC and other psychedelic centres O'Brien, Hollingshead and the others had played straight into the media's hands. By claiming he was "Mr. LSD", O'Brien had unwittingly painted himself as a criminal "Mr. Big". Irrespective of O'Brien's eloquence in describing the positive uses of LSD, the frightened British middle classes felt something they didn't understand was taking place, and they were only too happy to believe anything the popular press told them. Bob Dylan had summed up what the LSD users thought of the straight world on his 1965 LSD inspired album *Highway 61 Revisited* when he wrote: "Because something is happening here/But you don't know what it is/Do you Mr. Jones?"[12]

Despite their urbane cleverness in tricking the first wave of LSD proselytisers, the police and press had also made errors. In their haste to warn that LSD use caused insanity, "visions of hell" and immorality, they had inadvertently highlighted a crucial fact. At each of the properties infiltrated, observed or raided the LSD dealers had a non-stop stream of customers. Yet no one was forcing these people to use LSD, it was a conscious decision. As LSD was non-addictive it was clear that young people were using it repeatedly because they liked the experience and gained something from it. It was also clear to LSD users that despite the press hyperbole LSD did not automatically cause insanity or immorality. Firsthand reports from LSD users almost always stressed the positive effects and qualities of the drug, while the "bad trips" were simply accepted as a necessary part of the experience, to be dealt with as they arose.

London Life, the *People* and the *News of the World* were read by hundreds of thousands of readers. In their pursuit of public outrage and sales figures these news sources had also raised the public profile of LSD to an unprecedented level. Prior to March 1966 the British public had little knowledge of LSD and these exposés were the first time most young people had read anything about the drug. Now the letters LSD were a household name, and to anyone curious enough to read beyond the hyperbole the clear message was "LSD exists, it is easy to get, and it will blow your mind". What better advertisement could a drug and a subculture have?

In the same edition the *News of the World* revealed another psychedelic menace to the British public: morning glory seeds. While fulminating against their misuse, the paper explained exactly how to prepare the seeds for use as a psychedelic drug. As evidence of how popular the seeds were becoming they cited a shop owner in Richmond who had sold his entire stock of seeds to one young man. As with the media revelations about LSD, most young people were similarly ignorant of the fact that morning glory seeds could be used to get high, but following the scare story it was public knowledge. Garden centres began to notice an influx of a much younger clientele who just wanted to make the one purchase.[13]

There was an immediate knock-on effect from these revelations. The Home Office rapidly issued a statement requesting the seed trade observe a voluntary moratorium on sales of morning glory seeds. The Pharmaceutical Society of Great Britain took an immediate interest in the seed buying habits of Britain's youth and initiated an investigation. As with LSD, the press was trying to use its muscle to have a drug legislated against. That no deaths or serious illness had resulted from the use of morning glory seeds appeared to be irrelevant. The simple fact that young people had discovered a cheap, legal and effective way of getting high was enough to outrage the tabloid press.

On 7 April the Pharmaceutical Society of Great Britain reported to the Home Secretary, Roy Jenkins that "... some species of the plant could, if seeds were eaten, produce hallucinations and well-being". Could a substance that produced feelings of well-being, with no serious medical contraindications be legislated against, and if so on what grounds? The Home Secretary needed time to consider and it was noted that, "... the organisations concerned would consider separately the implications of the report and have further consultations."[14]

Throughout 1965 and 1966 Sandoz Pharmaceuticals, the Swiss

chemical manufacturer responsible for discovering, producing and distributing LSD, had become increasingly worried about the recreational use of the drug. On 15 April, after a spate of lurid LSD press stories from America, Sandoz announced it was ceasing to distribute LSD to the medical profession there, believing this would prevent LSD from leaking out to the hippies. This may have been a good public relations exercise for Sandoz but it was a futile gesture – too little, too late. The vast majority of LSD being manufactured for recreational use in America and Britain was now being made by legendary underground chemists such as Augustus Owsley Stanley III, known as Bear. It would not be long before maverick chemists would be producing Britain's own illegal LSD.

On Wednesday 6 April, Britain's first LSD court case opened when John Esam stepped into the dock at Bow Street Magistrates' Court, charged with conspiracy to distribute LSD. George Shindler, acting for the prosecution sounded unconvincing in court when he outlined the legal issues, noting that the drug did not yet come under the Misuse of Drugs Act, but hoped it would soon. Some of those in the public gallery wondered why Shindler was so hesitant and why, if LSD wasn't covered under the Misuse of Drugs Act, there was no mention of it being covered under the Poisons Act. Shindler added, perhaps in an attempt to have Esam remanded in custody, that: "It is clear that Esam is in touch with people all over the world who are taking this drug." But the magistrate was minded to grant bail to Esam and his co-defendant Russell Page, until 19 April.[15]

Following the revelations by *London Life*, the *People* and the *News of the World*, it was inevitable that LSD would come to the attention of the BBC. When it did they immediately commissioned a freelance producer, Jack Bond, to film a piece on LSD for its *24 Hours* programme.

Bond decided to film an LSD party at the home of Chelsea antique dealer Christopher Gibbs on April 16. Gibbs was well-known on the LSD scene, having been a visitor to the World Psychedelic Centre, and his Chelsea flat played host to many LSD sessions. Gibbs was an enthusiastic LSD user and for him it, "blew away the cobwebs and removed lots of layers of armour."[16] With its sumptuous decorations and view of the River Thames, Gibbs' flat was not only beautiful, it was regarded as *the* place to take LSD. The wealthy and socially mobile Chelsea set took LSD there many times and film maker Nigel Lesmoir-Gordon recalls taking LSD there with Mick Jagger.

The *People* paid £100 for a tip-off about the party's location and sent a couple of reporters to cover the story. Their report, splashed across the front page the following morning, was predictably sensational. The BBC and *People* journalists witnessed what appeared to be a wild "happening", with numerous people under the influence of LSD and other drugs. "A happening is a party at which people do whatever comes into their heads – self-expression, man" one guest at the party told the *People*. Self-expression was just a tad too much for the journalists who could make no sense of the event. Sensory overload was the order of the day, with many attendees decked out in what appeared to be fancy dress. Some people stared transfixed at temporary sculptures in one room. In another room there was a traditional psychedelic light show; and in another a surreal film was being projected. While some of the *People* article sounded plausible, other parts appeared to be fresh out of the book of drug clichés. One such questionable quote was: "Look at me, I'm high on LSD. I'm a baby again." The *People's* traditional prurience shone through in the accounts of how "Men danced with men – women danced with women" and its observation that in a darkened room where the LSD trippers were watching a light show, men and women were embracing.[17]

The BBC filmed what they could and fled, one of the crew saying, "I've had enough – that was too much for anyone to take". When the BBC saw the front page of the *People* they back-pedalled, a press officer stating, "What part of the film is used is an editorial decision. It is still not certain when we shall include this material in the programme or how much of it or in what form."

At Esam and Page's court appearance on 19 April the prosecution introduced new evidence into court. Alongside the charge of selling LSD Esam and Page were also charged with sale of DMT. DMT, or dimethyltryptamine, is a fast acting psychedelic drug several times stronger than LSD. The effects of DMT are difficult to describe but some DMT users have likened it to being launched, seemingly for eternity, into a million alternate universes, though the effects last in reality for no more than thirty minutes. DMT was available throughout the Sixties in London but due to its dramatic and unpredictable effects it was taken by relatively few people, most preferring the much more manageable and user-friendly LSD.

Once again there was some confusion in court as to just which law Esam and Page had transgressed. Esam now believed he had not broken any law and pleaded not guilty to the charges against him, reserving his defence. None of the newspaper reports about the case mention which law they were being prosecuted under and, looking at the case in retrospect, it is hard to understand why the magistrate did not discharge the pair.

John Ryman, for the prosecution, argued: "We are dealing with the use of a type of drug not considered by the courts to any extent." Here, Ryman was being disingenuous as he knew full well that until now LSD had not been considered in *any* court. He added: "We must, therefore, have the best considered judicial interpretation of these matters." The magistrate gave Esam and Page bail to allow the prosecution to organise its case. It was to be several months before they would be in court again.[18]

History shows Esam to have been correct in deciding to challenge the law. Others weren't so prescient. The first successful prosecution for LSD took place in late May when Roger Lewis, a freelance photographer, appeared at Marlborough Street Magistrate's Court charged with possessing thirteen LSD-laced sugar cubes and aiding and abetting the sale of LSD. Lewis' defence was that he had become interested in LSD after reading about it in *London Life* and that he had bought some in a Chelsea coffee bar. He pleaded guilty and was discharged on the count of possession but fined £25 for aiding the sale of LSD. It was clear to London's judiciary that Chelsea was becoming well-known as a place where LSD was frequently used and could be easily bought. In an LSD prosecution in August, involving a King's Road boutique owner, the magistrate noted: "There are too many drugs going about in Chelsea."[19]

Michael Hollingshead was sentenced on 24 May. Legal Aid had been refused and, though he could have paid for legal representation, Hollingshead's ego and megalomania got the better of him and he decided to conduct his own defence. He compounded this folly by arriving at court high on LSD which, as he notes in a classic piece of understatement, "… enhanced the unreality of the scene …" Hollingshead accepted the charges relating to cannabis, but denied being in possession of heroin and morphine, saying they had been left in his flat by a man named Arthur. Needless to say, the judiciary was unimpressed with his defence and he was sentenced to twenty-one months in custody. [20]

As prisoner 4380, Hollingshead settled down to life in London's Wormwood Scrubs and tried to make the best of a bad situation. While in prison he noted: "I myself had a reasonably steady supply of hashish, and a stash of LSD which Richard Alpert and Owsley had left during their visit to the Scrubs."[21] Hollingshead might have had LSD in prison, but once again it seems his ability to mix fact with fiction got the better of him. Owsley, a.k.a. Bear, (now living in Australia), utterly refutes this claim; "I'm sorry – your source is false about me … I never met Michael Hollingshead."[22] This is yet another example of Hollingshead's disingenuity, a mixing of fact with fiction to create a mask of public identity. All his stories, unless backed up by third party evidence, must be treated with a degree of suspicion.

Hollingshead's time in prison was uneventful, with one major exception. The MI6 agent, George Blake, imprisoned for forty-two years after it was discovered he had been passing on secrets to the Soviets, was also a prisoner in Wormwood Scrubs. During conversations with Hollingshead, Blake expressed an interest in taking LSD and one Sunday afternoon when the prison was quiet and inmates had free access between cells the pair took the drug. Initially everything was all right but Blake soon began to tense up and became paranoid that Hollingshead was working for the intelligence services and had given him a truth drug. Blake eventually calmed down, spending the final hours of his LSD experience in deep thought, reflecting to Hollingshead that he might not be able to cope with his long prison sentence. Blake escaped and fled to Russia a few weeks after his LSD trip and Hollingshead's account of his LSD trip has never been corroborated. Hollingshead, thought to be a model prisoner, also left Wormwood Scrubs, but by a more conventional transfer to the open prison at Leyhill in Gloucestershire.

With Hollingshead under lock and key and the World Psychedelic Centre closed down, the London LSD scene had lost some of its focus. Now Leary was not coming to Britain to market his brand of drug-induced religion, and in the absence of any other psychedelic gurus in London, the LSD subculture was free to develop in its own way. The purposes people used LSD for were limited only by the number of LSD users but some deserve special mention, if only to illustrate that LSD use was not all motivated by a desire for peace and love.

Terry Taylor had left England in 1963 to live in Morocco, where he pursued the life of an expatriate beatnik. He returned to London in 1966 and introduced a new strand of thought into Britain's burgeoning psychedelic culture: magic. Taylor is a fascinating character, about whom little is known. He is noteworthy in the history of LSD in Britain because his 1961 novel *Baron's Court, All Change*, featured the first fictional reference to LSD in Britain: "'Really?' my junkie friend said, sounding interested, 'What's it now? Bennies, L.S.D., or Nems?'"[23]

Taylor had been encouraged to take up writing by Colin MacInnes, and became the role model for the hero of MacInnes' tale of emergent youth culture, *Absolute Beginners*. Through MacInnes' patronage Taylor was introduced to a world of bohemian creative types such as surrealist painter Ida Kay, who would influence his interests in art and the occult. At the time of writing the novel Taylor had not yet taken LSD but his interest in it would have far reaching consequences for him as the 1960s progressed.

Baron's Court is a classic novel of London beatnik life, its nameless protagonist rebelling against straight society through fringe religion, drugs, multi-culturalism, jazz and sex. Yet it would be just another genre novel were it not for the fact Terry Taylor was thinly fictionalizing the life he lived.

In the early Sixties Taylor left Britain for Tangier. There, with other Europeans and Berber tribesmen he formed a group practising drug-induced magic. American poet Johnny Dolphin was involved in this group and in his travelogue *Journey Round an Extraordinary Planet,* describes how Taylor's magic circle used marijuana to materialise thought forms: "Each one would concentrate, projecting his inner scene. The one with the most power would make the scene that would take over the night in the Magic Room ... Terry, lean, deft and poised, prepared the kif from the dried plants, carefully selected from the Berber women's stocks. Then he would pass out the majoun cookies ... We sat backs to the wall in silence, focusing on making the scene appear."[24]

Dolphin continues: "Terry wanted to turn all London on and later helped start the process with street acid together with his tall, thin-nosed call-girl friend from Chelsea." This was an aim Taylor would soon achieve.

When Taylor returned to London he vigorously pursued his interest in the occult, now combining his rituals with LSD as well as marijuana. He formed a magic circle in Notting Hill Gate involving, among others, two hippie call girls, Bernadette Whybrow and Julia Callan-Thompson. Magic rituals are incredibly powerful psychological events in their own right. When magical practice is combined with LSD the effects of both are exponentially intensified. Taylor's group soon discovered the potent mix of magic and psychedelics to be highly effective in the evocation of thought forms to reality. But the aftermath of these sessions was physically and mentally exhausting, and the group began smoking heroin to dampen their over-stimulated imaginations. What began as an occasional calming smoke of heroin led inevitably to intravenous use and years of addiction for several of the group's members. Taylor's magic group operated in London for a few years and he and his hippie girl friends would soon become involved in Britain's first illegal LSD manufacturing and distribution network.[25]

There was a general perception among the police and public that LSD was already covered under the Poisons Act, but LSD's exact legal position was unclear. Roy Jenkins, Britain's Home Secretary, believed LSD was dangerous and wanted the drug brought under the umbrella of the Misuse of Drugs Act 1964, so events were set in motion to achieve this. Jenkins' decision to deal with LSD had been influenced by a variety of factors. The increasing number of ill-informed scare stories in the media, plus pressure from some sectors of the medical establishment, contributed to a general sense of unease that LSD was a problem which needed dealing with rapidly. If Jenkins allowed LSD to remain legal it would call into question the reason for legislation against other consciousness-altering drugs. This would open a debate the government did not want and so Jenkins found himself in a situation where he had no choice but to support legislation curbing the possession and use of LSD.

In June the *British Medical Journal* published a leading article calling for LSD to be made illegal. Citing a study of 129 people who had received LSD therapy, the *BMJ* claimed that two patients committed suicide and four others attempted to take their own life. The study was flawed though as there was no attempt to determine whether or any of the deaths and attempted suicides was as a result of taking LSD or whether there was a predisposition to suicide. For this study to have had any validity, a control group of subjects without identified mental health problems would have been needed, as well as a group who took no LSD at all.[26]

On 21 July, Roy Jenkins laid before Parliament a draft Order adding LSD to the Misuse of Drugs Act, which would make it illegal to possess, manufacture or deal LSD. This announcement was widely reported in the media, leading to an irate memo to the Home Office from G.P. Clements of H.M. Customs and Excise. Clements was annoyed he had only discovered that the importation of LSD was to be made illegal after it had been discussed on BBC's *24 Hours* news and current affairs programme. In a phone call to R. Bamfield, head of the Home Office's drugs branch, Clements also learned that the Home Office only planned to tell Customs and Excise about the new legislation *after* it had been passed! It is uncertain whether this was a measure of the general lack of communication between government departments or an intention to present Customs and Excise with a fait acompli which they had no choice but to accept. [27]

During the amendments to the Misuse of Drugs Act 1964, an

interesting discussion took place when the law was put before the House of Lords. Lord Stonham introduced the debate by summing up the drug's medical and social uses, surprisingly failing to mention any of the alleged dangers. An air of nervous jollity attended the brief debate, with the Conservative Lord Sandford noting, "... the government, with all their troubles did not want to contend with hallucinations as well." This prompted widespread laughter in the House. Lord Saltoun, recalling a snippet from a newspaper article on one of the effects noted by psychiatrists, asked, "Does not LSD enable you to remember what happened when you were born?" Lord Stonham replied, demonstrating his ignorance of the effects and reasons for taking LSD, "The effect of creating hallucinations is not to enable you to remember back, but rather to forget and to imagine you are otherwise and otherwhere than you are. LSD is not the only substance which can create that illusion. I have known people who felt they could fly on four pints of bitter." By now the House was in an uproar of laughter at Stonham's childish humour and the motion was agreed without further debate.[28]

Media reports about the looming illegalization of LSD triggered a furore in the world of LSD therapy, provoking several people to speak out in the drug's defence. Dr. Bhattacharya, who had treated 581 patients with LSD, wrote to the *British Medical Journal* vigorously defending the medical use of the drug. "I do not consider LSD to be a 'miracle' drug, but certainly consider its assistance immensely valuable in certain forms of psychiatric illness ... There were no cases of suicidal attempts and at no time did any patient produce any bizarre behaviour which was beyond our control."[29]

Other commentators applauded the coming change in the law and were scathing about the alleged benefits of LSD. Writing in the *Sunday Times,* Alan Bestic launched into a tirade against LSD. He compared the drug to heroin and suggested that heroin addicts, "that raggedy army", and LSD users were one and the same. Bestic argued that LSD was liable to severely damage the minds of those who took it and that claims LSD provided insight or illumination were "almost certainly untrue". Bestic offered no evidence to support his assertions and the article was little more than an attempt to give conservative *Sunday Times* readers what they expected to hear. His final paragraph was a call to arms against LSD and a rather paranoid warning about the future, "If action is not taken quickly – and by that I mean within the next few months – that raggedy army will have grown so large that it will be unbeatable; and by that time it could well be receiving its arms from the professionals, who know a good market when they see one."[30]

Meanwhile, the correspondence between the Home Office and H.M. Customs continued. Customs, now reconciled to the fact they were expected to police importation of LSD into Britain, protested that they had little knowledge of what form LSD came in or how to identify or find it. The Laboratory of the Government Chemist, part of the Ministry of Technology, was called upon to provide Customs with facts about LSD, which they did in a lengthy and detailed letter. But even the Home Office were not above repeating unverified facts about LSD and one internal memo claimed: "As to identification, we hear that LSD is now stored on toast as well as sugar lumps or blotting paper!" The origin of the LSD on toast rumour is unknown, and there is certainly no evidence toast was ever used as a delivery system, but the canard was repeated several times in Home Office memos, thus making it Britain's first official LSD urban legend![31]

LSD became illegal to possess or distribute on 9 September 1966, a month before it was outlawed in the USA. The only exceptions to the law were doctors, who could still prescribe the drug and use it in psychotherapy. To do that they had to go through a licensed importer, soon to be limited to only one company. Shortly before it was outlawed Jonathan Aitken, then a minor figure in the Conservative party, made headline news when he took LSD and reported his experiences for London's *Evening Standard*. Unsurprisingly the story was splashed across the front page. Aitken told of seeing "visions of hell. Continents dripping with blood. Black men fighting brown men, fighting yellow men." These negative quotes have become attached to his LSD experiment, but Aitken also noted that he had considerable positive insight into his problems and into his future. Aitken didn't record exactly what he saw in his future but it's unlikely that he could have foreseen the fall from political grace which culminated with him being sentenced to prison for perjury in 1999.[32]

As part of the LSD criminalization process the Government also took a long look at who was licensed to import LSD into Britain. In April 1966 thirty-one companies were issued with licenses which would allow them to import LSD if they wished. These companies were mainly chemists and drug manufacturing firms. The Home Office changed the law so that licenses to import drugs would no longer include LSD by default, and a specific requirement would be needed to import it. By early 1967 only Brocades GB were licensed to import LSD into Britain. This meant that any LSD used recreationally after 9 September was made illegally and imported from overseas. America and Holland were the main producers of illegal LSD at this time but now a clandestine LSD laboratory had been set up in London, producing large quantities of high quality LSD for distribution in Britain and elsewhere.

John Esam's conspiracy to sell LSD case finally came to trial at the Old Bailey in October. During the two day trial the jury could not reach an agreement as to Esam's guilt or innocence and a re-trial was planned for January 1967.

Commercial enterprises connected to the rapidly expanding hippie subculture had been springing up throughout 1966. Barry Miles' Better Books and Indica gallery had proved there was a place for shops selling reading material and art geared towards the broad spectrum of counter culture interests. The logical next step was a counter culture newspaper, "... a paper for the 6000 at the Albert Hall, a paper for the people living in cheap rooms in Notting Hill Gate, Covent Garden, Ladbroke Grove, Chalk Farm." These areas were known to the hippies simply as the Gate, the Garden, the Grove and the Farm and were the main constituencies of LSD users in London during the Sixties and Seventies. Miles, Hopkins and others put their heads together, drew on their many contacts and connections and created *International Times,* or *IT* as it was often called.[33]

The paper was launched at 11.00 pm on 14 October at the

Roundhouse in Chalk Farm. The gig, organised by Hoppy, featured Soft Machine and Pink Floyd and drew over 3000 people. In a nod to the zeitgeist, those in the queue were met by a figure offering sugar cubes from a tray. Some said all the cubes were dosed with LSD, others that one in ten were. In fact none were. In any case LSD was in plentiful supply once inside, but the inference was obvious, *IT* was *the* paper for LSD users. Rock musician and writer Mick Farren later wrote of the event that it was more than a rock show it was "the germ of a new way of life".[34] The first issue of *IT* carried a round up of the year's main LSD-related news, and until the paper's eventual demise in the mid-Eighties it provided news and opinion about many facets of LSD culture.

Paul McCartney's curiosity about LSD had been growing steadily throughout 1966. He'd visited the WPC in Chelsea in 1965 and fellow Beatles John and George had told him about their wonderful experiences with LSD. In fact, most people he knew had become "experienced" to put it in the hip jargon of the day, but he'd been putting it off. Eventually, more out of peer pressure than anything else, McCartney took the leap.

At the end of an evening of nightclubbing he found himself at Guinness heir, Tara Browne's hip mews house, where a small party was underway. "Tara was taking acid on blotting paper in the toilet. He invited me to have some … And that night I thought, well, this is as good a time as any, so I said, 'Go on then, fine.' So we all did it."[35]

McCartney had a good time that night. He told his biographer Barry Miles it was "quite spacey". The Beatle went on to have many more LSD experiences but was never as attached to it as John Lennon. McCartney concedes though, that he was never the same after LSD and was later to make a very public statement about his use of the psychedelic.

Not long after his LSD trip with McCartney, socialite Tara Browne tragically died in a car accident. In the early hours of 18 December he rammed his Lotus Elan into the back of a parked car. The twenty-one year old had been a habitué of Swinging London's nightclubs and was popular with various members of the Beatles and the Rolling Stones. Browne was a frequent LSD user, often tripping the night away with the Stones' fill-fated guitarist Brian Jones. Keith Richards and his girlfriend Anita Pallenberg were also among the circle of rock aristocracy in which he moved, and Pallenberg vividly recalls driving round London with Browne one LSD-drenched night. "He had a Lotus sportscar and suddenly near Sloane Square everything went red. The lights went red, the trees were flaming and we just jumped out of the car and left it there."[36]

Hoppy Hopkins' success with the Spontaneous Underground and events such as the *IT* launch led him to realise there was a market for larger and more regular psychedelic events. Teaming up with American record producer Joe Boyd, they rented a struggling Irish drinking establishment, The Blarney Club on Tottenham Court Road, and turned it into London's most successful club for the psychedelic generation. The club later became know as the UFO club, UFO standing for Unlimited Freak Out, or Unidentified Flying Object. But in its early days UFO was only part of the club's name. The main name on the flyer for the club's launch on 23 December was Night Tripper, an obvious reference to LSD users, over a gyrating female hippie dancer. UFO would be the home for the LSD subculture's London adventures until its closure. Boyd summed up the essence of a visit to the club "... at UFO the grinning crocodile of psychedelics wrapped its lips around your ankle, dragged you in and licked you all over."[37]

As 1966 drew to a close there was a final blast of authoritarianism when the United Nations commission on narcotic drugs made a public announcement. The UN called on all world governments to put stringent controls in place to prevent manufacture, sale or use of LSD. The days of legal LSD were ending not only in Britain and America, but across the world.

The year 1966 was pivotal in the history of LSD. Close scrutiny of the LSD subculture by the media and police led to the drug being legislated against and its users demonised. In the space of twelve months the drug had risen from being an obscure chemical, used as a religious sacrament by a few psychonauts, to a household word that filled "straight" society with dread. Though the media and political establishment tried to give the public the impression they had the measure of LSD, its users and their aspirations, in reality they were ignorant. Legislation against LSD had been rushed through Parliament and was not driven by medical evidence or the result of any medical trial or study. There is no evidence in government documents to indicate that the legislation was driven by anything other than fear of the unknown, media hyperbole and international pressure.

If the authorities seriously believed that legislation would curb LSD use they should have looked at their existing drug policy, which had done little to stem the increase in recreational drugs. In treating LSD as just another recreational drug such as the opiates, heroin and marijuana the establishment had overlooked many crucial factors which influenced and informed the growing LSD subculture.

LSD was a new drug, whereas existing recreational drugs had a long history of recreational use across a range of countries and social contexts. None of these drugs had a philosophical underpinning in western society in the way that LSD had, first with Heard and Huxley and later with Hollingshead and Leary. Unlike existing recreational drugs, LSD was advocated as having a purpose other than simply to get high. For LSD users the psychedelic experience was about enhanced and expanded perception, a way to see the world as it really was, the Blakean vision of seeing "a world in a grain of sand and heaven in a wild flower, hold infinity in the palm of your hand and eternity in an hour". In short LSD provided a numinous experience unmediated by a religious hierarchy or sacred text.

In the early days of LSD use those who were primarily attracted to it were creative individuals who sought out novelty, change and insight into the human condition. LSD provided this and much more. LSD radically altered one's perception of the world and many users found they could not easily step back into the grey three dimensional worlds of work and superficial social relationships. The remaining years of the Sixties would see the LSD subculture develop further but the halcyon innocence of pre-legislation LSD were gone. The committed LSD users, whether rich Chelsea socialites such as Christopher Gibbs or working class street hippies such as Dave Tomlin and the thousands in between, would need new sources of LSD. And that meant illegal LSD laboratories and the rise of the outlaw LSD chemist.

8

SENSES WORKING OVERTIME

> You know what happens when you take acid; your conceptual framework gets sort of ripped apart for a few hours. I think really the acid wave hit in 67.
>
> Hoppy Hopkins[1]

The year 1967 is the one people most closely associate with hippies, the counter culture and LSD. It is a time often referred to in cultural shorthand as the "summer of love", conjuring up images of flower-bedecked youth, the "love-in", happenings and drug fuelled bacchanalia. At the start of the year LSD was still only of relatively minor interest to those not actively involved in its use. But there was a slowly intensifying background media buzz about the drug which, by the end of the year, would ensure no adult in Britain was ignorant of what "LSD" meant or what the drug represented.

Anyone intrigued by LSD may have spent the dying days of 1966 being mildly amused by the record given away with 23 December issue of the satirical magazine *Private Eye*. Mystery vocalist Whispering Jim Narg wrote and sang one of the tracks, "Psychedelic Baby", the lyric imploring:

Psychedelic baby, won't you take a trip with me
Dip your lump of sugar in the LSD
If you want a kinky caper
Then suck the blotting paper
Psychedelic baby, with me.[2]

The significance of this little known song is that it is the first time the term LSD or psychedelic appears in British music. The Pretty Things had cut a song the year before called "£.S.D". The chorus ran "yes I need LSD"[3] and though clearly about the drug both the lyrics and the way the title was written were done to make people think it was about money, not drugs. Narg's song, therefore, was the first to refer directly to the drug. It is also noteworthy for being the earliest public reference to blotting paper being used as a carrier for LSD. That *Private Eye* was satirizing the drug was proof positive that it was now a well-established part of the swinging London scene. Whispering Jim Narg was Dudley Moore, one of the new wave of young, university-educated English comedians. Moore, incidentally, was a patient and friend of John Riley, the private dentist who turned John Lennon and George Harrison on to LSD in 1966. In January 1967, Moore, together with comedy partner and *Private Eye* founder Peter Cook, released the single "L.S. Bumble Bee" of which he said: "Peter Cook and I recorded that song about the time when there was so much fuss about LSD, and when everybody thought that 'Lucy in the Sky with Diamonds' was a reference to drugs. The exciting alternative offered to the world was L.S.B!"[4]

On 17 January, while the Beatles were in the studio putting the finishing touches to their forthcoming LP *Sgt Pepper's Lonely Hearts Club Band,* John Esam and Russell Page's trial for distributing LSD came to a dramatic conclusion in London's Central Criminal Court. The prosecution was confident that the discovery of LSD allegedly worth over £100,000 would result in conviction and a lengthy sentence for the defendants. They had even engaged the services of Dr. Albert Hofmann, the creator of LSD, who flew in from Switzerland to give evidence at the trial. But Esam, equally confident he had done nothing wrong, mounted a vigorous defence. He engaged the services of Professor Ernest Chain, who had won a Nobel Prize for his work in developing penicillin as an antibiotic.

Chain took the witness stand and argued that LSD did not conform to the poison rules in existence at the time of the raid, and therefore Esam could not be found guilty. Hofmann claimed LSD could be termed a poison and therefore came under the Poisons Act. Neither side would back down, so the decision was left to the jury who accepted Chain's evidence. The judge had little option but to acquit Esam and Page of conspiring unlawfully to sell LSD. After the trial Judge Graham Roberts was at pains to point out to the press that LSD was now illegal to possess or sell and that: "It is important that this should be known so that other people do not think the jury's verdict is a licence to use this drug, because it is not."[5]

The popular media were disappointed. They had been watching Esam's trial with interest, hoping he would be found guilty so they could run yet another series of self righteous LSD exposés on the back of his court case. Esam's acquittal took the sheen off the media's zeal but didn't deter them from bringing LSD to the public's attention again. Just as they had done in the early months of 1966, journalists had once again been scouring London's pubs and clubs in an attempt to dig some dirt on LSD users. Now they were focusing on the use of LSD by musicians, a quest stimulated by several pop musicians' reference to LSD in their lyrics and in interviews.

Donovan, the psychedelic troubadour who had already made oblique reference to LSD and the Cromwell Road scene in a 1966 song, was their first target. On the last Sunday in January the *News of the World* ran a two page investigation into his drug habits. "Sunshine Superman", the title track from his as yet unreleased LP was heading up the pop charts in Britain and the *News of the World* immediately seized on the opening line: "Sunshine came softly through my window today, could have tripped out easy but I've changed my ways." The fact that this was a song recorded over a year previously and the lyric claimed he'd changed his drug taking ways was immaterial to the paper as they delved further into the song. "I'll pick up your hand and slowly blow your little mind" was also evidence to the journalists that Donovan was actively trying to corrupt the morals of his listeners.[6]

Journalists were dispatched to chat, incognito, to Donovan at a "happening" at 101 Cromwell Road. Their alleged conversations with the singer were earnestly repeated verbatim for the readers, Donovan claiming he used LSD regularly. The paper also found a fan, Suzanne Lloyd, who claimed she had fallen under Donovan's spell and lived at his flat for a while where she saw Donovan and friends often taking LSD.

Though there was some truth in the *News of the World's* exposé of Donovan's lifestyle, the tone was one of pure sensationalism. The Move, another pop group who were turning psychedelic, were also fingered as LSD fiends in the same article. Their single, "Night of Fear", which reached number two in the pop charts, was examined and lyrics such as "Your brain calls out for help that's never there/The silent night has turned to a night of fear" and a chorus of "Just about to flip your mind, just about to trip your mind", were offered up as evidence of The Move's interest in LSD.[7]

For their investigation in the following Sunday's edition, the *News of the World* changed their target and went after the Moody Blues. Once again they delved into interviews and lyrics, pulling out anything which even hinted at drug use. The group's house close to the River Thames at Roehampton was identified as a place where they and other musicians regularly took LSD. This exposé had little impact on the band whose manager, Phil Robertson, was open about their use of LSD, freely admitting the band used the drug. LSD philosophy began to permeate the Moody Blues' lyrics and song titles; their 1968 LP *In Search of the Lost Chord* featured the track "Legend of a Mind", written about Tim Leary and with lines like, "To the little man who sells you thrills along the pier. He'll take you up, he'll bring you down".[8]

In their third portrayal of the music and LSD scene in Britain the *News of the World* dug a little deeper. They correctly identified the London Free School and *International Times* as being focuses for LSD use and information and linked Pink Floyd with the emerging psychedelic drug scene. Tim Leary's role in the psychedelic

Left: God is alive in a sugar cube badge

Below: Dr. Ronald Sandison, the first person to bring LSD to Britain and pioneered its use in psychotherapy

Above: Michael Hollingshead's hand made card with psychedelic text/art. Christmas 1965

Above: Timothy Leary (left)

Above: UFO club advertisement from the *International Times*

Above: Victor Kapur's LSD laboratory in London, 1967

Above: Michael Hollingshead, Nepal, 1969

Left: A 1960s LSD party, London

Right: Granny Takes a Trip, London boutique

Above: American poet, Allen Ginsberg on LSD in the Black Mountains, Wales, 1967

Right: Publicity flyer for *The Trip*

Above: Movers and shakers: author John Michell (left) and DJ Jeff Dexter (right)

Right: A late Sixties LSD poster, popular with acidheads

TAKING A TRIP?
GO LSD
THE ONLY WAY TO FLY!
SEE YOUR
TRAVEL AGENT

Below: Hampshire Drug Squad at the Isle of Wight festival, 1970

Above: Bill Dwyer, London LSD dealer and organizer of the Windsor Free Festivals

Above: Sign outside a tent at the Stonehenge Free Festival

Above: Acidhead, Jeremy Dunn holding the newspaper giving details of the sentences passed on the Operation Julie chemists

Above: Christine Bott – Operation Julie

Above: Operation Julie graffiti on an Edinburgh building

Above: Graffiti relating to Operation Julie, on a west London building

Above: Operation Julie police chiefs being commended, 1978

Above: Casey Hardison's LSD laboratory, 2004

Above: Casey Hardison's LSD laboratory, 2004

Above: Blotter LSD seized at Hardison's laboratory

Above: Sheet of LSD blotter art, signed by Albert Hofmann

revolution was also acknowledged, his book *The Psychedelic Experience*, being referred to as "... a sort of text book for the LSD cult ..."[9]

As they had done in 1966, the *News of the World*, under the guise of informing their readers about the growing use of LSD, had actually acted as an advertisement for the drug. Even in early 1967 there were still far fewer users of LSD than the media imagined. By explaining exactly what LSD was, its cost and its effects, *News of the World* gave thousands of teenagers a glimpse into a way of life they desperately wanted to be part of. Associating LSD's use with pop and rock musicians and explaining the drug references in their lyrics enabled any adolescent with a sense of adventure easy access to all he or she needed to know to get involved in psychedelia. To an extent the unwitting media promotion of LSD led to thousands of young people throughout Britain becoming more knowledgeable about the drug than they would otherwise have been. As the winter of 1967 thawed into the warmer months, many of them trekked to London and other large conurbations to seek and join the LSD scenes there.

The power of the press in promoting LSD use cannot be underestimated. The media may not have actually caused anyone to take LSD against their wishes but their detailed reporting of its effects, prices and availability did everything but that. Record Producer Dave "Boss" Goodman recalls that as a mod he first came across LSD in the *News of the World* and the report he read made him immediately want to obtain some of the drug. Within a short period of time he was heavily involved in LSD dealing: "Down in the basement we've got the bottles we used to mix the crystal acid with distilled water and drip it in single trips onto sugar cubes or blotting paper."[10]

LSD was available to the *News of the World* reporters at between 30 shillings (£1.50) and £2 per dose, either on sugar cubes or on blotting paper. LSD powder in capsules and pill form was also on offer and it was clear from the media coverage in the first few months of 1967 that LSD could be obtained easily in most of Britain's major cities. Sandoz's decision to stop supplying it to the medical profession seemed to have had no effect on the supply so it was clear that LSD for recreational use wasn't coming from them. But just where the drug was coming from was a mystery to the media and the police. No LSD had as yet been seized by customs and no British LSD laboratories had been located. But the Metropolitan Police's Drug Squad had picked up vague hints and rumours that a major LSD laboratory was operating in London and was supplying not only much of the high quality LSD available in the capital but was also exporting it to the USA. All they had to do was find it.

In their attempt to alert the British public to the supposed dangers of LSD the *News of the World* made a serious error in the 5 February edition of the paper. Among the truths, half-truths and speculations about the drug habits of pop musicians was a paragraph which read: "Another pop idol who admits he has sampled LSD and other drugs is Mick Jagger of the Rolling Stones. He too was a visitor at the Roehampton home of the Moody Blues."[11]

Jagger was horrified and immediately issued a statement: "I am shocked that a responsible paper like the *News of the World* can publish such a defamatory article about me. I want to make it quite clear that this picture of me is misleading and untrue, and therefore the only way left for me to prevent this libel being repeated is for me to ask my lawyer to take action in the High Court immediately." The Rolling Stones appeared on the Eamon Andrews show that same evening and Jagger made clear his intent to sue the paper. Two days later Jagger's lawyer issued a libel writ against the *News of the World*.[12]

By issuing a legal challenge to one of Britain's most powerful and wealthy newspapers Jagger must have known he was taking a risk. Not a financial risk – the Rolling Stones could easily play the money game – but the risk of further tabloid attention being focused on the Stones' bohemian lifestyle. As a consequence of the writ, Jagger and the Rolling Stones were pursued by journalists even more than was usual for the next few days. The following Saturday after an evening recording session Jagger, his girlfriend Marianne Faithful and Keith Richards, together with several others from the Stones' inner circle, drove down to Richards' moated country residence, Redlands, in Sussex. George Harrison and his girlfriend joined them later.

After partying long into the night the Stones and their entourage were woken the following morning by one David Schneiderman and offered a tab of white lightning LSD with their cup of tea. Several of the group accepted the offer and the day dissolved into a psychedelic haze as they drove round the wintry Sussex countryside. Richards: "The weird twist is that we were all on acid … and I'm seeing bursts, angels flying around." In the evening as they were coming down from the LSD, the police arrived with a warrant. All the guests were searched and questioned and a variety of substances were taken away for analysis.[13]

David Schneiderman was new to the Stones' inner circle, having met Richards only once before, a year earlier in New York. He turned up in London a week before the Redlands drug raid and was invited to join the party there by Richards. Schneiderman was known as the "acid king" and according to Christopher Gibbs: "Schneiderman had a swag bag overflowing with every kind of mind-altering substance, including white lightening and dimethyltriptamine [DMT], which was a real revelation to all of us …"[14] During the raid, Schneiderman dissuaded the police from opening his attaché case by claiming it contained exposed film for a New York newspaper. Had they opened it the police would have found a treasure trove of psychedelic drugs.

At the trial in June the Stones' defence lawyer, Michael Havers QC pointed the finger firmly at the *News of the World,* claiming they had tipped the police off about the drug party at Redlands. Richards agreed and, going a step further, alleged that Schneiderman had been a *News of the World* plant in order to get Jagger arrested for drug use, thus undermining the writ he had issued against the paper. Schneiderman, the only person found by the police to be in possession of cannabis and the supplier of the LSD for the party, was not in court to defend these allegations. He left the UK within a day of the police raid and did not return for his trial. No one seems to have known who he really was and he has not surfaced since the police raid. Speculation is rife that he may have been an undercover agent employed by US or British intelligence services, but there is no hard evidence to support that. Yet his sudden appearance and disappearance, together with his access to large amounts of LSD, casts a shadow of mystery over him.

The description of him given by Christopher Gibbs paints a picture of a typical intelligence service operative or "spook": "The infamous David Schneiderman, on the other hand, was a pied piperish character, who the hell he was and where he came from, nobody knew, he had just popped up. He was able to tune into everybody's wavelength and was seductive, satanic, the devil in his most beguiling of disguises. After the bust he vanished as devils do, in a puff of smoke, and was never seen again."[15]

Though Jagger refused to acknowledge his LSD use at the trial and the *News of the World* denied being involved in tipping off the police, both parties were being somewhat disingenuous. Ex-Police Constable Don Rambridge, who was part of the police team who carried out the raid, said later: "It was the *News of the World* story that put us on the boys, backed up with some other information from a reliable source." Rambridge also noted that Stan Cudmore, the Detective Sergeant in charge: "… had the link with the press."[16]

If true this is yet more evidence that in the middle years of the Sixties the popular press and police were working together to bring drug cases against leading musicians, and focusing specifically on their LSD use. Rambridge's claims were given further credence by the strangely coy account of the raid published in the 19 February edition of the *News of the World*. Though the paper knew who had been at the party the report gave no names or even an indication of where the party had taken place. That they knew the intimate details of what had taken place at Redlands was evidenced by their knowledge that, minutes before the raid, "… one pop star and his wife drove off and so quite unwittingly escaped the net". This was George Harrison and his girlfriend, clearly allowed to leave before the raid took place. The Beatles, at this stage, were still enjoying a positive image in the media, while the Rolling Stones were the bad boys of rock when it came to drugs and sex.[17]

The paper also understood that, "… at least one person present is believed to have been in possession of the drug LSD, a tiny dose of which gives up to 16 hours of hallucinations." No LSD was found and nor was anyone charged with its possession. The *News of the World* could only have known LSD was present if they knew of the contents of Schneiderman's attaché case. And if they knew about that, whoever Schneiderman was working for, he was at the very least in touch with journalists at the *News of the World*.

Jagger, meanwhile, had spent some of the intervening time between the drug raid and the trial in Marrakesh. There he met up with the photographer Sir Cecil Beaton, Jagger claiming LSD was: "… like the atom bomb. Once it's been discovered it can never be forgotten, and it's too easy too make."[18]

LSD was rapidly permeating all levels of society. It was coming out of the private house parties and becoming entrenched in the nightclubs frequented by the glitterati of swinging London. Record producer Simon Napier-Bell noticed the increase in LSD use in 1967 when the atmosphere at South Kensington's Cromwellian Club, normally full of noise and gossip, changed. The regulars there were now often silent: "… they just stared into space and said how beautiful everything looked. It was acid."[19]

While pop stars, minor aristocracy and the rich and famous were happy to take their LSD in exclusive clubs, and private country retreats, the growing numbers of hippies in London were attracted to clubs such as UFO, Middle Earth and Happening 44. LSD was a feature at these nightspots, available cheaply or even given away. Dave Tomlin, a regular at UFO, recalls the acid ambience: "Foxy girls with heavy mascara slink in the candlelit shadows, where sugar cubes receive their globule of nectar from the tip of a glass dropper, to be sucked like lemon drops by hopeful trippers intent on adding spice to the night."[20]

Inevitably the media were infiltrating the hippie nightspots to file reports for their outraged readers. When the *People* discovered that the Electric Garden club was in Covent Garden, just round the corner from their offices, they immediately sent reporter Patrick Kent to see what was going on. Somewhat predictably he saw lots of hippies involved in a happening, many of them under the influence of drugs. The hippie cult, Kent opined in his last paragraph, was: "… degrading, decadent and just plain daft."[21]

Occasionally, presaging the festivals to come, hippie celebrations broke free of the subterranean clubs. At one-off events such as the

"14 Hour Technicolour Dream", held on 29 April 1967 at Alexandra Palace, they gathered in large numbers. Over thirty bands spread across two stages took the hippie masses through the night until dawn. A huge light show projected coloured bubbles and abstract patterns onto billowing white sheets, while fairground rides and inflatables added to the sensory overload.

The cream of London's psychedelia was at the event both as performers and participants. John Lennon wandered freely through the audience and the bands included Soft Machine, the Crazy World of Arthur Brown, and of course the band that perhaps most represented the experience of LSD at the time, Pink Floyd. Pink Floyd manager, Peter Jenner remembers the experience well: "That really was the most psychedelic experience that I've ever been to. At least half the audience was doing acid. I was doing acid … I did some acid before we went, and by the time I got to Alexandra Palace the old acid was beginning to go and trying to drive the van was getting quite exciting."[22]

As dawn broke the sun's light began to filter through Alexandra Palace's huge windows, transforming the Victorian "People's Palace" into a psychedelic cathedral. For many hippies there it was the moment they had been waiting for. Pink Floyd, Syd Barrett high on acid, was playing and it was a high point, in all senses of the word, for psychedelic culture. Peter Jenner recalled: "The band played at dawn with all the light coming through the glass at the Palace, the high point of the psychedelic era for me. It was a perfect setting, everyone had been waiting for them and everybody was on acid; that event was the peak of acid use in England ... Everybody was on it: the bands, the organisers, the audience, and I certainly was."[23]

But the idea of putting almost ten thousand people, even hippies, together for several hours had its faults. Pink Floyd lighting engineer, Peter Wynne-Wilson saw another side to the hippie dream: "I can remember thinking that the drug situation had got extremely messy and perverted because there were people completely in a state because of drink and drugs. And it seemed to me to be a real falling apart, I didn't like it at all."[24]

Wynne-Wilson's observations were astute. When taken in

controlled circumstances LSD was a powerful but usually harmless experience. But when taken with strangers in huge venues, accompanied by disorientating lights and music, the experience was much less predictable. LSD use at the "14 Hour Technicolour Dream" showed the crossroads use of the drug had reached. Numbers of LSD users were increasing daily and were becoming bolder in going out to pubs, clubs and gigs. Entrepreneurs, both hippie and straight, saw an opening in the market and sought to provide venues for large numbers of people, many of whom would be under the influence of LSD. In their enthusiasm, whether driven by ideology or profit, to create environments in which people could enjoy the LSD experience, the organisers had ignored the absolute importance of set and setting.

After all the negative publicity surrounding LSD in the first half of 1967, its supporters received a boost in June when Paul McCartney admitted on TV to ITN's Keith Hadfield that he had taken it four times. The revelation reverberated through the UK. Where once the Beatles had been the clean cut antithesis of the Rolling Stones, after McCartney's frank disclosure it was obvious to all they had crossed the great divide between "straight" society and the psychedelic pioneers.

Coming as it did only weeks after the release of *Sgt Pepper's Lonely Hearts Club Band* the cynical might have viewed McCartney's bombshell as a cynical marketing move, a trick designed to get maximum publicity. But the Beatles didn't need the publicity and McCartney's candour was such that he seemed to have been genuine in his desire to share his experiences with his fans.

For McCartney, taking LSD meant mind expansion and the ending of all social evils: "We only use one-tenth of our brain. Just think what we could all accomplish if we could only tap that hidden part! It would mean a whole new world. If the politicians would take LSD, there wouldn't be any more war, poverty or famine." Not only did the Beatle admit to enjoying LSD he was clear that: "My personal opinion is that LSD is not dangerous." For anyone still hesitant about using LSD McCartney's admission he had taken the drug was as near to a celebrity endorsement as was possible. And for many *Sgt Pepper's* was the ultimate psychedelic album, made by acidheads for acidheads.[25]

The album's iconic sleeve photograph was conceived by pop artist Peter Blake and photographed by Michael Cooper at his London studio. According to McCartney two of the Beatles had taken LSD for the event. *Sgt Pepper's* has come to define psychedelic music and the summer of 1967. From its release on 1 June the album was everywhere, playing on the radio, TV, in shops and in hippie pads across the UK. It became, for a while at least, the album to listen to while on LSD. Its bright, colourful splashes of sound and inventive lyrics made it almost impossible to have a bad experience.

Several tracks on the album appeared to be about drugs, although whether they actually were or not is a matter for conjecture. Speculation has raged to what degree socialite Tara Browne's death inspired "A Day in the Life", the closing track on the album. Because of his penchant for LSD, rumour spread that the phrase, "he blew his mind out in a car" referred to the possibility Browne was on an LSD trip at the time of his death. Lennon claims the song's lyric grew from stories in the *Daily Mail* for 17 January 1967 ("I read the news today, oh boy") which juxtaposed details of Browne's inquest with a surreal filler about the number of road works in Blackburn, Lancashire. McCartney allows that while he didn't connect the lyric with Browne he accepts that Lennon did.[26]

Though the record buying public received *Sgt Pepper's Lonely Hearts Club Band* ecstatically, the British cultural establishment wasn't at all happy that some of its lyrics might be affecting the nation's youth. Prior to its releases some broadcasting mavens within the BBC already had severe doubts about the lyrics to "A Day in the Life", mainly because of the line, "I went upstairs and had a smoke, somebody spoke and I went into a dream". They may also have heard the rumours about the cause of Tara Browne's death. On 19 May the BBC Press Office issued an internal statement relating to the song: "The Beatles new LP 'Sergeant Pepper's Lone (sic) Hearts' Club Band' contains one song which the BBC has decided not to broadcast. It is called "A Day in the Life'".[27]

It seems from this statement that the BBC wanted to ban the song and for the ban to remain secret if at all possible: "This information is on no account to be volunteered but it may break from other sources in which case you may talk as follows." The statement went on to describe that if challenged about the existence of the ban it was to be acknowledged but qualified with: "The BBC takes a pretty liberal attitude these days ... however, we have listened to this particular song over and over again and we have decided that as far as we are concerned it appears to go a little too far and could encourage a permissive attitude to drug-taking."[28]

The BBC went a step further on 25 May when they issued a statement to the heads of every major record label in Britain. Frank Gillard, Director of Sound Broadcasting issued a two page statement in which he wrote: "I am writing to tell you that we are increasingly concerned over the allegations that some pop records contain references to drug taking, and could be construed as giving encouragement to unfortunate habits and perhaps even to vice." Gillard insisted the BBC would be ultra vigilant even to the point of banning some records that may have entirely innocent lyrics. Somewhat amusingly Gillard suggested that: "... these references are often obscure and couched in language not readily understood by ordinary people." Clearly, in the eyes of the BBC LSD takers were not "ordinary"![29]

Rolling Stones' guitarist Brian Jones took off for America in mid-June to attend the Monterey Pop Festival. There were few British bands on the bill but this was the first multi-day rock festival ever to be staged and Jones wanted to be part of it. While there he hooked up with his old friend Dennis Hopper and the pair took LSD together. The Monterey Festival was notable for "Monterey Purple", a bespoke batch of LSD created for the festival by noted San Franciscan LSD chemist Augustus Owsley Stanley III. A large quantity of this LSD was destined for Britain and Owsley recalls: "Brian Jones had a photographer in his entourage who brought a telephoto lens which had been gutted. He took it back filled with Monterey Purple. I asked Brian to share the stash between his Stones and the Beatles. So far as I am aware he did so."[30]

Throughout 1967 there was a dramatic increase in LSD

availability in Britain. Quantities of good quality "outlaw chemist" LSD were being brought from America and there was also a supply from an as yet unidentified UK laboratory. The rapidly growing counter culture, combined with the long hot psychedelic summer created an almost insatiable demand for the drug.

In July 1967 Allen Ginsberg, the American beatnik poet, arrived in Britain. He had been invited by R.D. Laing to speak at the Dialectics of Liberation conference held at the Roundhouse in north London. While in the capital Ginsberg did several poetry readings and was interviewed extensively. He spoke in depth about LSD and how useful it was for breaking the bounds of social conditioning. Ginsberg stressed that LSD was not an end in itself but should be used to regain the lost awareness written about by poets such as William Blake. And he was clear that LSD had set in motion a movement of altered consciousness and perception which would continue even without the drug: "Even if LSD disappeared and all the beards and the hair disappeared the awareness would spread … Even if the police captured all the LSD manufacturers like Owsley, put everybody in gaol, I think ZAP, everything would spread anyway. YOU CAN'T STOP IT NOW."[31]

Interviewed by film maker and poet Iain Sinclair, Ginsberg offered a series of practices he felt would be useful during an LSD trip. These were basically techniques borrowed from Eastern philosophies and included breathing and posture exercises: "A little five minute ritual is a very good form of meditation when you are going up on a psychedelic. Also a good place to come back to at any point during a trip when you want a simple place to lay your body against."[32] Ginsberg also stressed that getting out into the countryside among nature's solitudes was also an excellent way of preventing problems on a trip.

These were all ideas taken for granted among the early LSD community in the USA, now starting to filter through to the psychedelic scene in Britain. Ideas of minimal consumption, voluntary poverty and the possibilities of consciousness expansion without LSD were coalescing in the minds of many LSD trippers. For some the LSD vision was enough to give them the realization that western consumerism was a pointless waste of time, designed only to enslave mind and body. Many left on the "hippie trail", overland to the East in search of a genuine spirituality. Others travelled east to continue the counter cultural lifestyle in countries where living was much cheaper and the pursuit of consciousness expansion was less restricted.

After the Roundhouse conference Ginsberg travelled to the Black Mountains of Wales to stay at the country retreat of his English publisher, Tom Maschler. On 28 July, both men took LSD and wandered the hills around Llanthony Abbey, marvelling at the amplified sensory intricacies of the natural world. The experience inspired Ginsberg to write "Wales Visitation", a glorious evocation of the inter-connectedness of everything. The poem demonstrated that for all his New York City beat-speak Ginsberg was a nature mystic at heart.

Ginsberg wanted to create, "… an artwork comprehensible to people not high on acid, an artefact which could point others' attention to microscopic details of the scene … It might transfer the high consciousness of LSD to somebody with an ordinary mind".[33]

No imperfection in the budded mountain,
valleys breathe, heaven and earth move together,
daisies push inches of yellow air, vegetables tremble,

Stare close, no imperfection in the grass,
each flower Buddha-eye, repeating the story,
myriad-formed.[34]

Maschler recalled the trip as being a "… superb experience but I never wanted to take it again."[35] The poem was published in book form a year later with photographs of a clearly intoxicated Ginsberg communing with nature on the damp, cloud-wreathed Welsh hillside.

Another poetic reference to LSD came in the form of Roger McGough's "Poem For National LSD Week", published in the 1967 anthology *The Mersey Sound.* The poem is actually shorter than its title and is a clever play on words, adding a comma between the first and second words of the phrase "mind how you go"; thus encapsulating both the effect of LSD and a warning about its use in four words.

Psychedelic lyrics and the widespread knowledge that many pop musicians were taking LSD caused policy makers within the BBC to sit up and take notice. In July Huw Wheldon, controller of programmes, issued an internal policy statement that summed up the current legal status of drugs and mused on the moral and social implications of songs with drug related lyrics. Wheldon was staunchly against the idea of the BBC playing any part in condoning drug use in any way whatsoever: "The programmatic considerations are these: that we can condone by default. We can help make the thing a commonplace. This we cannot allow ourselves to do."[36]

In retrospect these statements appear amusing. The idea of the BBC trying to prevent drug use by banning certain songs was never going to work. Many songs slipped through the BBC's net and it was clear that the Corporation hadn't even gone to the trouble of bothering to ask anyone from the counter cultures which songs were and which were not about drugs.

"Itchycoo Park" by the Small Faces, released on 4 August, is just one example of an LSD song the BBC failed to spot. With its subversive lyrics about playing truant from school, "why go to learn the words of fools" and its knowing invite to Itchycoo Park, "over bridge of sighs, to rest my eyes in shades of green" where the participants would get "high", the song was as obvious a hymn to LSD as there could be. The closing refrain of "It's all too beautiful" left the listener in no doubt as to what they thought of the LSD experience.[37]

The Small Faces were one of the bands who took LSD a little less reverently than many of their contemporaries. Instead of using it primarily to explore the mysteries of mind and matter, they took LSD mainly to have a laugh, a good time. People were beginning to realise that once you were used to taking the drug you could get out and about, visit pubs, clubs and the countryside, all seen through a colourful LSD prism.

However, bands like the Beatles and the Small Faces were really mainstream psychedelic musicians. Numerous groups jumped on the psychedelic bandwagon and sang vaguely drug suffused lyrics dressed in the latest paisley fashions. It was a good marketing tool but hardly true to the spirit of the drug or the counter culture. Record company heads soon realised that drugs, like sex, sold records and promoted their acts accordingly.

The true musical psychedelic pioneers weren't the brash popsters but were small groups of friends who enjoyed playing LSD inspired music together. Donovan was popular among serious LSD takers, his filigree musical arrangements and lyrics about relationships and the wonder of the universe being to many acidheads' tastes. But even Donovan was classed by some as having "sold out", sacrificed his principles in favour of a pop musician's lifestyle.

Bands such as the Incredible String Band were regarded as making authentic LSD music. The String Band, as they were known, had developed out of Edinburgh's beatnik scene, later taking easily to drugs and a semi-communal LSD-inspired lifestyle. In December 1966 their original banjo player, Clive Palmer, had been the first person in Scotland to be arrested for possession of LSD but left the group after the first LP. Palmer was not a drug taker and didn't appreciate LSD at all: "People used to tell me you could write fantastic music on LSD, but it didn't affect me at all. It was rubbish, I couldn't do anything. I just wanted to sit down."[38]

The two principals of the String Band, Mike Heron and Robin Williamson were rather keener on the drug and in July 1967 released *5,000 Spirits or the Layers of the Onion*. This was challenging, barely describable music, which polarised opinion in those who heard it. It was clear to any LSD takers who heard *5,000 Spirits* that Heron and Williamson had also taken the drug. Their acid folk songs of hyper-awareness, talking clouds, death and Williamson's desire to reflect "the sheer unspeakable strangeness of being here at all" echoed and amplified the odd perceptions experienced by LSD users. The musical accompaniment was of strings bowed, plucked and strummed, sitar, eastern drone and pattering clay drums. The overall effect was of music from a luminous multiverse where lysergic logic made perfect sense.

The cover art clearly spelt out the contents to prospective buyers and provided LSD-inspired listeners with hours of study. The Fool, a group of Dutch artists much beloved of the Beatles, had been commissioned to provide the cover art. They came up with a psychedelic classic: a kaleidoscopic organic vision of vegetation, sun, moon and stars complete with hermaphroditic human faced winged creature. If you were a teenager, whereas your parents might just tolerate the Beatles, you could expect a bang on the bedroom door telling you to "turn that rubbish off" if you slipped *5,000 Spirits* onto the turntable.

As did many other musicians, the Incredible String Band later eschewed the adventure of psychedelic drugs. But for a few years in the late Sixties their LPs were psychedelic hymnals for the dedicated LSD tripper.

While the LSD takers in Britain were exploring the inner and outer universe the entertainment industry was slowly realizing there was money to be made from the psychedelic scene. This process began in America and a series of low budget films were produced to cash in on the media hype surrounding LSD. The most significant to impact on the UK was director Roger Corman's *The Trip*, subtitled, "A big thrill in a little pill", scheduled for release in October 1967.

The British Board of Film Censors however, had other ideas as they followed in the wake of the BBC's attempts to surreptitiously protect the nation's morals from even a whiff of LSD. When confronted with *The Trip,* John Trevelyan secretary of the BBFC, made no attempt to hide his feelings: "Bearing in mind the dangers of the drug we have decided to ban any film which could conceivably encourage taking it. It is a question of balance … we decided in advance that we will not admit this as a subject for films." The BBFC file from 1967 no longer exists but a file note from 1971 gives the primary reason for rejection: "The deterrent episodes (e.g. the nightmare quality of a bad trip) are not strong enough to counterbalance the pleasurable effects of the LSD."[39]

Despite the fact that *The Trip* was in fact a cautionary tale about the effects of LSD, which it portrayed somewhat luridly, the film did not get a UK release until 2004. It co-starred Peter Fonda and

Dennis Hopper in what was to be a dry run for the definitive LSD film, *Easy Rider,* in 1969.

The Beatles, already at the forefront of psychedelic music and fashion, proved in the fading summer of 1967 they were also in the vanguard of spirituality. Their LSD experiences had caused Paul, John and George to ask themselves questions about their identity and purpose, giving them a glimpse of other realties they found difficult to assimilate. Eastern religion, especially Hinduism, seemed to offer answers or at least some understanding and on 25 August the three musicians boarded a train bound for Bangor in North Wales to study with the Indian guru Maharishi Mahesh Yogi. They were accompanied by other LSD taking pop stars with spiritual leanings, including Mick Jagger. This very public excursion and display of piety garnered huge amounts of media attention and brought to the public's attention the links between psychedelics and spirituality.

Though individuals and small groups continued to use LSD as a religious sacrament or for self development, a growing number of people were using it just for the effect; to be witness to and part of a psychedelic Disneyland of the mind. Taking LSD in clubs and pubs or as part of large crowds at rock shows didn't suit everyone and "freak outs" were becoming more common. The counter culture realised this and began to issue information about the effects of what they were taking and how to deal with it. In October *International Times* ran the Acid Report, a two-page spread giving basic chemical, legal and sociological facts about LSD. This was intelligent and well presented, although how effective it was in preventing bad experiences with LSD is unclear.[40]

Record producer Joe Boyd was a dispassionate observer of the LSD scene. He had seen the drug destroy Syd Barrett and other musicians and had harsh words for the psychedelic summer of 1967: "By that summer when school was out and people were flocking to London, the sudden surge in demand for drugs meant that quality deteriorated ... So after that wonderful atmosphere of the spring, by August or September there was an awful lot more aggression and problems."[41]

LSD had begun to flood London in increasing quantities during the spring and summer of 1967. The police were frustrated because they had no clues as to who was producing it or how it was being distributed. Then, in August 1967, came the breakthrough they had been hoping for: information that large quantities of LSD were being produced in north London. Drug Squad officers and officials from H.M. Customs worked together on this lead and on 27 September arrested Alexander Davidson at Heathrow Airport. He had LSD in his possession worth £10,000 which he was attempting to smuggle to America. From this arrest it was learned that the LSD originated from Victor James Kapur, proprietor of New North Chemist in New North Road, Islington.[42]

A team of Drug Squad officers were immediately assigned to the case and within a few weeks had a list of Kapur's associates. Kapur was seen to make several brief, late night visits to hotels and he was also followed to a house in London N8 where he spent time in the garage with the brother-in-law of the owner.

At the beginning of November the police received information that a large consignment of LSD was due to be distributed soon. Surveillance on Kapur was stepped up and he and his associates were put under round-the-clock observation from 8 November onwards. Police intelligence sources indicated that the transfer of drugs would take place at a hotel in Leicester Square and officers were duly posted on the streets, in coffee bars and in pubs and hotels. So confident were the police that their intense surveillance would bear fruit that they had already been granted search warrants for various premises.

At 12.15 pm on 12 November the waiting paid off. Harry Nathan, an antiques dealer, was seen to enter the Samuel Whitbread public house in Leicester Square. Kapur went into the pub shortly afterwards. The three police officers present witnessed Kapur hand something over to Nathan. Both men left the pub shortly afterwards and were arrested in the street by police officers.

When searched Nathan was found to be carrying a condom containing what analysis later revealed to be approximately 19 grams of LSD in powder form. This was the package handed to him by Kapur in the pub. When turned into tablet form or dissolved and dropped onto blotting paper this would make 95,000 doses of

LSD, each containing a hefty 200 μg. A quantity of LSD was also found under the seat of Kapur's car.

Various addresses were being searched at the time of Kapur's arrest and within hours ten people connected with the case were in custody. The police found two laboratories. One was in the back room of Kapur's chemist shop and another, larger one, was in a garage he rented from a friend of his brother-in-law. Police analysts found that the laboratory equipment from both locations had traces of LSD on them. However, other than the LSD seized in the initial arrest no further quantities of LSD was found.

Kapur had been observed by police to visit Bernadette Whybrow at her flat in Cambridge Gardens, Notting Hill Gate. When arrested she was found to have a small quantity of LSD in liquid form. Whybrow was clearly one of Kapur's distributors, selling the LSD on to smaller dealers. She was also using the LSD herself and with friends as part of the occult group she was involved in with Terry Taylor and others, described in Chapter 7. Whybrow was also a prostitute, although at the time of her arrest was trying to get out of prostitution to concentrate on drug dealing.

As police investigations continued it became obvious that Whybrow was central to the Kapur case. Among items found in the garage used by Kapur as a laboratory were large quantities of negatives portraying him and several women engaged in sexual activities. One of the women was Whybrow.

In court on 13 December Whybrow claimed she had no knowledge of Kapur. This was despite the candid photographic evidence to the contrary and regardless of Kapur having been observed at her flat on a number of occasions. A police file note also suggests Whybrow was well- known to the police: "Although there is no evidence to support this, it is known that Whybrow sells LSD to the artist-beatnik type of person and to Americans."

By following the paper trial left by Kapur, police discovered that he had made numerous trips to Germany to buy Ergotoxine, the key raw material from which he would make LSD. Kapur had actually bought the chemical from a British company, but claimed it was for sale to a continental business and he would take delivery of it there. The police were surprised to find that the first purchase of Ergotoxine was in September 1966. This suggested that Kapur had been manufacturing significant quantities of LSD since at least the autumn of that year.

The police failed to get to the bottom of Kapur's distribution network because none of the defendants were prepared to discuss this. However laboratory tests conclusively proved that the LSD Davidson was trying to smuggle to America had the same chemical composition as that seized during Kapur's arrest. Information presumably gleaned from informers led the police to speculate: "While there is evidence that Nathan was engaged in transporting the drug to the United States of America, it has been learned the girl, Whybrow, was responsible for its distribution to London buyers, although we are unable to prove this."

Kapur, unlike other LSD chemists, appeared to have got into making LSD almost by chance. He had no previous criminal convictions, was not motivated by any ideology, and appeared to have made very little money from manufacturing LSD. His connection with Bernadette Whybrow came as the result of him using her services as a prostitute. When she discovered he had the necessary skills to make LSD she talked him into it. The presence of Kapur, Whybrow and others involved in sexual activities suggests the relationship could have been sustained by blackmail; Kapur was unable to stop making the drug even if he had wanted to. Had Kapur wished he could have cooperated with the police and given them information which would have led to further charges being laid against his associates and a more lenient sentence for himself. But he made it clear to the police he would not give them any useful information, saying: "I need to protect myself, my wife, and my children." Kapur was remanded in custody until his trial in May 1968.

The Metropolitan Police believed that Kapur's arrest had a major impact on LSD: "It is significant that since the arrest of these people only minute amounts of LSD are known to be available in the London area. It can be concluded therefore that Kapur was one of the main suppliers of the drug and that the timely apprehension of his team has prevented the corruption of thousands of young people." There was a slight dip in availability of LSD in London but the law of supply and demand soon meant fresh supplies were coming in from abroad. The gap in the market and potential for huge profits also meant that new LSD laboratories were already becoming operational in Britain to meet the growing demand among young people for LSD.

The police found it hard to believe that such large quantities of LSD could have been produced for so long without them being aware of it. The Kapur arrests brought home to them the problems associated with policing LSD manufacture, distribution and usage. Whereas marijuana and cannabis were bulky, obvious and easily detected by smell, LSD was the exact opposite. The colourless, odourless drug could be manufactured in vast quantities, and enough to intoxicate the whole of Britain could be hidden in a shoe box. These problems would plague police investigations into LSD for decades.

Kapur's arrest had alerted the police to the scale of LSD use and manufacturing and they stepped up their investigations accordingly. Some police officers were determined to smash the production and distribution of what they saw as a threat to society. Others, such as Norman Pilcher, one of the detectives on the Kapur investigation, saw the opportunities offered by LSD as yet another chance to make money from criminals while pursuing their quest for career glory.

In LSD the media had found a new moral panic with which to bait the public, politicians had a new drug on which to blame the corruption of youth, and commerce had found a new market to manipulate. 1967 had been a watershed year for LSD use. Although the drug had only been illegal since late 1966, an organised pro-LSD movement might have been able to lobby the government for a change in the drug laws. But the lack of any such movement, coupled with the media's dogged pursuit of LSD scare stories, meant the public and politicians largely saw psychedelic drugs as a dangerous influence on young people and a possible threat to the fabric of society.

The summer of love was over. LSD had permeated all levels of society and its culture had created and fuelled a revolution in music, fashion and lifestyle which was to echo throughout

British society for evermore. Irrespective of the media's hatred of the drug, LSD or, more often than not, the imagery of LSD was being used as a marketing tool to sell almost any product. LSD culture was now self-perpetuating, the drug experience itself driving ideas about lifestyle which were brought to realization often within days. As Joe Boyd commented: "The more tabs of acid there were circulating, the more freaks you saw, the more boutiques, macrobiotic restaurants, the more tie dye sold – and the music evolved."[43]

LSD had become widespread during 1967, its use no longer confined to major cities. Earlier attempts by the psychedelic movement's founders such as Michael Hollingshead, David Solomon, Hoppy Hopkins and others to frame the drug's use as a primarily religious experience had been only partially successful. For many the sheer sensory joy of LSD was good enough reason to take it. However, there was still a grass roots movement which believed LSD had the capacity to cause a major change in individual consciousness and also to be used as a springboard to create a new society. This movement was unfocused and had many strands, some interlocking, some entirely discrete. But it was this subtle, almost invisible, movement that would drive psychedelic culture forward, out of the Sixties, into the Seventies and beyond and which would lead eventually to the destruction of the LSD dream.

9

ALL YOU NEED IS LOVE?

If one is able to live with oneself …
then acid holds no surprises.
Chris Huhne[1]

The years between 1968 and 1973 were a transitional period which saw LSD move from being an artefact of the swinging Sixties to a widely available, cheap drug. Tens of thousands of people had now tried it and the hippie counter culture was becoming increasingly LSD oriented. Yet, as the acid scene grew, it also became fragmented. LSD was now central to the lives of many individuals, but the philosophies held by the elders of the psychedelic community did not immediately catch on with the growing number of LSD users. If there was to be an LSD inspired revolution among young people, it was going to take a great deal more thought and effort than people had first anticipated.

Britain's first trial for the manufacture of LSD began on 16 May 1968 and lasted to 31 May. Victor Kapur was sentenced to nine years imprisonment for his role as the chemist, to run consecutively with five other sentences of up to two years. The others involved received lesser sentences. Kapur was struck off the Register of Pharmaceutical Chemists, while the detectives who had worked on the case received commendations. Detective Norman Pilcher, who would achieve notoriety in his own right in the coming years, was one of those commended.[2]

Bernadette Whybrow, the person who was responsible for Kapur starting to manufacture LSD, was dealt with in a most unusual fashion. On the specific directions of the Director of Public Prosecutions, she was summarily sentenced at Bow Street Magistrates' Court on 25 January. After pleading guilty to the charges of possession of LSD and amphetamine, Whybrow received two years probation. Considering the depth of her involvement with Kapur the light sentence suggests she was either an informant or had supplied the police with valuable information during the investigation. Circumstantial evidence to support this contention comes from the Metropolitan Police file on the Kapur case, which notes: "… it is thought she was one of the main distributors of the LSD in London."

Based on the amount of Ergotoxine purchased, the police estimated Kapur may have produced up to fifteen million 200 μg doses of LSD. Even allowing for mistakes and failures, Kapur's output had been prodigious. However, his arrest did nothing to stem the flow of LSD in Britain. Other manufacturers both at home and abroad were keen to supply the growing demand and LSD was no harder to obtain after Kapur's arrest than before.

After the 1967 self-styled summer of love, 1968 was a much colder, bleaker time for the counter culture. Large numbers of young people who had left home to join the psychedelic revolution were now facing their future; should they return home to the small towns and small minds they had escaped from, or should they make a stand and try to create the new society their acid visions had shown them?

Accommodation in London and the provinces was at a premium, both for young people and especially those whose longhaired appearance suggested they might be drug users. This meant real effort had to be put into finding somewhere to live, and for those who could not find a flat to rent squatting seemed a viable option.

The London Squatters Campaign was set up in November 1968 to coordinate the growing squatting movement. Suddenly, squatting was a way of life, quickly adopted by the hippies. The first big hippie squat took place in November 1969 when the London Street Commune created headline news after hundreds of people invaded 144 Piccadilly, a privately owned mansion at Hyde Park Corner. The media railed against what they saw as an infringement of basic property rights; the *People* opined: "Drug taking, couples making love while others look on, rule by heavy mob armed with iron bars, foul language, filth and stench. THAT is the scene inside the hippies' fortress in London's Piccadilly. These are not rumours but facts, sordid facts which will shock ordinary decent family-loving people."[3]

The idea that hippies could create their own communities simply by squatting in derelict houses, or in some cases whole streets, was anathema to the British way of life. This was a direct threat to society's most closely held values. Living communally, not working at a nine-to-five job and taking psychedelic drugs called into question notions about the nuclear family and the work ethic. In truth, this media-created moral panic was never going to amount to a real threat to mainstream society but it was regarded as such and squats did provide a fertile breeding ground for the development of counter cultural ideas. And wherever hippies gathered LSD was bound to be present.

The squat at 144 Piccadilly lasted less than a week, but the principle had been seen to work and hippies spread their wings, looking for buildings to occupy on a more permanent basis. One of the earliest large squatting communities developed in the empty Eel Pie Hotel on Eel Pie Island on London's southern fringes. Chris Faiers lived at the squat, known as the Eel Pie Commune, from 1969 to 1971. According to Faiers' *Eel Pie Dharma,* LSD was a mainstay of the lifestyle there, with large groups often taking the drug together. "Many of the communards were heavily into LSD trips. I was wary of the group trips, both because I didn't trust the motives of some involved, and also because the effects of too much acid were becoming apparent to me."[4]

Initially, the group acid trips were successful and helped bond people to each other and to the communal lifestyle. Gavin Kilty also remembers the group trips and the ethos of the commune: "We ate, danced, sang and tripped together trying with a seriousness that belied our age to forge a consciousness anew amid what we saw as the ruins of Twentieth Century Schizoid Man."[5] But as time passed, Faiers noticed: "The commune was changing for the worse, and much of the problem was the acid. Acid had a freeing effect on most people for the first few trips, but for those with mental problems, the acid quickly worsened their state. It had a similar effect on group dynamics. The effects of a strong hallucinatory trip were so overwhelming that some people looked for leadership at any cost to free them from the confusion. A few of the Eel Pie regulars, such as Magic Mike, were only too happy to assume the mantle of acid guru."[6]

Many other squats quickly sprang up and by the mid-Seventies tens of thousands of young people were squatting in London alone. By 1970, a thousand squatters were occupying Elgin Avenue in Notting Hill Gate and by 1972, Camden's Prince of Wales Crescent was home to 280 squatters, one third of them holding qualifications at degree level. Squatting became highly organised; there was even a London based squatters' estate agency. In 1974, a group of London-based activists created the idea of a network of independent collectives and communities under the name Albion Free State. Groups such as The Diggers, who were later to become the core of the early hippie travelling community, motivated much of the early squatting movement.

Those who could afford or find a flat tended to settle in the same enclaves favoured by the squatters. These locations tended to be in run down inner city areas where property was cheap to rent and where the neighbours were working class or immigrants. From the late Sixties and throughout the Seventies the counter culture almost developed a city within a city in London. Notting Hill Gate, Ladbroke Grove and similar areas in the west of London were becoming home to thousands of young people, many of them LSD users. This neighbourhood had already been home to many of the first wave of LSD users in the mid-Sixties, and so it was natural the counter culture would increasingly congregate there. It became a hippie stronghold, a fertile breeding ground for new music, new drugs and a new way of life that encompassed both.

In *Soft City,* Jonathan Raban gave his impressions of Notting Hill and its hippie denizens: "Their parents are lower middle-class clerks … 'straights' who, in their children's version of them, live in a state of amazingly ingenuous incomprehension." Raban is condescending toward the acid-based counter culture, believing "… its claims to being a counter culture are both pompous and impoverished."[7]

For Raban, the inhabitants of Notting Hill and other hippie enclaves had withdrawn from the world to focus on themselves – more counter-productive than counter culture. He is scathing about the hippie preoccupation with bodily health and spiritual illumination via the agency of drugs: "Just as the body is perceived as a vessel that must be kept clean with yoga exercises and elaborate diets, so the head is the ultimate casket of the self. The pursuit of *satori*, of 'inmost happiness', is an epic journey into self-hood; and the illusion, at least, of this inward drift is made dramatically real in the acid trip …" Despite his opinion that this way of life was juvenile and affected, in Notting Hill Gate's alternative scene Raban could still catch a fleeting glimpse of "… a state of magic to which the fragmented industrial city unconsciously aspires."[8]

The growth in "elaborate diets", as Raban puts it, was intimately linked with LSD use. The dramatic psychological effects of LSD often caused users to examine not only their spiritual life but also their physical one. The common revelation on LSD that "all is one" was enough to lead many people to decide they could not eat animals that once lived and breathed as they did. Senses amplified by LSD could also make flesh and fat look and taste gross, while fruits, vegetables and cereals appeared wholesome. These perceptions frequently lasted when the drug had worn off, and there are numerous instances of LSD users becoming vegetarian overnight.

The desire to purify the mind with LSD led logically to the purification of the body and whole food shops and cafés sprung up in the areas where hippies lived. How and what we eat helps determine culture, and vegetarianism marked another way that hippies were able to set themselves apart from the rest of "straight" society. Living on fruit, vegetables, cereals and pulses was also relatively cheap and very healthy, a major factor when living on state benefits or low paid jobs.

One of the major proponents of whole foods in the LSD counter culture was Greg Sams. From selling macrobiotic snacks at the UFO club in 1967, Sams moved on to open various cafés including, in 1969, Notting Hill's Ceres, to cater for the soaring demand for unprocessed foods. Sams cogently summed up the effects of LSD on the counter culture's day-to-day existence: "We don't ever talk about it, but the natural foods industry was largely founded by people who experimented with LSD ..."[9] The insights temporarily afforded by these mind-expanding drugs inspired a more spiritual approach to life and a search for a new way of living. They created a lifestyle where food was your best medicine, prevention replaced cure, the environment was valued and protected and people lived in harmony and peace.

"The natural foods pioneers realised that the political process offered little hope so they chose the path of creating an alternative society. Some went off to Wales and bought small farms and turned them organic, some opened natural foods stores, some went on to be wholesalers and manufacturers, some studied alternative therapies and became practitioners. They knew in their bones they were on the right track, despite ridicule and hostility."[10]

Purifying mind and body as a response to insights bestowed by LSD was one thing but when under the influence the majority of LSD users liked nothing more than to fill their minds with music. Music was yet another way acidheads sought spiritual truths, and certain bands were identified as producing psychedelic music: music created by acid users for acid users which revealed fundamental truths and spiritual insights if listened to when tripping.

Some musicians liked to have fun at the expense of the spiritual leanings common among LSD takers. One of the most pertinent examples was the Small Faces' LP *Ogden's Nut Gone Flake,* released in June 1968. The band was a bunch of former mod pleasure seekers, amphetamine ravers who had turned on to LSD and found they liked it very much indeed. Nevertheless, and despite their jack-the-lad image, the drug brought them to a state of humble introspection. Instead of throwing their lot in with eastern gurus as the Beatles had done, or writing facile songs about love and peace, their experiences led them to conclude that LSD was whatever you made of it. From that realization came the idea for *Ogden's*.

The first side of the record was a collection of off-kilter songs about, among other things, bakers and dockside prostitutes. Swirling organ and crashing cymbals added psychedelic counterpoint to Steve Marriott's soulful vocal to create one of the most unique and underrated psychedelic albums of the era. The closing track, "Lazy Sunday" described perfectly the feeling of coming down from a trip: "Lazy Sunday afternoon, I ain't got no mind to worry, close my mind and drift away."[11]

Side two darkened the mood and invited the listener on a cod-psychedelic quest. The idea for this came from the bizarre notions and thought patterns that often gripped people during LSD trips. When this happened, the most ordinary event could be instantly transformed into something of frightening and portentous significance. For the Small Faces it was the quest of their protagonist, Happiness Stan, to find the missing half of the moon, narrated by surreal comedian Stanley Unwin. Unwin twisted phrases and invented words to create a universe that fitted exactly with what the band was trying to do.

With a nod to Stan being in the LSD induced state of "hours slipping by while time stands still" our hero gets obsessed by the half moon and "absolutely smashed and flaky" sets out on his quest on the back of an insect, "Tripily how on the back of a fly". Stan goes through a series of adventures in which his perceptions are further distorted until he is eventually taken to Mad John, a cave dwelling guru. Rather than an austere eastern guru who demands obeisance and restrictive living practices, Mad John is friendly and humorous and gently chides Stan for the futility of his quest. John explains to Stan that whatever he believes, everything works out all right in the end (shades of Huxley's belief that the Universe is All Right). The album reinforces this message with the concluding philosophical sing-along: "Life is just a bowl of All Bran, you wake up every morning and it's there," which advises Stan to live the best life he can and to enjoy himself.[12]

At the other end of the spectrum, for those who preferred their psychedelia unusual, austere and freighted with portent, the Incredible String Band provided the era's darkest musical excursion. Recorded during the winter of 1967 and released in 1968, *The Hangman's Beautiful Daughter* catered for acidheads who relished a challenge at all levels. *Hangman's* has no peer musically, inviting the listener to sidestep daily existence and enter a music that appears to come straight from a faerie dimension.

The album's centrepiece is "A Very Cellular Song", a thirteen-minute odyssey that takes the listener into a strange and distant world, where one can meet amoebas who are "living the timeless life". The idea for the song came to the Incredible String Band's Mike Heron while he was tripping: "All it was, was a trip, and that was the music I was listening to."[13] For some the Incredible String Band's music only made sense when they were on LSD and although the band later eschewed the freedom of acid in favour of the strictures of Scientology, they have come to be seen as the archetypal acid folk band.

In May 1969, an article in the *Evening Standard* alerted the Home Office to the possibility Timothy Leary might try to gain admittance to Britain later in the year. This news quickly reached the Home Office and a flurry of internal correspondence was generated, reviewing and updating the reasons Leary was denied admittance in 1967. A memo dated 15 September noted that immigration officials expected Leary to land at Heathrow later that day. The decision to uphold the 1967 decision and refuse him entry to Britain was made while he was in transit from Tangier via Madrid.[14]

Leary duly arrived at Terminal 1 at 7.00 pm. He was met by immigration officials and denied access to the UK. His reason for wishing to enter the country was to take a short holiday and to attend a party. The Home Office were already aware of his intentions to attend a party as they had received an anonymous telephone call from a woman who said she believed Leary was coming to attend a "LSD party". The caller appeared to have specific knowledge about the party, telling immigration officials that Leary wouldn't be carrying any LSD but that, "... supplies would arrive another way from the United States for the party."[15]

Arrangements were quickly made for Leary to return to Tangier or Madrid. However, Leary stated he did not wish to return to either

Morocco or Spain, but "... wished to go on to a more civilised country – America". While Leary was waiting, customs officials tried to get a decision as to whether he ought to be searched. Consideration was given to the fact that if he were found to be in possession of LSD it would cause a stir in the press, and the Home Office wanted to avoid that at all costs. Luckily, seats were found on a flight leaving for America in a few hours and customs decided against a search. After a few hours wait Leary was taken to a Securicor bus and, escorted by an immigration official, boarded a flight for New York that took off at 11.45 pm.[16]

The Home Office file refers often to the press and it is clear they did not want the media to know Leary had attempted to gain access to the UK and had been refused. Leary's attempt to come to the UK, claims of holidays and parties notwithstanding, may have been manipulated by him to glean some media attention. One of the officials, Mr Geenyer, who dealt with him during his wait at Heathrow, commented, "From his manner it appeared that Mr. Leary fully expected to be refused leave to land. It also seemed that he was a little disappointed that his presence failed to attract any public notice."[17]

Though the LSD party to which Leary had been invited was not identified, it was almost certainly the event held in September by the staff of *Rolling Stone* magazine's London edition at a venue in Hanover Square. In his analysis of late Sixties counter culture, *High Sixties*, Roger Hutchinson notes: "Possibly the most extravagant mass 'bad trip' of the decade took place late in 1969, in Hanover Square, at a party held by the newly-launched London edition of the American rock magazine *Rolling Stone* to entice advertising from the music industry. The drinks served at the party had been laced with LSD, and the LSD had in its turn been laced (unbeknown to the *Rolling Stone* staffers) with strychnine."[18]

According to DJ Jeff Dexter, "For some reason someone had laced a lot of the food and the alcohol had been laced with some substances."[19] Dexter was used to the effects of LSD but his friend, pop star Marc Bolan was not. Indeed, Dexter, who knew Bolan well, believes this was the first time he had taken LSD. This might surprise many Bolan fans as Tyrannosaurus Rex, Bolan's group, was a favourite of acidheads and he commanded a large following with his fey, Tolkien-esque lyrics, colourful clothes and alternative lifestyle. Other guests at the party, many of them journalists from the mainstream press such as *The Times* and the *Evening Standard,* were also getting ill on the spiked food and the party was rapidly descending into chaos.

Bolan completely freaked out on the drug and had to be driven home by his girlfriend June, overwhelmed and terrified by the LSD: "By that time Marc was going crazy ... and then he bit June and started flailing and I had to hold him down in the back of the Mini. He started to cry and he really just didn't know what was going on. June called a friendly doctor who came round and tranquillised Bolan."[20]

Dexter discussed the experience with Bolan a few days later. The singer was afraid he was a faker because he had not been able to cope with the experience and could not understand how his friend was able to. "It certainly made him think a lot about who he was," concludes Dexter.[21]

The Home Office may have thought it politically expedient to prevent Leary from entering Britain, but they couldn't prevent the counter culture reading his books. Leary's impact on LSD use and philosophy in Britain cannot be underestimated. Once LSD was legislated against, mainstream and underground books, magazines and newspapers followed his every move and pronouncement. His books were required reading for the committed acidhead, even if they weren't always understood; many more people talked about Leary than read or comprehended him. Some LSD users found them helpful, both in navigating their course through an LSD trip and in providing a philosophy for the use of acid.

Reviewing *The Politics of Ecstasy for The Times,* Richard Holmes noted the American's self-obsession and found his naïvety about the dangers of drugs disturbing. Nevertheless, he also found it an "enthralling piece of American documentation". Holmes saw Leary's advocacy of LSD as "just the counter used again and again in the attempt to answer one enormous overall question, which is never posed: what the hell has gone wrong on this Americanised planet? What blessed vision of the spirit will lead us all home again?"

Holmes admired Leary's message of spiritual self-reliance and reverence for the planet, equating it with the vision sought by the American transcendentalist philosopher Thoreau. However, Holmes "... could not overlook the LSD vendor either. As a marketer of dream solutions for my generation I have for him nothing but scorn."[22]

"Dream solutions" was one way of describing the visions of change offered by LSD, but Holmes was wrong to think that acidheads weren't actively considering the "blessed vision of the spirit". Religion and spirituality had been at the heart of LSD use since the Fifties and the drug set many people on a path of spiritual development that they saw as a natural conclusion to their LSD use.

The early acidheads who had travelled the hippie trail to the East in search of enlightenment were now beginning to return. With them, they brought religious trinkets, tales of ashrams where gurus offered enlightenment and a clutch of spiritual practices and techniques. This mix 'n' match spirituality was highly attractive, particularly to hippies who could not bring themselves to subscribe rigidly to any specific belief system. The aura of spirituality permeated the flats and squats of London and spread out through the major cities and provinces. Alternative bookshops began to stock texts from Taoism, Buddhism and Hinduism. What had once been the interest of a small group of people spread to the growing numbers of LSD users. Acidheads began, in great numbers, to read books such as the *Tao Te Ching*, the *Bhagavad-Gita* and the Buddhist sutras. The Taoist divination system, the *I Ching* was particularly popular among LSD users and it was a common book to find in flats and squats, consulted and acted on with the utmost sincerity.

Quintessence guitarist Allan Mostert noticed this change in attitude: "There seem to be more and more people in London with altars in their pads. It's nice that people are starting to realise that their pads are shrines and temples. We're all walking palaces. Our senses are really the gates of the palace. Some people don't know there are gates there."[23]

LSD use and ideas from eastern spirituality became enmeshed, and for those who couldn't bring themselves to stick solely to either acid or meditation, a mix of the two seemed to be equally effective. For those who had been shaken to their soul by LSD, religious practice offered both spiritual salvation and an escape from the disorientating effects of the drug and the impact it had on their lifestyles.

One religious group that specifically targeted LSD users was the Divine Light Movement (DLM), founded in India in the early Sixties. The DLM was led by Prem Rawat, known originally to his followers as Guru Maharaji Ji. Rawat's teachings were an eclectic mix of various elements of Hinduism with the focus being on four meditation techniques that caused physical effects in the practitioner. Rawat believed himself to be "Lord of the Universe", the physical manifestation of the divine. His followers were known as Premies and Knowledge was the spiritual transmission conferred on those deemed ready to receive it, Knowledge being analogous with enlightenment.

Drug users of all persuasions were attracted to DLM in its early years because of its relative lack of structure compared to other religious disciplines. One study discovered that, when compared to a control group, those who joined the DLM in the early Seventies reported twice the incidence of drug use prior to joining the cult. Rawat noticed the appeal of DLM to the acid subculture and manipulated it to the cult's advantage.

One early DLM promotional leaflet focusing on LSD in relation to Rawat's teachings philosophised: "If a man takes LSD, as long as he feels the effects of LSD, he feels okay, but when the LSD finishes, he is not ok, because he is no longer in bliss." The leaflet continued with the claim, "What I have is a constant LSD. It's not LSD; it's like a built-in LSD, which God provided you with when you were born. When you get into it, you're always blissed out. There is no need to come down from it ... So come, leave these things and come to me. I've got a much better thing. Try it, you'll like it. It's much better and much more far out."[24] For anyone brought to the end of their mental and spiritual tether by LSD these words would have seemed like a lifeline thrown to a drowning person: someone who understood LSD and promised to take you further without it.

Rawat already had many followers in Britain when he visited for the first time in June 1971 to appear at the Glastonbury Fair. This event is covered in detail in the next chapter but suffice to say it was an event at which there was "bucket loads of acid", according to one attendee who later became a DLM Premie. Organiser of the festival, Andrew Kerr, was unimpressed by how Rawat's brand of spirituality was introduced to the festival: "I was on stage at the time listening to a band called Brinsley Schwarz ... when all his followers came along and pushed the band off stage. I walked off, disgusted."[25]

Though some festival-goers were highly impressed with Rawat and took Knowledge from him, others were less keen. Many of the grass roots hippies including Sid Rawle, who was running one of the free food kitchens there, were indifferent to the fourteen-year-old guru and his pushy followers. They believed he was out of tune with the spirit of the event and had virtually gate crashed the event. Rawle even believed that the pyramid stage had been specially designed for Rawat, which Andrew Kerr flatly refutes.

DLM ashrams quickly sprang up all over Britain, attracting those for whom LSD was either too overwhelming or who wanted a more organised spirituality in their lives. Many who joined the DLM and received Knowledge later became dissatisfied with the organization, regarding it as a dangerous cult. Having broken free, these ex-Premies now run their own email message boards on which they discuss their experiences. LSD is often mentioned as being one of the reasons they turned to DLM. They equated the effects of DLM practice and the Knowledge offered by Rawat as being synonymous with the LSD experience. One ex-Premie wrote, "... acid was absolutely key to me looking for 'knowledge', which was what our group of mates called it before I knew about Rawat."[26] Another recalled, "the line I remember from the guy who told me about the big K was – it's like the most gentle, most beautiful, peaceful acid trip you can imagine."[27]

In its early years in Britain DLM was not as tightly organised as, say, the Hare Krishna movement and didn't demand that its adherents dress differently or cut their hair. This was also one of the attractions of being a Premie, on the outside, you could remain a hippie. In fact, many Premies joined DLM and continued to use LSD and other drugs. One ex-Premie noted, "the number of ISB fans and Deadheads that were around was scary."[28] Both the ISB (Incredible String Band) and the Grateful Dead were regarded as hard-core acidhead bands, their lyrics often of the "cosmic" variety, their fans frequently serious LSD users and seekers after transcendence.

Other religious organizations, such as the Hare Krishna movement, Meher Baba and Transcendental Meditation, attracted LSD users in large numbers. For some LSD users these religious organizations almost certainly saved their mental and spiritual health. They gave the spiritually inclined but existentially shattered LSD taker a structured existence, a purpose and an extended and loving family. Despite this, large numbers who joined these cults and sects only briefly or who couldn't break free of their LSD habits came back into the LSD subculture and took up where they left off.

As a result, barely understood ideas taken from a variety of religions and beliefs were fed back into the LSD subculture. Books such as Tim Leary's *Psychedelic Prayers* and *The Tibetan Book of the Dead*, touted as being guidebooks for those on an LSD trip, bolstered these ideas further. These books helped consolidate the already widely held belief that an acid trip was about self-discovery, the experience of God or of supernatural powers. LSD users often found that a heavy trip could encompass all of those and much more besides, leaving them spiritually fragile for days afterwards.

Jeff Dexter, like many other acidheads, was a follower of the Tibetan Buddhist Chogyam Trungpa Rinpoche, and visited his monastery in southern Scotland. "One night there I had some acid and Trungpa said, 'Well, give me some then.' So I gave him some acid. Three of us in the room took acid, including him. After about forty minutes this bead of sweat appeared on his forehead, I looked at it, and I thought it was a crystal coming out of his skull! And he went, 'I see, little mouse'. That's what he called me, little mouse. 'This is something quite special. You have to realise that all your answers you are looking for …' and he put his hand on my shoulder and of course if he touched anyone up there they thought they had been immediately blessed, 'all your answers are already inside you. You're already there.'"[29] Shades here of Huxley's *Island* philosophy: "Here and now boys, here and now."

Going into an LSD experience with the idea and expectation that you were going to untangle your psyche, literally meet God or the devil and hang out with deities put an enormous strain on some individuals. These trips were frequently unplanned and unguided, the participants often disregarding or misunderstanding the importance of set and setting. Some people had the most amazing, positive, life enhancing experiences, while others were shaken to their core. Whenever LSD users gathered they would swap stories of their latest forays into the chemical unknown, often to the point where self-obsession eclipsed interest.

LSD stories had become the war stories of a generation of young people. Being an LSD user meant you were part of a secret society, for which the price of admittance could be your mind, your soul or both. The singular nature of the psychedelic experience meant only those who had experienced the lysergic long dark night of the soul were able to empathise with their fellow psychonauts. Sadly, this meant that people often took LSD because it was the thing to do, because they had heard the stories told by those who had been through the doors of perception and wanted to experience it for themselves.

This do-it-yourself chemically fuelled search for spirituality frequently led to people getting themselves into difficult existential states, or "freaking out". Poet and former acid dealer, Dave Cunliffe captured this state in "The Two Hour Assassination of God", the first and last verses of which are:

At 4 am, she entered the brain of God
And stumbled blindly through its convoluted
Swamps until reaching a clearing
In which was reflected the image of everything
that had ever happened
To anyone anywhere in time and space

At 6 am she clearly and directly saw
A myriad living things manifest
In joy and liberation upon the surface
Of a world which didn't really change
Except some skin and scales just dropped away [30]

This might sound trite and over exaggerated but is a very accurate description of what might take place on a powerful LSD trip. The experience Cunliffe describes would have been utterly, palpably real and loaded with life changing portent and meaning. Those unable to assimilate this kind of experience into their lives, or who couldn't laugh at the cosmic absurdity of it all, often turned to religion in an attempt to deal with the devastating effects of the drug. Others, those who dared admit their LSD use had gone wrong, made use of the mental health services or limped back into straight society, forever haunted by their psychedelic nemesis. No study has yet been carried out to determine the numbers of people whose mental health was damaged by unwise or excessive LSD use. But the acid casualties, as they became known, certainly existed, often living miserable half lives, their thought processes and quality of life dimmed by the dark side of the LSD experience.

Of course, not everyone's LSD trip was tinged with numinousity or dogged with existential doubt. There are numerous accounts of people taking LSD and having nothing but unadulterated psychedelic fun. Unfortunately, the government saw no political value and the media no increase in sales figures by reporting stories of individuals whose lives were changed positively by psychedelics. Shock horror accounts of madness, degradation and weird religions were the stories Mr. and Mrs. Average wanted to read in their daily paper. Yet for the vast majority of LSD users this wasn't the case and while some found fulfilment in spiritual and cerebral pursuits and others wrestled with their souls on LSD, others just had fun.

Pete Mellor spent the late Sixties and early Seventies as a hippie, living in London and Cornwall. His description of the sheer, unadulterated pleasure LSD could give is a useful antidote to the accounts of those who were mired in fear, religion and belief because of LSD: "I loved acid. Perhaps once a week, during the night, we would drive out into the Cornish countryside, or the woods, or just hang around the bays. I remember one dawn, after a clear starlit night. We watched the sunrise and saw the first rays lifting the morning dew off the ground, forming clouds in the air. Magic stuff ... A ramble in the country was turned into an adventure like nothing since. Colours, sounds, vision were super heightened. Normal, straight humanity was hilarious! On acid, we were cosmic. The sound of the sea was a symphony. Hours could be spent sat cross-legged on some prehistoric stone, meditating. Digging the vibes. A million things could get you spaced and wasted on the utterly incredible-ness of whatever your attention became fixed on. Acid was speedy and so your body pulsated with energy. You could walk for miles. Or a flat could become your total world. Nothing else would be real. Like the man said, 'nothing is real and nothing to get hung up about'. I never once had a bad time on the stuff, or got frightened or freaked out."[31]

Mellor's attitude and philosophy toward LSD use mirrored that of American author Ken Kesey, who wrote the classic study of mind games in a psychiatric hospital, *One Flew Over The Cuckoo's Nest*. Kesey was introduced to LSD via a US government sponsored test programme in the late Fifties. Kesey's attitude was LSD is a drug, it produces amazing effects and can bind people together, get out there and use it how you see fit, but most of all – have fun! In 1964, Kesey, together with a motley crew of psychonauts known as the Merry Pranksters, crossed America in an old school bus. This LSD fuelled excursion was chronicled by Tom Wolfe in the *Electric Kool Aid Acid Test*, and became the inspiration for the Beatles' *Magical Mystery Tour* film.

Kesey visited Britain in late 1969 together with his Pranksters, some Hells Angels and an offshoot of the Grateful Dead family known as the Pleasure Crew. Jeff Dexter believes there were also some of the people who were in the Brotherhood of Eternal Love, a loose knit group of LSD chemists and distributors. They were there because, somewhat patronisingly, "they were trying to turn on London". They had also come to visit the Beatles who were, to the US acid intelligentsia, the "sun kings", psychedelic deities who needed to be thanked for their contribution to the consciousness revolution. And to accelerate the revoluton "they brought with them thousands of acid tabs. I was supposed to share this with the people I thought were ok. I was given this huge bag of acid. It was orange. I was doing lots of shows at that time and whenever anyone I felt was deserving I would share it with them, pass on the sacrament to them, and it was brilliant, absolutely fantastic … I never sold it, I just gave it away."[32]

In the late Sixties, the government believed most LSD consumed in Britain was imported from America. This perception was based on a wealth of media reports from the US and an unwillingness on the government's behalf to acknowledge that a great deal was being made in Britain. The Kapur trial had shown that LSD was being illegally manufactured almost from the day it was outlawed. LSD was relatively easy to make and the formula for it was available in university libraries and in samizdat publications circulating in the counter culture. There was constant demand for LSD and the temptation to try making it was strong for anyone who was curious and had the money to finance a laboratory.

Peter Simmons was one of those who found the temptation too much to resist. After being on the periphery of the cannabis and LSD dealing scene for a few years, Simmons thought he would move into manufacturing. Money wasn't the motivating factor in this decision. "I was quite evangelical. Money was just something that enabled you to do things. I wanted people to trip".[33]

A friend gave him a partial recipe for LSD and when his dealing partner located a full formula for LSD at the Patents Office, he decided it was time to find a chemist who could turn his dream into reality. His first two chemists worked from a laboratory he set up in a caravan on a site outside London. This turned out to be a disaster. They were disturbed by a neighbour knocking at the door and, believing it to be the police, they flushed the drug away. This lab had cost Simmons £1000 to set up, no small amount in 1968.

The second attempt, using a chemist called Quentin Theobald, was initially much more successful. Another lab was constructed, this time at Theobald's house at Hythe in Kent. Theobald knew what he was doing and asked Simmons for the best equipment, including such items as a rotary evaporator. The cost of the lab caused Simmons to "go up several gears in my dealing" to provide the funds for this laboratory. The lab lasted for three production runs. The run produced a gram of liquid LSD that they sold on in 100 trip bottles. It was sold as liquid because the chemist couldn't manage to crystallise it. They managed to get the second run solid enough to put it into capsules for sale. Although Theobald was a competent chemist, the flaws in the manufacturing process meant that they were unnecessarily handling the LSD and were high most of the time.

The finished product sold well and gave them the impetus to continue making the drug. However, all was not well. Flushed with his success at being an acid chemist, Theobald began to boast about his unusual career at parties. Being an LSD chemist carried considerable kudos in the counter culture and it's easy to see the social advantages of his boasts. But his indiscretions meant that word of their activities was out and it was only a matter of time before the police got wind of their laboratory.

During one production run, the chemist and an old friend got blind drunk while trying to solve the problem of how to crystallise the LSD. The drunken evening ended with them falling asleep having forgotten where they had put the fruits of their labour. When Simmons arrived the next day, he found a filter paper on a windowsill covered with a chemical mess; the missing LSD, left exposed to the air and sunlight for over twelve hours. Simmons thought it would be inert but wanted to test it anyway. So with no knowledge of what the dosage would be he randomly cut a lump off the paper and ate it.

The LSD hit shortly afterwards as Simmons sat watching

cricket on the village green. He managed to stagger through the overwhelming hallucinations back to the lab where he retired to bed before losing consciousness. When he came round several hours later, still heavily under the influence, he estimated he had taken a dose between ten and hundred times the usual dose.

The third LSD production run had just been completed and the drug was in crystallised form when the police simultaneously raided Simmons' London flat and the acid lab in Hythe. At the trial, Simmons received five years in prison, Theobald the chemist seven years. Simmons believes his sentence was high because details of the Manson trial had recently dominated the media. This is unlikely. Though sentencing was inconsistent when it came to LSD, five years imprisonment for producing substantial quantities of the drug was light when compared to sentences in the late Seventies.

When the initial furore about LSD had died down the media needed a new way to present the subject to its readers. Between 1968 and 1973 the media seized on any scare story they could to demonstrate the evils of LSD. It was claimed the drug was responsible for individuals jumping from the roof of a house, drowning as the result of believing LSD allowed one to walk on water, dying in a car crash while under the influence of LSD and being run over while tripping. These were just a few of the stories published by the press during that period. But in each case, there was no evidence that LSD was actually responsible for the mishaps, only that the victim was using it at the time or had done so previously. This was selective reporting at its best.

Even if the scare stories were all true and directly related to LSD use, the numbers of such incidences, compared with the numbers of people taking the drug, were disproportionate to the press coverage. It would have been odd, for instance, to find in *The Times*, a report of someone running naked through the streets after a drinking session, yet that is exactly the story the paper ran in April 1971 when a youth on LSD did exactly that. The unspoken implication in all these reports was that LSD would always make you do things over which you have no control. None of the papers reported how many people had found spiritual salvation or changed their lives for the better by using LSD. For the media LSD always equalled misery.

More serious allegations were made in 1970 when the government's Advisory Committee on Drug Dependence published "The Amphetamines and Lysergic Acid Diethylamide". The paper suggested that the urge to kill is one of the mental states brought on by use of LSD. This suggestion was a very small part of the report and was not backed by any quantifiable evidence, but made good newspaper copy, even *The Times* reporting "LSD induces urge to kill".[34]

London's Drug Squad was, until 1968, quite disorganised. The majority of the fieldwork was done by two teams of detectives, one of which was led by Norman Pilcher who had been involved in the Kapur LSD ring. Pilcher was notorious in London for targeting the drug habits of rock stars; after a raid on John Lennon's flat he earned a mention as the "Semolina Pilchard" in The Beatles' "I am the Walrus".

LSD was a relatively new drug to the police and as such required a new way of policing. When Victor Kelaher became head of the Drug Squad in May 1968, his strategy was to target the LSD manufacturers rather than the street users. His first big case came in the spring of 1968 when a Hungarian student chemist by the name of Kalniczky was arrested at an LSD laboratory in the East End. Kalniczky's partner in crime told the police where they had obtained their raw materials, and by using phone taps the police were able to arrest Malcolm Sinclair, an industrial chemist, and John Conway, a nightclub owner. Unfortunately, Kelaher had not checked the statute books. If he had, he would have discovered that possession of the constituent chemicals of LSD was not illegal and so the case against them failed. Sinclair was also exporting the same chemicals to the US through a friend called Ken Lee. This information, when supplied to the American authorities, led to successful convictions for crimes relating to LSD possession and manufacture in various States.[35]

As LSD use increased so did arrests for possession, supply and manufacturing. But the methods some police officers used to secure their convictions was coming in for criticism from many quarters. In their first annual report Release, the civil rights group founded in 1967 to help those arrested for alleged drug offences, claimed that the police sometimes planted drugs on suspects to guarantee convictions. Worse still, there were rumours that the drug squad were paying off informants with seized drugs.

Rumour became fact when, in 1970, Kevin Healy, a London heroin addict, agreed to become a police informer. Healy agreed to act as intermediary in an LSD deal between an undercover drug squad officer and a major LSD supplier called Lewis. The subterfuge paid off and Lewis was convicted of possession of 13,152 LSD tablets. He received three years probation, a light sentence and one of many inconsistent sentencing decisions made by the courts when they have dealt with LSD suppliers and manufacturers.

All Healy had officially received for his trouble was £20. Unofficially he claimed that he was given 162 of the seized LSD tablets, with the promise of more to come. This didn't seem much to Healy who was now worried about the possible repercussions of being identified as an informer. Realizing he had evidence of corruption, he immediately went to see Rufus Harris at Release who took the story to Granada TV's *World in Action* team.

World in Action was a respected investigative TV programme of the 1970s. Using Healy's information, they began a covert investigation. In one secretly taped telephone conversation between undercover drug squad officer Nick Prichard and Healy, Prichard was caught on tape admitting that Healy could expect a cut of whatever was retrieved from a drug arrest, saying "... you know you get that from us."[36]

In July 1970 Ken Lee, who had been involved in the supply of raw materials used to manufacture LSD in the 1968 Kalniczky arrest, returned to Britain. Police intelligence discovered he had brought a gram of LSD with him and was looking for a buyer. Undercover police officer Nick Prichard posed as a hippie and negotiated a sale between Lee and undercover American drug enforcement agent John Coleman. So far, so good. During the deal, in which the LSD changed hands for £450, Coleman persuaded Lee to reveal the names of his American colleagues who were running LSD labs, leading to their arrest. The American Drug

Enforcement Agency was pleased, having secured several arrests for the outlay of £450.

In their book *The Fall of Scotland Yard,* authors Cox, Shirley and Short make the point, "LSD had been bought and sold in London with the full knowledge of the Drug Squad and without the arrest of either party: worse, a Scotland Yard officer had been present at the deal and had indeed conspired to bring it about. The Home Office, when they learned about the incident the following November, had a positive word for the operation: 'illegal.'"[37]

Despite this sting being organised by the London police and although Nick Prichard was present during the transaction, Lee was not arrested.

Another hint of police corruption came in the summer of 1970 when a London LSD dealer known as Bartlett was arrested at the Isle of Wight festival in possession of 430 trips. Bartlett claimed he was a police informant working for Norman Pilcher and that Pilcher had personally given him the LSD to sell at the festival. Bartlett could not provide any substantive evidence Pilcher had provided him with the drug, and initially it seemed like a weak ruse in order to receive a lighter sentence. But when Hampshire police checked with their London colleagues they were phoned by Pilcher himself, confirming Bartlett was an important police informant. So important, in fact, that the head of the drug squad, Victor Kelaher, appeared as a character witness for Bartlett at the Isle of Wight quarter sessions.

The fact that the Drug Squad was corrupt came as no surprise to the counter culture. They had known about it for years and published several articles in the underground press about the matter. But the level to which the Drug Squad were corrupt made several high ranking police officers think carefully how they would structure any large anti-drug operations in the future. When Operation Julie was set up in the mid-Seventies to target LSD manufacturing and distribution in Britain, the lessons learnt in the Drug Squad corruption trials were applied to the Julie team and corruption was avoided.

In March 1970, the Home Office report of the Advisory Committee on Drug Dependence reported: "Probably the bulk of

British LSD is smuggled in from the USA." Those responsible for compiling the report would have done well to look at the LSD seizures for the preceding years. Much of the LSD found in police raids was being manufactured in Britain, some of it being manufactured specifically for export to the USA. For instance, detectives involved in the Kapur LSD manufacturing case found evidence some of Kapur's product was made specifically for the American market.

Whatever the Home Office thought they knew about LSD in the early Seventies, they had no idea of a plot being hatched beneath their noses. A group of LSD idealists was coming together, motivated by their psychedelic experiences, certain that the drug could be a catalyst for radical change in society. Lief Fielding, one of the group's peripheral members, wrote: "In the 60s I was an 'acid freak' – one of a group centred around Reading University whose lives had been transformed by the powerful psychedelic. Acid had, we thought, given us a collective vision of a saner, safer future, one where human interactions would not be based on greed, fear and coercion."[38]

This sort of thinking was endemic throughout the LSD counter culture at the time, but Fielding notes: "Unlike many similar groups throughout the country we did not confine ourselves to talking. In 1970, together with a bunch of similarly-minded people from Cambridge, we began to manufacture and distribute small quantities of LSD. Our conspiracy was on its way."[39]

American author David Solomon was now resident in Cambridge and headed the conspiracy. He surrounded himself with like-minded LSD intellectuals and with a promising young chemist called Richard Kemp; Solomon initiated the production of LSD that would lead inexorably to the 1977 Operation Julie arrests.

The early Seventies saw acid guru Michael Hollingshead back on the British scene. Following his release from prison, Hollingshead had spent some time in Sweden before returning to London. He then sojourned in Nepal, living in Kathmandu with the hippies and editing *Flow*, a poetry magazine. On his return he noted many acidheads were also, "… looking for a way in which to re-enter the West. They found coming back to the West after years in the Himalayas just a very bad trip because there you've opened yourself out and then you have to come back to all this."[40]

Hollingshead resolved to found a psychedelic ashram for those who found western civilisation too overpowering. In late 1970, he struck a deal with the Cathedral of the Isles on Greater Cumbrae, an island off the west coast of Scotland, and founded a commune within its grounds. The Pure Land Ashram, as it was known, attracted a number of young people, mainly drug takers. It has been alleged that full moon LSD ceremonies were held there on a monthly basis. According to an ex-resident of the commune, who wishes to remain anonymous, this is rubbish. "From time to time, and more on an individual basis, people would take LSD, but it was never that available from what I remember."[41]

When the Cumbrae commune closed due to pressure from the church authorities, they left the island together in a van, intending to continue their communal existence in London. They broke their journey at a large manor house where Hollingshead knew the occupants well. He introduced the group to two "male psychologists" who claimed they were experimenting with LSD for clinical use. Most of the Cumbrae group decided to try this new LSD, and the "psychologists" observed as the trip unfolded.

The former communard wrote of the experience: "We ended up in London via a big house in Oxfordshire where most of the group overdosed on some extremely strong LSD and really flipped out. I at this stage was off it so I was watching the whole thing. This was given to us at this house as some kind of psychological experiment by the people who lived there. Michael knew them. It all went terribly wrong and they thought we were going to wreck their house and their reputation locally."[42] Hollingshead knew Solomon very well and this event might well have been a test run for the early Operation Julie LSD that was to dominate LSD use in Britain for most of the Seventies. When back in London, Hollingshead took the Cumbrae group to meet the noted painter, Felix Topolski who he had turned on to LSD some years previously. Topolski painted a large picture of the group.

By 1970, the heady days of flower power were over. LSD use was still on the increase but the LSD inspired Manson slayings in America had cast a dark shadow over the counter culture. The Altamont festival, at which one man had died, was the antithesis of the Woodstock generation and the film *Easy Rider* had shown both touching naïvety and the violent death of the hippie dream through the eyes of two young bikers. Harder drugs such as heroin and morphine were becoming more prevalent and LSD culture was slowly being subsumed in the wider arena of general drug abuse. In Britain, this darkness was made visible in the disturbing 1970 film *Performance* starring Mick Jagger. Warner Brothers expected a benign look into upper class hippiedom but instead were presented with a hippie gangster film that baffled them, causing some executives to walk out of the first screening. The film starred James Fox as Chas, a gangster on the run from Kray-like mobsters. Looking for a place to lie low he holes up in the basement of the rich and decadent rock star Turner, played by Jagger. The film plays with ideas of identity and power, shot through with drug taking both on and off set. The psychedelics used in the film were hallucinogenic mushrooms, presumably because they were more visible than LSD. Rolling Stones' groupie Anita Pallenberg, who took a leading role, recalls she "... used to tease James Fox by saying that I had spiked his coffee with LSD."[43]

Performance was a dark and edgy look at the drug subculture. Whilst the film industry could mirror the zeitgeist with such films, television shied away from using LSD in anything other than serious documentaries and news items. This situation changed in 1972 with *The Alf Garnett Saga*, the second feature film based on the successful TV sit-com *Till Death Us Do Part*. The star, jingoistic Alf Garnett, finds a tablet of LSD in his fridge, hidden there by son-in-law Mike. Mistaking the drug for sugar, Garnett takes it and embarks on a fictional LSD trip that rivalled the real thing for strangeness. Garnett harangues TV personalities Max Bygraves and Eric Sykes as well as celebrity footballer George Best at a football match when at the height of his trip. The portrayal of the old, racist Garnett on acid must have left anyone in the audience who wasn't already aware of LSD's effects even more perplexed about the drug.

In January 1971, the pages of *International Times* featured a letter from one Bill Dwyer "Dear Brothers and Sisters, I have been busted with what eventually may prove to be 1400 tabs of LSD". Dwyer, who lived in a commune and was soon to become a driving force in the free festival movement, planned to base his defence on his belief that, "… acid is a holy sacrament which greatly assists the individual in cleansing himself of selfishness and the various million inhibitions bestowed on us by an authoritarian, moralistic society."[44] Dwyer's letter was evidence the LSD counter culture was a powerful force and had individuals at its core who were committed to LSD as an agent of individual and political change.

All over Britain small communes, squats and shared houses were home to groups of people for whom LSD was a way of life. A letter published in *IT*, a year after Dwyer's, exemplified this. It was from "Roger & the Gang" in a Hackney commune who were trying to recruit female members: "Dear I.T., we are a psychedelic based commune … We believe in group marriage and the expanding of consciousness and also live on a vegetarian/health food basis."[45] Individuals such as Roger and Bill Dwyer were representative of those people who were committed to a full psychedelic lifestyle; one in which LSD permeated and drove every aspect of their existence. They believed a psychedelic life was possible and, if enough people adopted it, could lead to a psychedelic revolution among young people. There were thousands of such people, living in flats, squats and communes, an acid constituency with big aspirations but few people capable or willing to lead them.

Increased use of LSD and other drugs panicked the government to update the 1964 Drugs (Prevention of Misuse) Act, to which LSD was added in 1966. The new act, the Misuse of Drugs Act 1971, created three classes of drug, A, B and C and all illegal substances, derivatives and known analogues were encompassed within it. LSD was now a Class A drug. Possession of the drug became punishable with seven years imprisonment and/or an unlimited fine, and trafficking punishable with life imprisonment and an unlimited fine. This did nothing to stem the use of LSD, which increased rather than decreased in the Seventies. Prohibition was very definitely not working, but new laws and new penalties provided the media and politicians with useful rhetoric with which to worry their constituents and readers.[46]

For the government, Timothy Leary's name had become synonymous with all that was bad about LSD. He had been refused entry to Britain on several previous occasions and it was clear the British political administration saw him as a serious threat to the nation's youth. In 1973 Leary once again attempted to gain entry to Britain. On this occasion, Federal Agents were escorting Leary back to the USA from Afghanistan after a period on the run following his 1970 escape from a federal prison. When the plane from Afghanistan stopped over at Frankfurt, Joanna, Leary's wife, phoned her godfather Max Aitken, owner of London's *Evening Standard*, and told him "Timothy says as soon as we get to Heathrow, he's demanding political, philosophical, and spiritual asylum."[47]

Leary was met from his plane at Heathrow by Mr Greenyer, who had dealt with him on two previous occasions. Greenyer later commented dryly, "During the years since I last met him, Mr. Leary has developed much stronger belief in himself as the 'Messiah', though he backs this with highly intelligent, even logical speech. His words, possibly said jokingly, before departure were 'In this world's march I am one of the very few in step.'" Despite his voluble requests to immigration officials, yet again, he was refused entry to Britain. Leary, whose US identity card gave his profession as "philosopher", took the refusal calmly before being flown to Los Angeles in a specially cordoned off area of a Pan Am 747. On this occasion however, Leary did manage to court some publicity; a large photograph of him appeared in *The Times*. Leary and his wife Joanna Harcourt-Smith were pictured on the moving walkway as they left the flight from Kabul, Leary sporting his trademark grin.[48]

Even though only a small percentage of Britain's population had actually taken LSD, the drug, or more correctly the *idea* of the drug, was now firmly embedded in popular culture. It was so accepted by the majority of young people that in 1973 the future contender for the 2007 Liberal Democrat Party leadership, Chris Huhne, wrote an article on drugs while at Oxford University. His position on LSD, which he intimated was actually being made clandestinely at Oxford, summed up the attitude held by most young people of the time, "Acid [LSD] is manufactured in the labs and is the only drug which is getting cheaper ... The considerable number of students at this university who drop acid are well-balanced highly intelligent people ... if one is able to live with oneself ... then acid holds no surprises."[49]

As the idea of LSD permeated society, manufacturers and their advertisers employed psychedelic imagery whenever they could. Book covers, LP sleeves, clothes, even food and drink began to be advertised with a psychedelic gloss, the implication being that by buying that particular product you were familiar with or at the very least aligning yourself with the LSD experience. Hippie clothes styles, such as the Indian kaftan, were being sold in high street chain stores. The LSD counter culture was becoming commodified and sold back to young people by cynical capitalists. By adopting the right clothes and music anyone could easily lay claim to being an acidhead. These so called "plastic hippies" were loathed by the genuine LSD counter culture, becoming just another in a long line of youth fashion fads stretching back through mods, rockers, beatniks and teddy boys.

The authentic LSD counter culture was about to start mobilizing itself through the free festival movement and the Operation Julie LSD manufacturing and distribution network. These two strands were crucial to keeping LSD culture alive throughout the Seventies and were to mark both the death of the LSD dream and point the way forward into the final two decades of the twentieth century.

10

BRING WHAT YOU EXPECT TO FIND

> Naked she danced in the warm morning sun. Her hips swayed suggestively to the beat of the music. On her back was scrawled in ballpoint: "Got any Acid?"[1]

Free festivals were a response to a variety of emerging needs within the counter culture. Night clubs and commercial rock festivals did not appeal to the sensibilities of acid sensitised hippies who were questioning ideas of profit and control; wanting to be more than just consumers of entertainment industry product. There was a demand for events self-generated by the counter culture, which would provide hippies with gatherings where they could live out their lifestyle with like minded people in a spirit of celebration and purpose.

Another factor in the development of the counter culture was the growth of communes and the squatting movement in London. By necessity this had led to a more communal way of life; whole streets in London had been colonised by squatters and it was a natural progression from community in the cities to communality in the countryside.

During the Seventies, local authorities evicted thousands of squatters; many went on the road permanently, their lifestyle becoming intertwined with the free festivals. Writing in *Festival Eye*, Krystoff summed up the contribution of squatters to the free festival scene: "The Free City of Camden, which became the base for early Stonehenge festivals, was a loose, street-by-street network of squatters, revolutionaries and artists who subscribed to the philosophy of giving and practiced consensus politics rather than 'representative democracy', establishing an anarchic lifestyle and a sense of community feeling. The first festivals at Stonehenge were the expression of this kind of community feeling. They were spontaneous 'happenings' and quickly attracted other avant-garde groups and communes from around the country. The eviction of the Free City of Camden made tens of thousands of people homeless and many of them took to the road. The festival became the community's home, rather than its playground."[2]

The first multi-day free festival was Phun City, held on Ecclesden Common near Worthing in West Sussex on 24 July 1970. It was organised by Mick Farren and backed by *International Times*. The organisers made the purpose of the festival clear: "Phun City is attempting to provide a three day environment designed to the needs and desires of the Freak, not just a situation set up to relieve him of his money."

There was no entry fee, food was cheap or free and there was an endless stream of music from the cream of Britain's underground bands. For the 3000 people who attended, the festival proved to be enormous fun. Many went feral for a few days, living under tarpaulins and plastic in the woods. LSD was in great demand but was more than matched by the supply. One veteran of the event, "Tom" remembered: "A genuine Californian hippie in long white robes holding a plastic bag with thousands of hits of pure acid came along trying to give us some tabs, but all the people around the fire were surfing on lots of clean high quality acid and everyone had more than enough anyways."[3]

Bolstered by the music and sense of communality engendered by psychedelic drugs, many people who were camping in the woods resolved to stay there. But the West Sussex constabulary had other ideas. On 27 July those remaining were unceremoniously ousted and sent on their way. Though the organisers lost significant amounts of money, Phun City had been a success, showing the counter culture they could come together in the country for several days and make their own entertainment. There was now much talk of a far larger festival, a real gathering of the tribes. But for such a festival to take place an organiser and a location were needed.

The annual Glastonbury Festival is a unique British cultural institution. Each year, in June, on the weekend nearest the summer solstice, hundreds of thousands of people flock to Worthy Farm in the Somerset village of Pilton to camp for three days. They are there to experience the dizzying kaleidoscope of music, theatre and arts on offer on numerous stages. The festival caters for all ages, cultures and socio-economic backgrounds. It is often referred to by cynics as a holiday camp for middle-class hippies. Yet the origins of this quintessentially British event are rooted deep in the counter culture and closely linked with LSD. Had it not been for the psychedelic focus of the first major Glastonbury event, the festival in its present form would not exist.

But why and how did Glastonbury become the spiritual birthplace of the free festival movement? The growing awareness among young people that the LSD experience itself was not the destination, but a catalyst to a spiritual journey, had led to an explosion of interest in a variety of belief systems during the Sixties. As we have seen, psychedelic seekers often chose to explore Buddhism, Hinduism and other religions. Others found themselves drawn to the Western Mystery Tradition, Arthurian legend, magic and shamanism, wanting to discover at firsthand the legacy of spiritual traditions and beliefs of the British Isles.

The Glastonbury area is steeped in myth and legend; it is claimed Jesus visited Glastonbury Abbey, UFOs were seen flying over the Tor, ley-lines criss-crossed the area sending serpent power through the West Country, a terrestrial Zodiac could be discerned in landscape features and so on. These and many other legends had recently been re-vivified for the counter culture by John Michell in his books *The Flying Saucer Vision* and *The View Over Atlantis*. Michell wrote: "It was, I think, in 1966 that I first went to Glastonbury, in the company of Harry Fainlight ... We had no very definite reason for going there, but it had something to do with ... strange lights in the sky, new music, and our conviction that the world was about to flip over on its axis so that heresy would become orthodoxy and an entirely new world-order would shortly be revealed."[4]

Michell was the counter culture's resident philosopher, their Merlin; an Eton and Cambridge educated polymath who had taken the side of the hippies and was educating them about their spiritual heritage. Michell lived in the hippie enclave of Notting Hill Gate, as comfortable at counter culture events as he was hanging out with the Rolling Stones and minor aristocracy. His books were key spiritual guides for the British counter culture and could be found in every thinking hippie's pad, offering a source of discussion and speculation for those long LSD trips toward the dawn.

Michell showed there was no need to take the hippie trail to the East when the West Country was just down the M4. And the visual imagery of Glastonbury was everywhere in the underground press. One very good example is the cover of issue one of the Underground magazine, *Albion*, to which Michell contributed heavily. Dragons and UFOs teem in the skies over Glastonbury Tor, here stylised as a woman's breast, whilst swords, serpents and geomantic imagery are visible in the Earth below. Hippie travellers in search of enlightenment had settled in the area from the mid-Sixties onwards, fuelled by Michell's exposition of Glastonbury as a sacred place. It was against this backdrop that the Glastonbury festivals developed.[5]

The first festival at Glastonbury in 1970 was a low-key, commercial event attended by a few hundred people. The festival, organised by Pilton farmer, Michael Eavis, was not a financial success. To recoup his losses, Eavis left the organization of the 1971 event, known as Glastonbury Fair, to a rather unlikely group of people.[6]

Andrew Kerr first met Arabella Churchill, Winston's granddaughter, while working on Randolph Churchill's biography of the great political leader. In the late Sixties, like thousands of others, Kerr was taking LSD and enjoying being part of the counter culture. The seed of his idea to hold a free festival at Glastonbury was planted at the 1969 Isle of Wight rock festival.

Kerr was outraged that large areas near the stage were cordoned off for the press and privileged few. On the drive back to London he announced to his fellow passengers: "We've got to have a proper festival and it's got to have at least some cosmic significance. Let's have it at the summer solstice at Stonehenge."[7]

Kerr's intention to hold the festival at Stonehenge was put in abeyance when he was given Michael Eavis' telephone number. A meeting was arranged at Worthy Farm and Kerr prepared by spending the night before atop Glastonbury Tor on LSD. The meeting was successful. Eavis agreed to the use of his land and Kerr, assisted by Arabella Churchill and utilizing a small inheritance, formed Solstice Capers to organise the 1971 festival.

The *Observer* wrote: "Kerr has the intensity of a man with a deep spiritual obsession. He claims he is trying to recreate a prehistoric science, whose huge energies are not recognised by modern society. His ideas are based on the writings of antiquarian John Michell, who in a book called *The View Over Atlantis*, recently elucidated the spiritual engineering which, he says, was known over the ancient world."[8]

These ideas were transmuted into the location and design of the stage. Kerr dowsed the site and when he located a blind spring, with Glastonbury Tor in the distance, the stage was situated above it. John Michell told him the stage should be built to the proportions of Egypt's Great Pyramid. This suited Kerr's intention for the festival, which was to "… create an increase in the power of the Universe, a heightening of consciousness and recognition of our place in the function of this our tired and molested planet."[9] Bill Harkin, now a respected stage designer, designed and built the stage and a silver pyramid sprang up among the cows and hedges of Worthy Farm.

Jeff Dexter, veteran DJ from London's UFO club, organised the music, consisting of the hippie bands that had played at London's Roundhouse, including freak favourites Quintessence, Brinsley Schwarz, Hawkwind, Gong, Traffic and Arthur Brown. These bands were open about their use of LSD and strove to create music and atmosphere to be experienced while under the influence of psychedelic drugs. Dexter tried hard to get the archetypal LSD band, the Grateful Dead, over from America to play but this didn't come off, though they did send a financial donation to support the festival.

Psychedelics of all kinds, including mescaline, were freely available at Glastonbury, but LSD was prevalent. Author, William Bloom's impression of Glastonbury was that "… nearly everyone was tripping at one stage or another. Sometimes it was being given away … The festivals would not have been what they were without hallucinogens."[10]

David Bowie recalled being under the influence of magic mushrooms as he took the stage at five in the morning: "By the time I was due to perform I was flying and could hardly see my little electric keyboard or my guitar."[11]

Arabella Churchill didn't indulge, but knew "there was a lot of acid because this man came up with a large briefcase and said: 'This is full of acid, man. I was going to sell it but everyone's doing everything for free so here, give it to everybody.' I put it under a bed and I can't remember what happened to it in the end."[12]

Many clergymen visited the 1971 Glastonbury Fair attracted by this radical youth movement and their alternative brand of spirituality. Among them was the diocesan youth chaplain from Swindon, who was given some LSD (whether voluntarily or not is unclear). The confused clergyman ended up rushing headlong down the hillside, his cloak flaring like a giant bat behind him. However, his Christian faith wasn't enough to help him navigate under the onslaught of LSD, and he had to retire to the bad trip tent organised by Release where he was gently talked back down to earth.[13]

Though the majority of LSD experiences at Glastonbury were positive there were, as at every festival, some drug casualties. Bad trip tents became a feature of the free festival scene, often full of seriously confused teenagers who had been attracted to LSD by peer pressure and expectation, but who were unprepared for the effects of the drug. These tents were the downside of the free festival experience. Quintessence guitarist Allan Mostert remembers: "A rather shattering experience I had at Glastonbury was while wandering through the audience before our set, I took a look inside the so called 'bad trip tent', where they took the people who had dropped LSD and gone on bad trips. This experience strengthened the idea in me of what we were actually trying to do with our music and 'message.'"[14]

The mixture of free psychedelics and living out the hippie ethos made the Glastonbury Fair the prototype for subsequent events. LSD brought people together around the campfires at night, making the already otherworldly experience appear completely divorced from the twentieth century and western civilization. Mick Farren summed it up: "We might as well have been in the sixth or even twenty-sixth century as we told tall travellers' tales of intoxication, of outwitting the law, of the lights in the sky, lost continents, the lies of government, collective triumphs and personal stupidity, while the music of past, present and future roared from the pyramid stage."[15]

Following the 1971 Glastonbury Fair the area became a focus for travelling hippies. Small encampments sprang up in the country lanes and there were almost continuous gatherings on the summit of Glastonbury Tor. In the Seventies, there were people taking LSD on the Tor every night of the summer. To visit the Tor, take LSD and watch the sunrise over the Somerset levels was considered a hip thing to do, a psychedelic pilgrimage.

At one stage, the tower on the Tor had been broken into and turned into a hippie crash pad. Free festival poster artist Roger Hutchison and friends travelled to the Tor from Essex. He climbed to the summit at 3 am, to find the inside of the tower bedecked with cushions and lighted tapers with a group of hippies smoking cannabis and drinking wine. Such was the spirit of community and trust in those times that he was immediately offered LSD in blotter form by a colourfully dressed hippie, and settled down to watch the sunrise, accompanied by chanting and drumming.

This type of shamanic activity was prevalent among the mystically inclined at free festivals. Drums, chanting and psychedelic drugs have been used together since prehistoric times, each enhancing the effect of the other. This type of group behaviour had not only a strong bonding effect but served to help individuals navigate the LSD experience, either as participants or observers.

Large numbers of hippies and others seeking an ecological and spiritual lifestyle settled in East Anglia in the early Seventies and held their own festivals. Thirty such festivals, or Fairs as the organisers preferred to call them, ran from 1972 to 1985. LSD was an inspiring, though less central, factor at these events; the Bungay May Horse Fair was described as having a "... truly anarchic quality which put you up against yourself more than any amount of acid and street theatre could do at the 'Barshams.'"[16]

In sharp contrast to the free festivals, the East Anglian Fairs were the expression and celebration of a static community that tried to involve the local population. Free festivals sought to isolate themselves from the local communities, intentional outsiders setting up camp for a short while before dispersing and moving on.

Soon after the success of the 1971 Glastonbury Fair, free festivals were held in north Devon and south Wales. But moves were afoot to develop large scale festivals that would run throughout the summer, becoming a focus for Britain's counter culture. The huge festivals at Windsor, Watchfield and Stonehenge would be the events which came to define free festival culture. Yet these festivals didn't just occur, they were initiated and planned by three key people, without whom the free festival movement would not have developed as it did.

It's important to trace the roots and motivations of these individuals to see how crucial LSD was to the free festival movement; how LSD underpinned the creation of environments in which people could live unhindered by what they saw as petty laws and restrictions. It is also important to acknowledge that although LSD played a major part in the early free festivals, drugs per se were not central to their economies. In the Seventies psychedelic drugs were employed at free festivals as a means to an end: celebration, spiritual enlightenment and the strengthening of a community, sold at minimal profit or given away. By the Eighties LSD had become much more commodified and free festivals acted as drug marketplaces, their distribution, promotion and sale being organised in a way that could rival anything from the conventional retail world.

The free festivals held in Windsor Great Park, near London,

were the genesis of a free festival culture, which, building on the template set up at Glastonbury, has lasted in one form or another to the present day. This would not have happened without the efforts of Bill "Ubi" Dwyer.

In the mid-Fifties Dwyer emigrated from Ireland to New Zealand where he immersed himself in the burgeoning anarchist scene. After moving to Sydney, Australia, he continued his involvement with anarchism, but politics alone no longer satisfied him: "It was still a life from which I sensed something basic was lacking but I did not know what this something was, I had rejected religion as being a mere part of the unfree society in which we live ... but there are spiritual yearnings in man which cannot be denied."[17]

Dwyer became involved with the Sydney Anarchist Group at the Cellar, an anarchist hang out off the city's Oxford Street. He began to attract socially disaffected young people to the Cellar, which changed within six months from political meeting place to psychedelic drug den. Dwyer had begun to use LSD and had become evangelical about its use. As it has done with tens of thousands of others, LSD changed Dwyer's life. For him LSD was a mystic, spiritual experience that "cleansed (me) of the evil of the past".[18]

The Cellar was transformed with mattresses, music and psychedelic lights and up to 200 hundred people at a time could be found there. A cage was built from which Dwyer sold LSD, "tickets" in Australian drug argot, through a curtain. A friend of Dwyer's recalled her visits to the Cellar: "It would've been 67 or 68; I was eighteen at the time and thought the Cellar was unbelievable ... For a start, it was free; although you had to pay for your 'tickets' once you got in there. They were purchased from an old movie box office. You put your money down and a hand appeared from under a curtain with the appropriate number of tickets. He had all the best and latest music, and all the grooviest people hung out there – it was magic."[19]

Dwyer identified those who frequented the Cellar as "... the ones most likely to find the anarchist message true to their aspirations", and he took them to his heart. Foreshadowing the ethos of the 1970s free festivals Dwyer recalled: "To promote the cultural and hedonistic aspects we hired double decker buses and drove off into the country complete with psychedelic musicians, where city kids often had their first real taste of nature."

The police sent undercover officers to the Cellar but this did not seem to bother Dwyer. Friends believed this lack of concern was due to his faith in LSD. In fact it was because he was buying his LSD directly from the police, who largely controlled the Sydney LSD trade at that time.[20] When Dwyer began to buy his LSD from another source he was soon arrested and imprisoned, later being deported to Ireland before settling in London. There he began dealing LSD again and according to Sid Rawle, had a unique way of doing so: "He would take money from people for an order of acid and it would be delivered the next day by the Royal Mail."[21]

In London Dwyer once again became involved with anarchist groups. He helped produce *Anarchy* magazine and was instrumental in issue three being "The Acid Issue". The cover featured a graphic of the LSD molecule and ninety percent of the content dealt with LSD, its effects and potential, mostly written by Dwyer. His articles are well written and make a persuasive case for the individual's right to use LSD.

Dwyer was passionate about the causes he held dear. In London he was often seen in full oratorical flow at Hyde Park's Speakers Corner eulogizing about, among other things, LSD. As a committed squatter, he also ranted against paying rent. His idea for a free festival came when he was tripping on LSD in Windsor Great Park. There he had a vision of a "… giant festival in the grandest park in the kingdom."[22] Windsor also appealed to the anarchist in Dwyer; it was on royal land, within spitting distance of the Queen's residence at Windsor Castle.

The 1972 Windsor free festival (slogan: "pay no rent") was the first of what were known as the Peoples' Free Festivals. A few hundred people partied for several days in Windsor Great Park, causing no problems. LSD was freely available to anyone who wanted it. Bolstered by the success of the first and of the growing numbers of other small free festivals, the second Windsor festival, in 1973, was a much larger affair.

LSD was not only sold cheaply at the Windsor festivals, large quantities were given away. Roger Hutchinson recalls an incident at the 1973 festival when he "… was on stage when this chap came up with a brief case, quite smartly dressed, and said: 'Is there anyone I can talk to about the distribution of the contents of this. I've got all this acid that I want to give away.' It was microdot in strips of sellotape." Hutchinson was acting as stage manager at the time and made an announcement over the PA: "'Does anyone out there fancy getting a bit higher tonight, we've got some little tablets here, yours for the taking, free,' and literally the audience just came up as one and went straight at the stage. It wasn't a very clever thing to do. The idea of it was sound I suppose, in a way, but it was already well into the festival and people were pretty wrecked and then to put on some extremely good microdot of 200 µg plus … was an absolute bloody disaster. There were people who had never tripped before, people who were used to London microdot, which was half the strength, so they were expecting one thing and they got something that took them to a completely new level, some people had taken more than one, and it was just chaos."[23]

Hutchinson didn't partake of the free LSD, having been tripping the previous night and needing some sleep. The next day he woke "… and found the site strewn with tripped out knackered folk, entangled with mangled tents."[24]

Following the 1973 event, word spread rapidly among Britain's grass roots hippies and through the growing network of communes, shared houses, squats and travellers, that the 1974 festival would be huge. The event was planned for the August Bank Holiday period and over 30,000 flyers and posters were distributed to advertise the festival. Hippie entrepreneur, Richard Branson paid for a Virgin Records stage to showcase his new acts, and individuals and hippie-friendly businesses made financial donations to the cause.

The poster for Windsor 1974 had tantalizingly advertised the presence of "psychedelicatessens". As the event unfolded, it was clear that though there were no psychedelicatessens there was a great deal of LSD.

Release set up a "bad trip" tent and prepared themselves for the inevitable onslaught of the first acid casualties. One of the staff there wrote: "A lot of us were running on natural speed by now and the first wave of heavy trippers inundated us fairly early. An inordinate number of them seemed to be 'wankers' i.e. sexually repressed individuals liberated in a bizarre kind of way by the acid."[25]

Windsor veteran Allan Staithes recalls, "there was a vast amount of acid at Windsor in 1974. Everyone was talking about it and it was obvious it was the focus of the festival. Around lunchtime on the Saturday a guy came to our tents and asked if we wanted to score any acid. We did. He produced a bottle containing tiny brown microdots at 50p each. It was the strongest acid we had yet encountered and the afternoon dissolved in a blur of wild dancing and celebration. Luckily we met up with some experienced acidheads from Wrexham who looked after us. We thought we were experienced but the acid at Windsor 74 was something else! It wasn't a bad trip but it was powerful, disorienting and shook me to the core of my being."[26]

The effects of the extremely strong LSD took its toll on the first day at Windsor. The Release report continues: "By late afternoon the area around the Release ambulance was reminiscent of a scene by Hieronymus Bosch. Yea, there was lamentation, weeping and gnashing of teeth." Those unprepared for the psychic and spiritual upheaval LSD caused were unable to keep their thoughts to themselves and, as the Release report dryly notes: "Worst of all were the juvenile philosophers who bellowed tedious cosmic observations about the state of the universe."[27] The festival newsletter published on the Sunday concurred on the strength of LSD available, "WARNING brown acid is very strong don't drop more than one tab."

Though many people took LSD during the day, the evening at free festivals was the optimum time to take acid. Staithes remembers a notice board appearing at Windsor each day with suggested "dropping times", the time of day at which LSD was best taken to enjoy the bands later in the evening. As the shadows lengthened, the real weirdness began.

To enhance the LSD experience several light shows had sprung up in Britain. They projected heated oil slides, films, cartoons and images of spirituality and nature on screens behind the stage. Even ordinary light sources could be a source of fascination for the LSD user and so these specially designed light shows became a valued contribution to any free festival as a backdrop to the live music.

The most celebrated of the British light shows was John Andrews' Acidica, a professional set up using up to thirty projectors. As the name suggests, the Acidica crew were well aware that the drug of choice at free festivals was LSD. Being LSD users themselves, they knew exactly how to tailor the light show for best effect: "We cater in the main for trippers. When we started we'd been every heavily into acid – the whole psychedelic thing and I knew that hints rather than specific designs would prompt a reaction from our audience. Most of our material is purposely ambiguous to allow individual interpretation of what we're up to. Now this is interesting because most people get off, but others freak out, it all boils down to where their heads are at – cos we're just putting up patterns!"[28]

Nigel Ayers, who as a teenager spent the summer of 1974 travelling round the free festivals, remembered LSD being given away in 1974 at Windsor when he was "… nearly crushed in the handout of hundreds of tabs of free acid in the final Windsor … There was a whip-round for a few days for 'free dope and acid', but only the acid materialised. Distribution wasn't from the stage but the stage probably announced it. Maybe six to ten people gave it out, scattered around the periphery under cover of darkness. The tabs were sandwiched in long strips of sellotape, which the distributor was biting off into individual tabs as he handed them out. There were loads and loads but a hell of a scrum to get them."[29]

Though the intent behind the distribution of free LSD may have been philanthropic and in keeping with the free festival ethos, the consequences of giving out quantities of strong LSD were ill-considered. Most of those who clamoured for the drug had already been at the festival for a few days, not eating or drinking enough and exhausted through lack of sleep and cumulative drug use. This combination of physiological and environmental factors intensified the LSD experience and, stuck in a field with minimal comforts and facilities; there was no way of moderating the drug's effects. This set of circumstances – the setting of an LSD trip – paradoxically, strengthened the sense of community and created a "Dunkirk spirit" atmosphere. Friends helped each other through difficult trips and older, more experienced LSD users were on hand if needed.

Not all the LSD dealers were particularly concerned about the effect LSD could have on the young and inexperienced user. For instance, Ayres saw one LSD dealer's tent at Windsor painted with: "I WANT TO DISTROY YOUR BRAIN CELLS" [sic]. Even among the largely mystically inclined free festival attendees there was a hard core who were just there to party and to get as intoxicated on whatever they could, with no thought for the consequences. It was this attitude, uncontested by the majority, which eventually brought the free festivals to the point of extinction and gave the authorities a good excuse to hound the counter culture.

There was also a hard core of free festival attendees for whom LSD was an essential tool in the goal of creating a society run on anarchist principles. Squatting, drug laws, the back to the land movement and a certainty that an alternate lifestyle could supersede the status quo were principles held dear by thousands. Though few did very much about it, their intent was certainly there, summed up in the Windsor newsletter *Maya*, as: "We shall celebrate with such fierce dancing the Death of your Institutions."

Several religious sects were in evidence at most free festivals, offering friendship, advice, and free food. They were also ever-hopeful of gaining converts from the ranks of those hippies left spiritually bereft by the LSD experience. The Divine Light Mission, followers of Guru Maharaj Ji, attended Windsor in 1974. Pat Conlon was a Premie or devotee: "I did service in the bad trip tent. I got stuck with one guy for most of one day. He was really freaked and two sisters in those ugly long dresses gave him satsang [devotional speech, chants, etc.]. He ripped his clothes off and wanted to fuck them … He was masturbating furiously and unashamedly. Being in pharmacy, I knew that he needed Thorazine but there was none to be had. I was told to give him satsang but could not bring myself to tell him as he was not in the mood for it."[30]

Another Divine Light Premie who worked in the bad trip tent had this to say: "I was in and around the tent for three days. There were always at least three or four people being cared for at a time, when I was in the tent. I suppose I saw fifty to sixty people over the three days."[31] Given that the festival ran for six days, it would appear that at a rough estimate, a minimum of 120 people had LSD experiences bad enough to warrant spending time in the Divine Light bad trip tent. Factor in the Hare Krishna people, the Release ambulance, other organizations who dealt with bad trips at the festival and the many individuals who were cared for by their friends or people they had met and it's clear that hundreds of people had problems dealing with the strength of LSD on offer at Windsor.

Windsor 1974 seems to have had more acid casualties than any other documented free festival. Set and setting, as we've seen, would have contributed to the situation to a certain extent. But, by all accounts, it was the sheer potency of LSD that caused the problems. This has led to speculation that it was the "super LSD" that had been developed by LSD chemist Richard Kemp, later to be arrested in the 1977 Operation Julie raids.

It is perhaps unfortunate that bad LSD experiences are the ones most often recorded in the media and in memory. For every bad LSD experience there were many more good ones; trips which changed peoples' lives irrevocably and pointed them down their career and life path. One person who underwent such an LSD experience at Windsor was author Graham Hancock: "I took LSD once in my twenties, at the Windsor Free Festival in 1974, and had a fantastic, exciting, energizing twelve-hour trip in a parallel reality. When my normal, everyday consciousness returned – and it did so quite abruptly, like a door slamming – I felt grateful for such a wonderful experience but so much in awe of its power that I vowed never to do it again."[32]

Hancock went on to become a best selling author and explorer in the field of fringe archaeology and consciousness studies. His website doesn't record whether he took LSD again but in 2005 he reported, "Now, in my fifties I had to confront the psychic challenges of major hallucinogens again", and has frequently taken psychedelic compounds, such as ibogaine, used by indigenous tribes. There was no formal police presence on the actual site of the Windsor 74 festival but the roads around and leading to the site were thronged with police, on foot and in vehicles. Many festival-goers were stopped and comprehensively searched but due to police ignorance about LSD, and how easy it was to hide, very little was discovered. It turned out that the purpose for the strong police presence wasn't primarily to find drugs; it was to ensure enough police were present to decommission the festival when the order was given. As cultural commentator, George Melly wrote after the event: "The last bastion of all that was the free festival occurred at Windsor last week and anyone rash enough to prefer to go there was at risk. Free food, free music, people peeing in bushes and whatever and poking wherever and whenever they felt like it, and on Royal ground too and without permission – there'll be no more of that!"[33]

And there wasn't. On the morning of 29 August, after more than a week of often violent confrontation on the festival's perimeter, hundreds of police moved in. Campers were told they had ten minutes to gather their possessions and move off. Many were given much less time than that before the police brutally attacked unarmed men, women and children, trashing tents, stages and possessions. This was the first serious attempt by the authorities to damage the counter culture, but it wouldn't be the last.

At the same time as the Windsor festival another, much lower key, event was taking place at Stonehenge. This was the first in a series of free festivals at Stonehenge which continued until 1984. Like Windsor, they were instigated by one man driven by his LSD experiences.

"Wally" was a cry heard at festivals and music gigs throughout the Seventies, often to people's annoyance as shouts for Wally echoed around camping sites through the night. Whether taken from the name of a lost dog or a lost soul, Phil Russell took Wally as his name, adding the surname Hope, in his campaign to hold free festivals at the ancient monument.

Wally Hope has become a free festival icon and his name lives in free festival legend as a dream of what could have been. His story is a sad tale of enthusiasm and naïvety. Wally came from a wealthy background – his legal guardian was the BBC newsreader John Snagge – and until he came into his inheritance he had a trust fund which allowed him to live as he chose. Early involvement with hippies, drugs and a group of street anarchists in London called the Dwarves embedded Wally firmly in the counter culture, but it was on a visit to Cyprus that the idea for a festival at Stonehenge was formed. There, he had a vision under the influence of LSD, a drug which he regarded as a sacrament. He saw the sun as God and he realised his mission was to reclaim the sun temple of Stonehenge from the authorities and turn it into a place of living celebration and worship.[34]

Wally attended the 1973 Windsor free festival but was unhappy with what he saw there. As an idealist, the idea of hippies demanding money from commercial traders clashed with his belief in the concept of "free". Wally's friend Tim Abbott noted: "He was disillusioned by what was already happening at the 'People's Free Festival' … As well as being a psychedelic anarchist, he had a strong traditionalist streak, and was upset that the Queen's back garden should be littered and fouled. He had a vision that it could be done in a purer way."[35]

Wally set up camp at Stonehenge in the summer of 1974, in good time for the solstice, and he and his followers occupied a site near the stones until the winter. Officials from the Department of the Environment, who came to investigate who was squatting on their land, were told that everyone there was called Wally. When asked their names by journalists or at the court proceedings to evict them from the site Wally's followers always gave their name as Wally.

Nigel Ayers spent several weeks at "Fort Wally", as the camp was dubbed, and was able to observe it closely. There was a hard core camp "… of thirty or so people … There were many different motivations behind the people at the camp. Some were obviously from highly privileged backgrounds, some were minors who had run away from abusive parents, some were petty criminals and addicts, some were mentally ill, some were hardcore mystics and some were teenaged hedonists."[36]

For all Wally's psychedelic dreams, the camp was a drab affair, with people sitting around doing very little. His followers were very keen on LSD and much time was spent talking about it, having discussions about such ludicrous questions as whether children should be given LSD. Nor was this a theoretical discussion. A couple at the site was actually giving their children LSD on a daily basis, believing it to be the "religious thing to do".

Giving any non prescribed drug to children is an unwise thing to do; giving them acid is totally irresponsible. Yet it's a measure of just how committed to the psychedelic lifestyle some LSD users were. In November 1974 Leonard Burkes, a squatter and LSD dealer from Kentish Town pleaded guilty to giving acid to his nine-year-old son. It was also suggested in court that he had given the drug to his four- and six-year-old children. Under questioning Burkes told the police he had been giving LSD to his children since they were four, giving the nine-year-old half a microdot twice a week. The boy was interviewed and said he had been taking LSD for a long time and it made him "happy". [37]

Wally and his tribe spent some time at the 1974 Windsor free festival before returning to their Stonehenge camp until the winter. His foot soldiers wintered in a squatted house in nearby Amesbury and Wally retired to Cyprus for the winter. On his return he threw himself headlong into the preparations for the 1975 Stonehenge festival. But it wasn't to be. In May 1975 he called in at the Amesbury squat and was caught up in a police raid. They said they were looking for an army deserter but instead found Wally with some LSD in his pocket.

Bruce Garrard, in his unpublished *Legacy of Wally Hope* suggests the LSD didn't even belong to Wally: "The theory goes that there was this young kid, run away from school, who had some acid, and Wally Hope took the rap for him. He was arrested and brought before Amesbury magistrates where he not only didn't deny possession of LSD, he enthused about it, told them it was wonderful stuff which opened the mind to all kinds of visions ..."[38]

Eulogizing about LSD in a court of law is a bad idea for anyone. For Wally, dressed outlandishly, with a reputation as a fervent anarchist, festival organiser and thorn in the establishment's side, it was positively suicidal. The magistrates thought Wally was suffering from a mental disorder and had him detained under the Mental Health Act and committed to the Old Manor psychiatric hospital in Salisbury.

Wally was held until two days after the 1975 Stonehenge festival had finished. He was medicated to such an extent that it took him two days to return to his guardian's home in Epping. LSD was Wally's sacrament, the chemical that drove his dreams, but the fire had been burned out of Wally with chemicals forced into him by the establishment.

Wally managed to get to the Watchfield festival in late August where he was cared for in a tipi. The Tipi People wanted him to return with them to Tipi Valley in Wales but he refused and returned home. Shortly afterwards he was found dead, choked on his own vomit. The coroner's inquest was adjourned twice before it took place and when it did much of the evidence was missing. Conspiracy theories abound concerning Wally. Was he targeted and destroyed because of his desire to hold free festivals at Stonehenge? Author Chris Stone received a letter from a solicitor, Trevor Helm, who had been hired to investigate Wally's death. Helm was of the opinion that Wally had been deceived by the authorities who told him if he didn't plead guilty to the possession of LSD charge, he would be remanded until after the 1975 Stonehenge festival had taken place. But the plea of guilty played into the court's hands and they were then able to section him under the Mental Health Act.[39]

Stonehenge 1975 went ahead without Wally and was a huge success. Between two and three thousand people attended and hundreds sat in cross-legged meditation to welcome the sun's rays on the summer solstice. One of Wally's friends, Sid Rawle, the media styled "King of the Hippies", had taken up the Stonehenge cause and for the next decade was the prime mover in organizing free festivals there. Though Rawle had stopped taking LSD, he was aware that the vast majority of his constituents did and needed somewhere to party and celebrate. Rawle was also heavily influenced by the native spirituality of Britain, and many of the free festivals he organised were focused on prehistoric sites. In 1978 he wrote to *The Times*, arguing: "The evidence is indisputable that Stonehenge and the surrounding area is one of the most powerful spiritual areas in Europe. It is right that we should meekly stand in the presence of God, but it is proper that we should sing and dance and shout for joy and love and mercy that He shows us ... Holy land is Holy land and our right to be upon it cannot be denied."[40]

The rout by police at Windsor in 1974 meant there was no chance of another People's Free Festival being held there in 1975. But the free festival movement now numbered tens of thousands and Sid Rawle negotiated a deal with the Labour government for land on which to hold one. The Home Secretary, Roy Jenkins, was involved and eventually an old airfield at Watchfield in Oxfordshire was offered. Rawle has made the point that part of the deal not to attempt another Windsor festival included the government promising not to break up festivals held at Stonehenge. For the first time this gave the new breed of hippie traveller a central focus, both physically and spiritually, in the seasonal round of free festivals.[41]

The Watchfield festival began on Saturday 23 August 1975 and ran for nine days. More people flocked to Watchfield than to any of the Windsor festivals, and with the increase in numbers came more instances of trouble. Several people were selling counterfeit LSD, in one case pieces of spaghetti dyed black, and it initially seemed that Watchfield was going to suffer an acute shortage of the drug. On Saturday, issue one of the Watchfield Freek Press put an urgent message on its front page: "Serious acid shortage – send urgent messages out – the acid must get through." This was an unequivocal statement from the festival organisers about just how important LSD was to free festival culture. Sunday's issue of the festival newsletter quoted Release as saying there weren't many drugs on site and LSD was the least available. But their information was wrong and the organisers' panic unfounded. LSD in several forms was available throughout the festival: blue blotter, blotter with the image of a strawberry, orange blotter and red and green microdot were all available. One festival attendee fondly remembered: "Window panes, red, white and blue blotters, mountains of microdot." The Freek Press's mention of LSD in blotter form, marked with an image, is almost certainly the first written reference to this type of LSD in Britain. Within a few years blotter LSD would overtake microdot as the preferred vehicle of LSD delivery.[42]

The Watchfield Free Festival was notable for having the largest contingent of undercover drug squad officers at a free festival to date. Martyn Pritchard's memoir of his time as an undercover policeman, *Busted*, notes the amount of LSD at Watchfield and also his frustrations at not being able to arrest any of the dealers. Numerous undercover officers, posing as hippies, infiltrated the festival. Others were more covert, engaged in secretly filming drug deals from a stationary van. Some undercover police had even managed to get themselves involved in the festival's organization and the production of the festival newsletter.[43]

The frustrations of the undercover police were understandable. But the decision not to arrest anyone at Watchfield for selling or possessing LSD had not been taken lightly. In November 1974, Detective Inspector Dick Lee of the Thames Valley Drug Squad had been analyzing the amounts of LSD seized at various festivals, both free and commercial. What he found surprised him. Although around 20,000 units of LSD were being seized each year, the evidence gleaned from festivals indicated the amount actually being used was several times that number, contradicting the general police opinion that LSD use in the UK was confined to a relatively small number of people.

In April 1975 Martyn Pritchard, the undercover police officer, was offered a thousand microdots for £250 with the promise of more, as much as he could handle, up to 10,000 dots per week. This was a staggering amount of LSD, evidence that the manufacture, sale and distribution of the drug in the UK were much more organised and widespread than previously thought. This realization was the first glimmer of what quickly developed into the largest drug operation ever mounted in the UK, Operation Julie. The Watchfield free festival was D.I. Lee's first opportunity to closely monitor the grass roots LSD culture. Lee's ghost-written account of Operation Julie noted: "Lee assembled a large team of men and women detectives to work undercover on the site. Their brief was to extract as much evidence and intelligence as possible regarding drugs, including LSD."[44]

As the decade progressed, the numbers of free festivals increased. Besides the large events like Windsor, Watchfield and Stonehenge, several smaller, low key affairs took place deep in the countryside. Rural property was inexpensive in the Seventies and numerous free festival organisers had moved to the country to live a back-to-the-land existence. Large numbers of hippies were now living in remote rural areas of Wales and the South West and it was a natural progression that localised festivals would be held.

These festivals, often developing from large parties also served the growing numbers of hippie travellers who made their living by trading at festivals. The further away from urban conurbations the events were, the less chance there was of police interference or of attracting unruly elements. And judging by the recollections of those present at these rural festivals, bad LSD experiences were rare. This is probably because of a combination of factors; smaller audiences, an idyllic environment (setting) and because the hard core of free festival attendees was, by and large, very experienced LSD users.

Of the minor free festivals held in the Seventies, the Meigan and Trentishoe Fairs stand out as exemplars of the LSD-fuelled counter cultural lifestyle. The first three Trentishoe free festivals, in 1972, 1973 and 1975 were held on top of the high cliffs overlooking the Bristol Channel in North Devon. For over three weeks a small alternative community was created, offering free organic food, alternative energy sources and a wide variety of metaphysical groups. Around 1500 hippies grooved to the sounds of Hawkwind, Here & Now and the cream of Britain's free festival bands. Drugs were plentiful; a vast amount of cannabis had been donated to the festival by local dealers and LSD was freely available and indeed often given away. Boss Goodman recalls "Everyone was eating pink micro dots by the handful." Bristol record store owner Nasher remembers "... the Chemists giving away bags of acid".[45]

By 1976, the Trentishoe site had moved inland and grown in size. But it was still untainted by the problems that plagued Watchfield, Windsor and Stonehenge. The only people prepared to make the trek to the moorlands of the West Country to live simply and communally were those within the counter culture who genuinely wanted to create their own society. Tipis and geodesic domes were the favoured accommodation, LSD the preferred drug. In the words of one happy attendee: "It was a hell of a show, everybody in the whole cell block (field) was playing with Lucy's Diamonds or Sam's Dice apparently, except me as I'd given up this hobby some months before. But I can still remember the utter madness of it now. It felt great."[46]

The local press concurred that the hippies had, for a short time at least, realised their acid fuelled dreams: "There may well be Marijuana at Pinkery Field and there is squalor in the conventional sense, but those present have contrived, in the face of middle-class pressure, to maybe create a culture of their own."[47]

The Meigan Fair was held in several years, notably 1974, 1975 and 1976 in the Preseli Mountains of west Wales. Originally a traditional hiring fair, in 1974 people involved with the Cwm Meigan commune decided to hold a free festival. The accent was on expanding the free festival ethos and providing multi-cultural events, from electric and acoustic music to meditation, theatre and games. By 1975 up to 8000 people, the majority of them being hard core members of the counter culture, attended the Meigan Fair. The Tipi People were out in force and the festival site saw a wide variety of tents, benders, live-in buses and vans and tipis, foreshadowing the travelling hippie convoys of later years.

Meigan's organisers announced: "We do hereby proclaim to artists, poets, craftsmen, musicians, storytellers that the third Meigan Faire will take place on the days of 25th, 26th and 27th July 1975, to entertain or to amuse."[48] Local people were friendly to the festival, a farmer loaning the land for the 1974 and 1975 Fairs in exchange for help with the harvest. Even the press were favourably disposed to the festival, though it was obvious they realised the LSD focus of the event, the local paper opening its report with: "Naked she danced in the warm morning sun. Her hips swayed suggestively to the beat of the music. On her back was scrawled in ballpoint: 'Got any Acid?' On a rock nearby were chalked the words, 'Reality is an illusion caused by lack of LSD. Please, where can I score?'"[49]

The amount of LSD available at the 1975 Meigan Fair has gone down in free festival legend. Meigan attendee Chris Church remembers that on the first day of the festival: "... almost all of them were incapable due to the huge consumption of psychedelics. It was the only event I ever went to where it seemed as if the lysergic state was the normal state to be in."[50] Musically it was slightly chaotic. So chaotic in fact that free festival synthesiser band, Zorch were unable to play because one of their musicians, Basil Brooks, was "incapacitated by LSD".[51]

Another Meigan veteran, Tim Rundall, recalls: "... a very unhealthy quantity of liquid LSD which emanated, I believe, from the cottage that would later be raided by the Julie squad."[52] In many recollections of free festival attendees there is an assumption that the LSD they were taking was that made by Richard Kemp or Andy Munro, the chemists arrested in the Operation Julie events. After his arrest Kemp admitted that he had timed LSD production runs to coincide with the summer festivals and he also claimed to have donated some of his profits to free festival organisers. Sid Rawle, however, has no knowledge of this and believes that it is unlikely it could have happened without his knowledge.

The Meigan Fair's organisers had thought carefully about the quantities of LSD that would be consumed and had tried to create the best setting possible. Deep in the countryside the festival-goers were untroubled by police or locals and there was always some music, theatre or other event to occupy the minds of those who had indulged in psychedelics. For those who found themselves in the middle of an LSD-induced existential crisis a "sanctuary" tent was provided. This was a tipi-like structure where people could be quiet, rest and read some of the metaphysical literature provided. There were no recorded bad trips, although some must have taken place, and the Festival Welfare Service thought it was a well-run and exciting festival.

When Margaret Thatcher and the Conservative Party came to power in May 1979 the free festival culture was in full swing. For young people with a sense of adventure and a DIY ethic it was possible to stay on the road and spend May to October at free festivals. The wealth of reminiscences now available on the internet leaves us in no doubt that LSD was available in large quantities and high strength at every one of the 1970s free festivals. Other than at Windsor in 1974 there had been relatively little trouble with the authorities. Free festivals were often allowed to run unhindered for several days before they were broken up by police. And, despite the best efforts of Operation Julie, there was no disruption in the supply of LSD. The free festivals of the 1970s were, for many, a halcyon period during which a new way of living, a new way of travelling and a new way of celebrating was forged and established within British culture. The problem was that this way of living and the substances which fuelled it were anathema to the vast majority and an easy target for right-wing politicians. The advent of Conservative rule would soon change the face of free festivals forever – and with that change came a change in LSD usage.

The final word on LSD and free festivals goes to Kevin Hagan, in 1981 a young musician who caught the tail-end of the free festival scene. He neatly sums up the effect of free festivals on the individual and the links between the festivals, anarchy and LSD: "It sounds corny, but going to the Stonehenge Festival changed my life. I couldn't believe my eyes when I saw it. It really was anarchy in action ... It was so different to anything I had seen before. It had the feel of a medieval encampment. There was so much going on – stages on every corner, stalls – and people providing weird tripping environments. It was like an activity camp for trippers! And everyone was doing it because they wanted to – not because they wanted to earn money ..."[53] This was the acid ethos writ large and lived out in day to day life. Free festivals were temporary autonomous zones in which the counter culture lived out their dream existence, the experience heavily influenced by LSD. This alternative lifestyle was antithetical to the materialistic, consumer society of the rest of Britain and would eventually be destroyed by the Government. But while it lasted, free festival culture and the lifestyle of those who supported it required large supplies of good quality LSD. This was supplied by an LSD manufacturing and distribution organization the like of which police had not seen before, or since and which became known as Operation Julie.

11

THE MIND ALCHEMISTS

> I have turned on a lot of people and got a lot of people high. I'd do it all over again.
>
> Richard Kemp[1]

During the early Seventies, large quantities of a new type of LSD became available in Britain. Media sources began to report increasing police seizures of tiny pills the size of a pinhead. Acidheads used to the drug in sugar cubes, blotting paper and capsules found they were now being offered small, often brightly coloured tablets known as microdots. Not only were the microdots tiny, they were inexpensive, between 50p and £1 each, much less if bought in bulk. But the most significant quality of microdots was their strength, at least 200 µg in each dot, enough to guarantee a powerful and consistent psychedelic experience lasting up to twenty-four hours.

A senior drug squad officer commented in 1972, "Microdots are the pushers' latest weapon in the drug war. In the past it was not too difficult to detect the evidence of LSD in sugar lumps or on blotting paper. But these new pills are so tiny they can be disposed of at a moment's notice."[2]

As seizures increased the media printed stories about the new variety of LSD; "Pinhead LSD 'a killer'" "Drug ring peddling LSD microtabs" "Extra strong LSD peddled" and "Report shows more LSD is available" were just a few of the headlines between 1972 and 1977. Journalists speculated that a "microdot gang" was responsible for the influx of powerful LSD. Microdots could be easily obtained in any town or city at any of the many clubs and pubs that had sprung up to cater for the large numbers of hippies and freaks. It was common on a Friday or Saturday night in one of these clubs for almost everyone in attendance, bar staff included, to be under the influence of the latest batch of microdots to hit town, the party continuing later at private flats, or on psychedelic country rambles. The drug's quality and strength were dependable and at a pound or less per trip, microdots represented extremely good value for money. But the qualities that made microdots so attractive; availability, price and strength, also caused problems for the unprepared.

Like thousands of other teenagers living a suburban existence in the early Seventies, fifteen-year-old Tim Lott was keen to experiment with LSD. When he first saw the drug, a blue microdot, he thought: "I had expected the LSD tablets to be about the size of paracetamol. I had intended, on this occasion, to take only a half or even a quarter. But the tablets are so tiny, they are virtually indivisible. It seems that I am bound to lose face if I try and divide it up. Anyway, something so tiny can hardly be very powerful."[3]

Believing the physical size of the LSD carrier had a relationship to the strength of dose was an easy mistake to make, and often led to novice LSD users taking more than they could handle. For Lott, having only preconceptions of what LSD might be like and with no experienced guide for the trip, his first microdot was simply too strong. At first he was impressed, amazed at a drug that made him feel he was "... in a state of the purest, most concentrated ecstasy and it is the most real, the most truthful thing I have ever experienced". Amazement soon turned to bewilderment as the drug's effect continued to increase, wave upon wave of sensory impressions washing over him, threatening to subsume him. Fearing he was losing his mind, Lott smashed up his parents' living room, ripped off his clothes and ran naked into the street, before being subdued by a neighbour and taken to the police station. His father rescued him and Lott spent the next twelve hours recovering in bed, the ghost of LSD flitting through his mind as he tried to piece together what had happened.[4]

Lott's experience was harrowing; a trip that spiralled out of control because he had no real idea what to expect. Although media and counter culture descriptions of LSD trips might make the psychedelic experience sound desirable, they could not accurately convey what a trip would actually be like. In Lott's case, he was ignorant of the crucial elements of set and setting and had no one to guide him on his journey. Of course, Lott's disorientating experience was not typical. The vast majority of LSD users enjoyed the experience enormously and benefited from it in a number of ways as accounts such as Pete Mellor's demonstrate (see Chapter 9).

Tim Lott's blue microdot was almost certainly made by chemist Richard Kemp; just one of millions of doses of LSD manufactured in Britain, and distributed across the world, by a group of psychedelic idealists. This tightly knit organization was nameless but their activities and produce would become known collectively by the name given to the police initiative that smashed their illicit enterprise: Operation Julie.

It is impossible to pinpoint the moment when the Operation Julie conspiracy began, but it can be traced back to 1967 when writer David Solomon, an acknowledged authority on LSD, settled in Cambridge. A year later, in 1968, Solomon met future Operation Julie chemist Richard Kemp. At the time, Kemp was living with Christine Bott, the pair having met and fallen in love while Kemp was working as a researcher at Liverpool University. While he was not central to the later production of LSD, Solomon was crucial initially in bringing the principles of the conspiracy together. Solomon was an "acid intellectual", a well educated man who had a sincere and reasoned belief that LSD should be used as a positive tool to alter consciousness. The writer was held in high regard by the worldwide psychedelic community and numbered many of its luminaries, including Timothy Leary, among his friends.

When he met Kemp, Solomon was involved in trying to synthesise THC, the active constituent of marijuana, and Kemp was happy to assist with this process. At some point in 1969, to finance further research into THC, the decision to manufacture LSD was made. One of Solomon's American friends, Paul Arnaboldi, supplied Kemp with 40 grams of ergotamine maleate and, being a brilliant chemist, Kemp had no trouble making three batches of LSD, albeit of a weak dosage, in the basement of his Liverpool flat. Curious as to what the fuss was about – Solomon had told him that LSD was a stronger version of marijuana – Kemp took a small dose. Under the influence, he accidentally knocked over a flask containing large amounts of the drug, ingesting enough LSD to catapult himself on a trip of cosmic proportions. Kemp was awed by the experience and slowly his ties to the world of formal academic research began to weaken.[5]

Solomon had many connections throughout the LSD underworld, one of whom was the enigmatic Ronald Stark. Much has been written about Stark's motivation for being involved in the international LSD trade and an entire book could easily be written on his exploits, most of which do not concern the British LSD scene. Stark's links with a group of Californian LSD dealers known as the Brotherhood of Eternal Love, who in turn had close links with Timothy Leary, has spawned a worldwide acid conspiracy with Stark at the centre.

There is no doubt about the depth of Stark's involvement with LSD, but his motives and who, if anyone, he was actually working for remains a matter for speculation. The major players in the international LSD market during the Sixties and Seventies all knew of each other and collaborated when necessary. However, the fact that Stark moved easily between these groups and individuals does not constitute a conspiracy as some have claimed. Nor has there been any proof of Stark's alleged links with the CIA and other intelligence agencies. Yet something about Stark gave people cause for concern. For instance, when Steve Abrams met him, he was convinced Stark was working for the American intelligence services; so convinced that he phoned Bing Spear at the Home Office to express his concerns about the man.

Solomon introduced Kemp to Stark, who in turn persuaded Kemp to leave his university job, to work full time on synthesizing THC. Pure THC is much stronger than cannabis resin or marijuana and, being in oil form, was easier to conceal and transport, meaning profits were high and risks low. According to Kemp, the deal between Solomon and Stark was analogous to that of a minor league football club player being transferred to the premier division. In exchange for Solomon being able to buy LSD at $900 a gram, Kemp was free to work on THC for Stark. While engaged on this project in laboratories in France, Kemp also made LSD, accidentally stumbling on a short cut that speeded up the process and resulted in an almost pure product.[6]

After a disagreement over money, Kemp split from Stark and returned to Britain. By early 1972, he had gone into LSD production. Kemp and Bott rented various flats for just long enough to complete a production run, before moving to the next destination. Solomon bought the precursor chemicals in Germany, later handing them to Kemp who kept them in a Swiss safety deposit box until needed. For each gram of LSD Kemp passed to Brian Cuthbertson for tabletting, he received £200. One of Kemp's early production runs, in Liverpool, produced 500 grams netting Kemp £100,000; a substantial sum of money in 1972.[7]

However, although it requires expert knowledge, producing pure LSD is only a small part of the process of getting the drug to the customer. First, it had to be turned into microdots by the tabletting process by Cuthbertson. Then it was passed by another dealer, Henry Todd, to several people from the Reading area who began to distribute the LSD for him. A network, capable of distributing tens of thousands of microdots a week, was slowly forming. Solomon, though, was no longer required to obtain the raw materials, Todd now handling that aspect of the organization.

At first, everything went to plan. Kemp made the acid, Cuthbertson tabletted it and their colleagues Henry Todd, Russell Spenceley, Alston Hughes and others managed the distribution chain. Then, in 1973, things changed. Kemp had always insisted that each dose of LSD was a minimum of 200 µg, to ensure the customer had a guaranteed full-blown psychedelic experience.

Something about Todd made Kemp suspicious and to test his integrity he bought some of his own microdots at a festival. The dealer assured Kemp that the acid contained a guaranteed 100 µg.[8]

To verify this Kemp asked a friend of Solomon's, chemist Andy Munro, later to become another crucial player in the Operation Julie events, to analyze the acid. Munro tested the LSD in the laboratories of a university and Kemp was horrified, but not surprised, to find the microdots contained 100 µg. He immediately confronted Todd who freely admitted his deception, but promised never to do it again.

Todd and Kemp were quite dissimilar individuals. Todd was a man's man, a *bon viveur* who enjoyed playing rugby and mountain climbing, paying lip service to the ideals of the LSD counter culture, more interested in profit than revolution. On the other hand, Kemp was seriously committed to social change through the agency of LSD. Kemp embraced the hippie ideal of self-sufficiency, at one point after his arrest telling the police, "I'd have everyone out in two-acre plots like ours, being self-sufficient".[9]

Todd and Kemp parted company in the latter half of 1973, a number of factors precipitating the split. Personality and ideological differences had existed for some time but Kemp was now realizing how central he was to the entire LSD conspiracy, "I was the goose that laid the golden egg", and wanted more of a financial cut. One source close to both men recalled that it was Kemp's discovery that Todd had invested heavily in General Franco's Spanish Highway Bonds that finally caused the rift between them.[10]

The consequence of the split was good news for the psychedelic community. Ideas for a new laboratory were mooted and Kemp once again took up with David Solomon and Paul Arnabaldi. Feeling the need to escape from London if they were to practise their hippie ideals and manufacture high quality LSD in seclusion, a suitable property was located in Wales. Arnabaldi paid £26,000 for the dilapidated manor house of Plas Llysyn near Newtown, Montgomeryshire in June 1974 and Kemp set about building a laboratory.

Kemp and Bott bought a property near Tregaron, some fifty miles from Plas Llysyn. It was a small and primitive cottage but it suited them and they fitted in well with the numerous hippie settlers in the area. Bott was a member of the Soil Association, an organic gardening group, and a keen member of the Goat Society. She owned two pet goats and the only known photograph of her shows her proudly exhibiting one of them at a local agricultural show.[11]

Todd, meanwhile, had been equally busy. He had recruited chemist Andy Munro and set him up with a laboratory, initially at unknown addresses and finally at 23 Seymour Road in the London suburb of Hampton Wick. Munro made LSD on the top floor and Cuthbertson handled the tabletting on the first floor. The Seymour Road lab was active for several months before Kemp's new lab became operational. By 1975, two laboratories were in production, making millions of doses of LSD. This period was the height of the free festival years and the market for the drug was huge in Britain, America, Australia and mainland Europe.

While the Operation Julie conspirators were busy setting up their manufacturing and distribution networks the forces of law and order were, at first, blissfully ignorant of what was taking place. Drugs, not least LSD, were relatively new to the police and it had only been since 1966 that drug use had become widespread in Britain. It was clear to anyone who studied the figures that LSD use and, by implication, manufacture, was on the increase. Convictions for LSD related offences rose sharply from 159 in 1969 to 1457 in 1972. Some police officers were very aware of this growing trend, one writing in his annual report "... this [1972] has been without doubt the year of the acid tablet."[12]

From September 1971, scientists at the Central Research Establishment at Aldermaston had been monitoring seizures of LSD and they too had commented on the rise of the LSD microdot. Microdots were one of a number of LSD types known to scientists as triturates – tablets formed from a mould. Other types included domes or, less frequently, squares. Microdots were made by mixing unadulterated LSD with calcium lactate or talc and with gelatine for bulk. A colouring agent was added and the mixture spread across a sheet of perforated metal or plastic. After the paste had dried, the microdots were pushed out by using a pin board corresponding to the mould. The Aldermaston scientists quickly realised that within a few weeks of a particular type of tablet becoming available in Britain it would appear in countries as far away as Australia. They concluded that 95 per cent of LSD in Britain and 50 per cent of the world's supply of LSD originated in Britain.[13]

Despite extensive knowledge of the differing types of microdot produced by the clandestine British LSD laboratory, the police were unable to gather any useful intelligence to indicate who was behind it or where it was situated. Then, in 1973, came a major breakthrough. Solomon's occasional partner in crime Gerald Thomas was arrested in Canada in possession of 7 kg of cannabis. Hearing of Thomas' arrest, Solomon panicked and destroyed all his possessions and the cocaine making equipment. Thomas took offence at this and in order to get both revenge and lighter sentence provided the Canadian police with the names of the major figures involved in the microdot gang. Thomas' information was accurate; he claimed the LSD was manufactured by a qualified chemist called Richard Hilary Kemp and his common law wife Dr. Christine Bott, while a man Thomas only knew as "Henry" carried out the tabletting. Thomas also named expatriate American author, David Solomon as the man initially responsible for acquiring the necessary precursor chemicals.

Thomas' information was passed to the recently formed Central Drugs Intelligence Unit where Detective Inspector Derek Godfrey followed it up. Godfrey soon found plenty to substantiate Thomas' claims. Kemp had been the subject of a Special Branch report in 1970 that established he had strong links with Ronald Stark. Godfrey knew that if Kemp had been consorting with the enigmatic Stark he was sure to be involved, at some level, in the manufacture of LSD. All the police had to do now was find him.[14]

As Kemp had now effectively dropped out of society, the police were unable to locate him immediately. It would be Kemp's notoriously bad driving that would be the cause of his eventual downfall. In September 1974, he was involved in a car crash and his distinctive red Range Rover, mentioned by Thomas to the police, alerted them. Perhaps knowing he might be under surveillance

Kemp gave his defunct London address but foolishly elected to produce his documents at Welshpool in mid-Wales, suggesting to police he was living in the area.

Drug Squads across Britain had been hearing rumours that LSD was being manufactured in Wales and Kemp's apparent residence there strengthened that suspicion. Additionally, an LSD dealer arrested in possession of a large quantity of microdots in Australia during 1974, claimed that the manufacturing source was in Wales but that one of the main distribution centres was a well-known restaurant in London, The Last Resort.

Although there was now strong circumstantial evidence of a Welsh LSD laboratory, there was no proof and Kemp's exact whereabouts were still unknown. It would take a death, a stroke of luck and good police work to begin to pull the strands of information together. In the spring of 1975, Kemp was involved in a fatal road accident near Aberystywth and, unaware of the CDIU's interest in Kemp, the local police allowed him to remove all personal effects and correspondence from the vehicle.

The distinctive red Range Rover was kept in police custody for a while, where it was noticed by a Thames Valley police officer who was in the area trying to trace Kemp. A painstaking examination of the vehicle revealed Kemp had overlooked several tiny scraps of paper which when pieced together showed a map of the area marking a number of locations. More significantly, another piece of paper bore the words "hydrazine tartrate", a crucial substance in the manufacture of LSD. Kemp's bad driving and the unfortunate death of a local vicar's wife had resulted in the police knowing his current address, the remote farmhouse near Tregaron.

This was the information the police needed and a conference was held in Carmarthen in April 1975 to plan the way forward, which was to initially place Kemp under surveillance. This soon confirmed that Kemp and Bott were away from their property for up to twelve hours at a time, often for several days. No direct evidence of LSD manufacture was apparent but a major LSD dealer from south Wales had been seen near the house and in the nearby village. The police seemed to be on the edge of a major breakthrough.

"It was at this point, when the momentum of the inquiry should have been reaching a peak, that it in fact began to flag." Those are the words of the 1978 post-trial Home Office Operation Julie report, noting the failings in the police system at the time. What should have galvanised the police into a major operation against the suspected laboratory almost caused it to fizzle away to nothing. Though the evidence was mounting, there was considerable resistance within the police force to any form of unilateral approach to the problem. When, in May 1975, Detective Inspector Godfrey, in conjunction with Detective Superintendent Gittus of the Metropolitan Police Drug Squad, sought permission and resources to mount a major operation against the laboratory they were turned down on grounds of cost. A meeting in June at Swindon saw permission granted for No. 8 Regional Crime Squad to mount a full-scale surveillance operation, but this too concluded without any breakthrough. The CDIU continued to gather intelligence about the major suspects and the Drugs Intelligence Laboratory analyzed and monitored seizures of LSD microdots but there were no further moves to locate or decommission the clandestine lab.[15]

But ignoring the problem would not make it go away and the Welsh connection came to the fore again in November 1975. Two officers from the Thames Valley Drug Squad working undercover in Chippenham, Wiltshire were offered quantities of up to 10,000 microdots from wholesalers who clearly belonged to a tightly organised LSD distribution network. Once again intelligence suggested the source of the LSD was in mid-Wales and another meeting took place in Swindon on 12 February 1976. Officers from six regional police forces plus representatives from the CDIU and the Home Office Drugs Branch were present. They reviewed all the evidence suggesting a major LSD manufacture and distribution ring was operating in Wales, concluding that a major initiative against the microdot gang was justified.

A meeting in Brecon on 17 February ratified the decision and Detective Inspector Richard "Dick" Lee (Thames Valley) took the role of investigating officer and Detective Chief Inspector Herbert (Avon and Somerset) was designated as officer in charge of the operation. Detective Superintendent Dennis Greenslade, also from the Avon and Somerset force, replaced Herbert almost immediately, and a squad of 25 officers was drawn together at Devizes police station. Such a huge operation needed a code name and during the discussion, Sergeant Julie Taylor entered the room. According to Dick Lee: "All attention suddenly turned to her and within minutes the decision was unanimously reached – the operation would be called 'Julie.'" Operation Julie was born.[16]

For the next thirteen months, the Operation Julie team worked flat out on the case. Eschewing normal working hours and practices and using cars and other equipment donated by various forces the team lived cheek by jowl in cramped surveillance conditions in Wales and London. A request to use phone taps was allowed by Home Secretary William Whitelaw and suspects were followed by car and on foot. The team quickly worked out the distribution chain was set up on the lines of a terrorist cell, which meant that each person in the chain only knew the one below and above him or her. Vast quantities of LSD, hundreds of thousands of trips at a time, were being moved round Britain, with about half being exported to the drug markets of America, Australia and Europe.

Desperate for some concrete evidence about where the LSD was being made the police broke into Plas Llysyn, finding that the cellar had been used as a laboratory. Although it was initially thought by police that there was no LSD laboratory at Seymour Road, by following Todd and Cuthbertson to a council rubbish tip officers were able to unearth paraphernalia connected to LSD manufacture. The full story of how the Julie team painstakingly stalked and eventually arrested the LSD conspirators is too detailed to go into here and those interested in the fine detail should read Tendler and May's excellent *Brotherhood of Eternal Love*[17] or Dick Lee's *Operation Julie*.

While the teams of police officers were working on the case the scientists at Aldermaston were busy analyzing seizures of LSD from Britain and abroad, trying to make sense of the methods used by the acid chemists and the extent of their distribution network. Neville Dunnett from the police forensic laboratory at Aldermaston was designated the scientist in charge of analyzing the LSD thought to be made by Kemp and Munro. Initially, Dunnett's task was to analyze seizures of LSD made throughout the world since 1971 and to look for patterns of manufacture and distribution. A graph produced for a Home Office report on the Operation Julie LSD showed the ratio of LSD microdots as a percentage of all LSD seizures increased from 5 per cent in 1971 to over 80 per cent in 1975. This was the impact Kemp and Munro's acid had on the world LSD market.[18]

As the spring of 1977 dawned, the police decided now was the time to act, before the principle conspirators managed to vanish into obscurity once again. The Seymour Road property had to be raided first because police found that Todd had cancelled the milk and the laboratory had ceased operation.

At 8.00 pm on 25 March 1977, a team of police smashed through the doors of Seymour Road, taking the occupants by surprise. "Ah, I suppose you've come about the television licence," Todd calmly quipped, before asking the police if they had come to give him the Queen's Award for Industry. Because the phone lines had been cut (and mobile phones had yet to become available), there was no quick or surreptitious way of Todd or his colleagues alerting their co-conspirators and the police were able to prevent news of the Seymour Road arrests from leaking out. A rapid search of the house revealed the top floor laboratory and the police were triumphant. Munro, Todd and Cuthbertson were taken into custody and settled down to their first night in the cells. As they did so, across southern England and Wales, police officers were gathering for the largest drug raid in British history.

At exactly 5.00 am on 26 March, over 800 police officers drawn from 16 police forces and 6 regional crime squads raided 83 locations in England and Wales. One hundred and twenty-two people were arrested, thirty-one of whom would later appear at Bristol Crown Court between 12 January and 8 March 1978, charged with a range of offences related to the conspiracy to manufacture and distribute LSD, as well as lesser charges of importing cannabis. The game was up.

The fall out from the Operation Julie arrests sent shock waves through Britain's psychedelic community. The police investigation was comprehensive and anyone believed to have been involved at any level with the LSD produced by Kemp or Munro was interviewed. Each of those arrested was questioned by pairs of police officers chosen either for their interviewing skills or for their specific knowledge of the prisoner's role in the conspiracy.

At first, none of the prisoners was allowed access to a solicitor, despite their requests. Dick Lee was concerned that once those in custody had seen a solicitor messages might be passed to others involved in the Julie conspiracy and valuable evidence could be destroyed. This was a calculated move on Lee's part. He knew the majority of those arrested were not hardened criminals and by restricting access to legal representation, they would feel even more alone and isolated, ideal conditions for softening them up for the rigorous interviews, which were soon to come.

A peculiar bond quickly arose between the Operation Julie police officers and those they had arrested. The prisoners had their clothes taken away for forensic examination and at first had to wear blankets for warmth and modesty. Several police officers took pity on them and brought in their own clothes for the prisoners. Food too was brought in for those who were vegetarians. Dick Lee was aware of this and the erosion of professional boundaries worried him. In time, he called a meeting at which he reminded his officers their relationship with the prisoners should show respect for their humanity but should not extend to acts of personal kindness.

Under questioning some of the prisoners, notably Kemp, Munro, Todd and Bott, gave the police the absolute minimum information. This situation was not true of the others though and many of those arrested quickly caved in, giving huge amounts of useful information to their interrogators. Several prisoners, either accidentally or in an attempt to receive more lenient sentences, implicated others in their statements and the police bounced one story off another to the point where those arrested were unsure what was true or false and who had said what. Dick Lee later told Steve Abrams that if David Solomon, arrested in the second wave of raids, had made no comment to the police, Solomon would have escaped conviction because they did not have enough factual evidence to convict him on. Even Richard Kemp, described by his inquisitor as "the hardest man he had ever interviewed", disclosed a great deal more than he needed to, giving details of LSD manufacture going back to 1971.

Even in custody, Kemp's natural arrogance and self belief didn't fail him. One interchange between him and Detective Superintendent Greenslade, gave some insight into his position:

Kemp:	You know nothing and you represent political repression.
Greenslade:	It's all very well to assume people have a wonderful time on your LSD. We have to clean up the mess. You have no appreciation of the amount of people all over the country having personal hallucinations.
Kemp:	You know nothing.
Greenslade:	I've travelled in the Far East and seen people on opium.
Kemp:	The opiates are something else. Acid is different.
Greenslade:	Whatever it is, it's against the law.
Kemp:	The law, and you, represent political repression.[19]

This exchange demonstrated the fundamental culture gap between the two sides. The police clearly knew little about what LSD was, what it did or how it was used by the counter culture. To them it was just another drug, albeit one that had more of a visible effect through its links to music, festivals, fashion and alternate life styles. Greenslade's attempt to sound knowledgeable by linking opium with LSD probably earned him Kemp's contempt, as the effects of the two drugs bear no relation to each other. Greenslade and his officers were rooted in the hard-core police drinking culture, and failed to understand LSD or its culture. Their ignorance must have come across strongly in the interviews with the Julie conspirators.

During his interviews, Kemp constantly reiterated his position on LSD, telling the police he had donated large sums of money and acid to causes he termed "head politics", head being slang for LSD user. The only such donation it's been possible to verify is his financial donation to Release, the counter culture drug and law information service. Kemp also claimed to have donated money and acid to the free festival movement, the main constituency besides the squatting movement for his product. Questioned by Detectives Spencer and Barnard, Kemp said of free festivals: "'You people have ruined them. I don't know why you don't leave them alone. The majority just want to turn on. It's a marvellous movement of unison when so many heads gather together.' 'Anarchy,' Barnard responded. Kemp was sympathetic, 'I'd like to turn you on. You don't understand.'"[20]

Books written about Operation Julie by Dick Lee and undercover officer, Martyn Pritchard amplify the fundamentally different worldview of the police to the Julie conspirators. Each new breakthrough in the case is cemented with a trip to the nearest pub and alcohol use, its devastating effects on the health and relationships of thousands of people notwithstanding, is frequently lauded as a tool for celebration or commiseration throughout the police version of events.

As the Julie defendants slowly caved in under the constant questioning large caches of acid were being discovered across England and Wales, culminating in a stash of 100,800 microdots being dug up in a wood. This was the world's largest seizure of LSD to date, more than had been seized worldwide throughout 1975. The Operation Julie investigators were making history. Almost immediately, in order to have his wife released, Brian Cuthbertson revealed the location of another cache of buried LSD containing over 600,000 microdots and after one of the conspirators informed on Kemp, police were able to remove 1.3 kg of LSD crystals from beneath the stone floor of Plas Llysyn, enough to make 13 million doses of acid. This caused considerable friction among the Julie conspirators because Kemp believed Solomon was the informer.[21]

The police seized a huge quantity of physical evidence. Besides what remained of the two LSD laboratories, vast amounts of personal possessions had been seized in the raids, including much that had nothing whatsoever to do with the LSD conspiracy. On 3 April, three detectives had firsthand experience of the consciousness altering properties of LSD after removing a carpet from the laboratory at Seymour Road.

After completing the task and eating their evening meal, the trio began to feel peculiar and decided to go out, get some fresh air and spend the rest of the evening relaxing in The Angler's, a local pub. As they settled down with a pint amidst the bright lights and general hubbub, realization dawned that the odd feeling was actually the onset of an LSD trip. Numerous LSD spillages in the Seymour Road laboratory meant the carpet was soaked with LSD and the three officers had inhaled enough LSD from the air to precipitate a trip.

Yet the trip they experienced on the Operation Julie acid was far from the parade of horrors the media and judiciary were to depict. As the officers' senses became enhanced, they "... could clearly hear people talking at the far ends of the room. The filled pint glasses were feather-like." They retreated from the pub and, "... walked out under the most brilliant moon (I've) ever seen. Our eyesight was sharpened so we could read the print on thrown-away cigarette packets as we passed."

Though the detectives weren't having a bad trip they knew they should report what was happening and get themselves checked out by the police surgeon. They were in a very jovial mood by this time, "... smiling and laughing about anything" according to one of the men. Their mood suddenly darkened when the police surgeon told them they would need to be examined at a psychiatric unit, remaining there until the effects of the drug had subsided. The officers reacted so badly to the news that their superiors believed they intended to barricade themselves in the room. Eventually they went to the Kingston Hospital but specifically asked for beds away from the windows "... in case it might give us that feeling which has affected others that they could fly. It was that scaring." Although the officers were ignorant of the principles of set and setting it is obvious that while they were in the pub and outside the effects of the LSD they had ingested were not too disturbing. Yet once in the clinical surroundings of a hospital they became nervous and agitated, reinventing the urban myth that LSD users feel the urge to jump out of windows in the belief they can fly.[22]

Though the officers suffered no harm whatsoever from their magic carpet ride there was no reason for it to have happened. While in custody, Andy Munro had warned the police not to touch the laboratory carpet because of the spillages, yet the authorities' ignorance of LSD's dangers meant they failed to inform those searching the house of the risk. One of the officers later spoke to a minor defendant in the trial, Nigel Fielding, telling him that he'd had "… a profound experience and it had left him shaken to discover that life was a deeper and more subtle business than he had imagined".[23]

Once the initial media furore had subsided, little was heard publicly of the Operation Julie defendants until the trial in 1978. But behind the scenes, at least one of the conspirators was trying to generate some public support.

A few weeks prior to his arrest, David Solomon met Lee Harris for the first time. Harris had recently launched Britain's first commercial drug magazine, *Home Grown* and Solomon planned to write for him. His remand in custody had stymied that idea but Solomon believed Harris could be a vital ally in getting the defendants' side of the story out to the counter culture in Britain and abroad.

On 29 April, less than a month after his arrest, prisoner F01468, wrote to Harris from prison. Solomon's letter was written as though to an old friend, despite their relationship being only a few months old. He claimed, knowing his letters would be intercepted by prison staff, he was not "close to the hub" of the operation but was worried that accusation would be levelled at him during the trial; a prospect he imagined as, "… facing some High Court judge, a rough beast, with a gaze as black and pitiless as the sea, whose only regret is that he can bury me for no more than the maximum of 14 years."[24]

Solomon suggested Harris might use *Home Grown* as a conduit for information about the case to reach the counter culture and the mainstream media: "I imagine you plan to give this affair complete coverage" he wrote, adding that such coverage would be extremely helpful. He recommended that Harris publicise the known facts about LSD and explain to the public that the drug's Class A status had evolved with no valid research being offered to suggest the drug was more dangerous than drugs of a lesser class or even alcohol or tobacco. This method of garnering support for the Operation Julie defendants was hardly the action of a criminal mastermind only involved in LSD for financial gain. Solomon's attempts to argue his defence from a factual and ideological point of view were in keeping with his philosophical beliefs about the drug.

Furthermore, Solomon indicated, it was time for the LSD counter culture to "... help our wives and children. It seems morally unthinkable that famous pop artists and groups – who owe much to Alice – would not cough up. Everyone – from Bob Dylan to the Stones, Lennon, McCartney *et alia ad infinitum* should be asked for sizeable contributions to help pay for our immense legal bills and keep our families fed and housed."

Solomon had hit the nail on the head. This was crunch time for the LSD counter culture. If the acidheads really believed their chosen drug was a sacrament, central to their culture of consciousness and lifestyle exploration, then now was the time to prove it. All the musicians Solomon cited had taken LSD and had written songs alluding to it. Some, like McCartney, had openly admitted to its use. LSD had been a major factor in their creative lives and their careers, to no small degree, were rooted in their and their audience's love of the drug.

Solomon's letter gives the sense that the Operation Julie defendants' trial could be a show trial between the establishment and the counter culture. A psychedelic standoff the defendants would still lose but which would send shock waves round the world, drawing attention to the British government's attempts to stifle an individual's right to alter their consciousness at will. On the last page of the letter, Solomon drove his point home, listing a number of heavyweight cultural mavens that Harris might persuade to publicly support the Operation Julie defendants. These included Francis Crick, the discoverer of DNA, novelists Henry Miller and Norman Mailer, playwright Arthur Miller and Humphrey Osmond, the authority on psychedelics.

Home Grown did run news pieces and well-written articles about the Operation Julie case. However, the magazine was published too intermittently to be of meaningful value in supporting those charged and later convicted and sentenced. *International Times* also covered the unfolding events and kept people informed about what was happening. But other than LSD users being self righteous and indignant about the arrests, the counter culture kept quiet. There were no demonstrations at New Scotland Yard, no marches on the Home Office and no attempt to organise a defence fund. After all, there was still a large amount of Kemp and Munro's acid on the streets, new manufacturers were coming on stream, the free festival season was starting and for the vast majority of the counter culture it was business as usual.

If the counter culture believed that the Julie conspirators could fund their costs from their reputedly vast profits they were mistaken. All money belonging to those arrested was immediately confiscated or frozen. The police removed even small amounts of cash found at the defendants' homes; in some cases leaving wives and partners with no source of income. On one visit to David Solomon's flat after his arrest, the police took £135 from his wife Pat without even issuing a receipt. This was money loaned by friends for her financial assistance and was not connected to the acid conspiracy.[25]

The *Daily Express*, among other media sources, managed to obtain copies of letters sent, prior to the trial, by Bott and Kemp to friends. Bott's letter reveals a woman driven by ideology rather than profit, prepared to speak her mind about her beliefs. She wrote, "I am sustained by the conviction of the righteousness of what we are into … all those we reached with our acid, lovingly produced, will feel united in support of truth and that vision we share of mankind living in harmony. The insanity of the world is becoming increasingly apparent even to the straight people … I'm certain a lot of people will re-examine their values before this trip is over."[26]

It must then, have come as a devastating blow to Kemp, Bott and Solomon when they realised that the millions of people who had taken their "lovingly produced" acid did not seem to care what happened to them.

Kemp's reply to Bott included: "We hope through our efforts our children will inherit a better world than we did. The forces of repression are firmly in control but I really believe we have started something no one can stop. It is so frustrating knowing they will call us evil men, destroyers of personality, purveyors of poison etc, and yet there is no scientific evidence to support their arguments."[27] Kemp was correct, there was no scientific evidence to support those arguments but scientific evidence was not under discussion at the trial where the prosecution was only interested in whether or not Kemp and his co-defendants had been involved in the manufacture and distribution of LSD.

For the main defendants the Operation Julie trial started on 12 January 1978 at Bristol Crown Court. The presiding judge was Mr Justice Park (Sir Hugh Park), an elderly judge with little knowledge of drugs or drug culture. Somewhat bizarrely, and in total contradiction of legal process, Park's twenty-year-old granddaughter sat on the bench with him for some of the trial. By the time of the trial, all the defendants, with the exception of Christine Bott, Brian Cuthbertson and Russell Spenceley, had pleaded guilty. For them the show was over and they could only await the judge's sentence.

All the national daily papers covered the trial, each trying to outdo their rival with theory and speculation. Was some of the acid destined for the IRA, the Angry Brigade or other international terrorists? There was no proof but it made for a good story. How much money had been made by the defendents? No one really knew but that didn't stop the press feverishly extrapolating millions of pounds from much smaller amounts. That the Julie gang made money seemed to horrify the press almost as much as their highly organised manufacturing and distribution system. The media was also obsessed with the fact that the majority of the Julie conspirators were university educated professionals.

And of course the media couldn't resist pulling some hoary old myths out of retirement. "We'll Blow A Million Minds" screamed the *Daily Mirror* on 9 March, going on to breathlessly report how the Julie plotters had planned to put vast quantities of LSD in the reservoirs serving Birmingham. There was no evidence to support this accusation either but the "acid in the water supply" made good, public frightening, headlines.

Christine Bott stepped into the witness box, her defence pivoting on her belief that LSD was a useful drug, both to individuals and for the world. She told the prosecution that she was not interested in money, a claim borne out by the simple rural existence chosen by her and Kemp. Bott admitted she knew Kemp had been involved in the drug's manufacture and though she claimed her personal experience of LSD was very positive, her "... philosophy as to its marketing and manufacture was a mixture of positive and negative". Her view of the legalities of the manufacturing and distribution of LSD was simple: "If I thought there was a crime, I thought it had more to do with making money than LSD."[28]

In response to further questioning, Bott told the court that LSD had been successfully used as a therapeutic treatment in psychiatry as well as to treat alcoholics. Though Bott agreed with the prosecution that LSD could be harmful to those who didn't understand how to use it properly this did not diminish her faith in the drug: "I thought it was an agent which if used in the right controlled conditions could have a beneficial effect on the lives of the individuals who took it."

It is probably this forthright attitude and ability to articulate her beliefs that cost Bott the sentence she was to receive. Gender politics in the 1970s were still very much confrontational. Park was a male judge from an alcohol driven culture. He must have been horrified to see the highly educated Bott defending the right to take psychedelic drugs while at the same time claiming disinterest in money. Bott was not arrested in possession of any LSD. Nor was there proof she had been directly involved in the manufacturing process, other than to support Kemp keeping him fed and comfortable. For her knowledge and support, she received a nine-year custodial sentence, only a year less than the other acid chemist, Andy Munro. As Munro commented, "Bott got nine years for making sandwiches. I got ten years for making acid."

Contrast this disposal with that of Russell Spenceley's wife Janine, who admitted to supplying large quantities of microdots, but at her husband's request. She received a two year suspended sentence and effectively walked from court a free woman. Had Bott put spin on her testimony, played the vulnerable female and claimed that Kemp had coerced her into a life of illicit LSD manufacture, the chances are she would have walked free from the court with a suspended sentence at most.

Though the principals in the Julie conspiracy knew they were not going to get away with anything less than a prison sentence they clung to the hope that a plea of mitigation might sway Justice Park's decision. In support of their plea Dr. Martin Mitcheson, head of the Drug Dependency Clinic at University College Hospital, London took the stand. Mitcheson argued that although LSD was a Class A drug he ranked it below the opiates, amphetamines and barbiturates in terms of its effects and only slightly more dangerous than cannabis. He also cited a BBC study from 1973 that indicated a minimum 600,000 Britons had taken the drug at least once, demonstrating how popular LSD was among the young. Furthermore, Mitcheson said, not one death certificate had ever recorded LSD as the cause of death. In response to questions from the judge Mitcheson agreed that he believed LSD should be moved to a lower classification.[29]

It was to no avail. Mr. Justice Park refused to accept the doctor's expert testimony. It was, he said, irrelevant. In law LSD was a Class A drug and to the judge it was immaterial whether it was less or more harmful than any other drug, legal or otherwise. Nor did he take note of Mitcheson's claims about the destructive effects of the legal drug, alcohol, and the number of hospital admissions it caused. Park interrupted Mitcheson with: "Alcohol is not a Class A drug."[30]

Though he was factually correct it seemed that the die had been cast and no argument however strong, however well supported by fact, was going to prevent LSD being officially denounced, its acolytes vilified and imprisoned. Justice Park, it seems, was interested only in the blind and unfeeling application of the law rather than interpreting the law based on the available scientific evidence.

During his time on remand, awaiting trial, Richard Kemp hand-wrote a long statement which he intended to read out in court as the basis of his defence. He eventually decided against this but only after sending the screed to Patrick O'Brien, a journalist on the *Cambrian Times*, Kemp's local Welsh newspaper. The *Cambrian Times* published an article based on Kemp's thoughts entitled, somewhat wittily, "Microdoctrine". In it, Kemp makes clear his own and the growing LSD culture's link between LSD, mindfullness and ecology. Although he kept the bulk of his beliefs out of court, Microdoctrine makes it clear that Kemp made LSD to change consciousness and to save the world from ecological disaster.

MICRODOCTRINE

Richard Kemp, the chemist of genius from Tregaron who was jailed for 13 years last week for his involvement in a conspiracy to manufacture and distribute the drug LSD, believed society would have to change rapidly if ecological disaster and social chaos were to be avoided.

In common with some expert scientific opinion he was convinced that, if Earth's raw materials were to be conserved and pollution reduced to a tolerable level, there would have to be a revolution in people's attitudes.

And he believed LSD could spark changes in outlook which would put the world on the road to survival. In an 8,000 word-statement which he had planned to deliver from the dock before being sentenced, Kemp declares: "I do have deeply held convictions as to the positive aspects of the use of LSD. It was these that provided the motivation for engaging in the activities for which I am before your Lordship and NOT the desire to make money by means of a criminal activity."

He prepared the handwritten document in order that his views would emerge clearly and because the "crazy media exaggerations" of much media reporting "really got me down no end". But his lawyers persuaded him not to deliver the statement in case it led the judge to pass a heavier sentence. Kemp says, "I am particularly anxious to counter the impression that I am an evil man so bound up in greed that I was uncaring or unmindful of the possible harmful effects resulting from what I did. I am not trying to ignore or excuse the fact I have broken the law. I wish only to put the crime in the perspective in which I see it."

On ecology and conservation Kemp believes it is obvious we are living on the world's capital rather than its income. He says that to achieve a level of consumption that is reasonable, taking into account the Earth's limited and dwindling resources, two things will be necessary.

"People will have to accept a lower standard of living by becoming content with having things which are necessary for survival, and luxuries will have to be kept to a minimum. Secondly, those goods which are supplied will have to be built to have the longest possible lifespan, at the end of which they must be capable of being recycled."

Kemp adds in the document he describes as "My LSD Philosophy": "Changes in policy by manufacturers will come about only if sufficient pressure for change is generated by the public. In as far as LSD can catalyse such a change in members of the public, it can contribute to this end." But he says that only if people find greater contentment within themselves and become free of trivial and outdated social pressures – he uses as an example advertising pressures to buy luxuries because these, it is implied, will bring social status – will they be able to accept the necessity of a life which revolves less around material things.

Kemp writes that he has taken LSD "over 200 times other than in the course of manufacture". He says "It has been my experience, and that of many of those I know, that LSD helps to make one realise that happiness is a state of mind and not a state of ownership." But he makes it plain that he has not yet freed himself from "the dependence on material things which we have been encouraged to develop throughout our lives". And he does not claim that this freedom is, "an inevitable result of LSD experiences. But I feel that I, and many of those I know, have started down the road to a greater reliance on our inner resources. Because the realisation that contentment is a state of mind, one compensates less for unhappiness by buying things. This is why I felt that, if a large number of people were to experience this truth, whether by means of LSD or by means of an appropriate discipline, such as yoga or meditation, the problems resulting from consumerism would be to a large extent solved."

Kemp practised what he preached in simple living. The £7,000 Blaencaron cottage he shared with Dr Christine Bott had few luxuries. There was no television or central heating, the sparse furnishings tended to be threadbare and the walls of the rooms were treated merely to an annual coating of white cement paint. A deep freeze stood in the lean-to but the ty bach (toilet) retained its original role. The only ostentatious touch in the two bedroomed home is a Victorian cast-iron spiral staircase, which Kemp bought in London and installed himself. They ate simply – an assortment of vegetables from the immaculately laid out garden, milk, cheese and yoghurt from their pedigree goats, eggs from half a dozen hens. He was committed to organic (non-chemical) gardening and belonged to West Wales Soil Association. During the 1976 drought, before sinking his own well with the help of a water diviner, he spent hours daily lugging water by truck to his vegetable beds from a river half a mile away.

Kemp claims that a sharp awareness of the importance of conservation is just one example of how clear sightedness through LSD can manifest itself. He believes the drug raises the barrier separating people from the unconscious part of their minds, and another benefit this can bring he says, is to alleviate or eliminate everyday neurotic problems. LSD, he adds, is often used as an end in itself because it enhances all the sense and "everything appears more beautiful. When people first use LSD they tend to concentrate on this aspect of the experience, but later they begin to use LSD as a means to learn about themselves, rather than as an end."

He adds, "If it were just a question of satisfying people's pleasure seeking desires, I would not have become involved. However, I believe that the end towards which LSD is a means is personally and socially beneficial. That is the way I and most of the people I know use it. I have never believed that LSD is a substitute for the hard work required to change oneself. One might say it is a signpost pointing a way to self-discovery."

Kemp's statement does not ignore the dangers of the drug. Anyone involved in the illegal supply of LSD, he says, is obviously running the risk of exposing certain people to negative experiences with which they cannot cope, and to which they may develop a panic reaction. He adds: "I must emphasise that in my experience of LSD use and in my observation of other LSD users, I have NEVER SEEN a person develop a reaction which has led to uncontrollable behaviour, aggressiveness or attempts to harm themselves or others. However, I do accept that this may have occurred but I am quite certain that it only happens where LSD is used in a circumstances far removed from those recommended by all concerned with the drug, and that such events are extremely rare." He adds: "I would like to contrast myself with the heroin dealer who sells to others something which he knows is addictive and does no good and which therefore he does not take himself. Chronic dependence on LSD is almost unknown and no-one believes that it is addictive."

But children, he says, should be protected. "It may be said that some of those under the age of majority have been exposed to something whose nature and proper use they did not fully understand. I would certainly support a system of social control, including a education about the nature and use of LSD, backed by laws where appropriate to protect those who are not fully able to take decisions for themselves, and to cover situations in which the use of LSD becomes a matter for public rather than private concern. One obvious example is driving a car on a public road."

He continues: "The present climate and opinion of law effectively forced me to make a choice between making LSD available without social controls, with the small risks inherent in this approach, or not making it available at all. Believing as I did that the benefits are so urgently necessary if we are to have any chance of solving the pressing problems of the modern world, I felt I had no choice but to adopt the course which has led me to the dock and your Lordship's judgement."

He maintains that other drugs, particularly alcohol, amphetamines, opiates and tobacco, are far more dangerous than LSD. And in a letter from prison: "We have been hunted down, not because of a few bad trips or LSD-associated deaths, but because of the dramatic political effects we have been having.[31]

The sentences, when they came, were harsh, and seemed to reflect Kemp's fervent belief that the social and political establishment feared the changes LSD wrought in people. The two LSD chemists, Kemp and Munro, received 13 and 10 years, respectively. Solomon, presumably because of his own admission compounded with the fact he was a public advocate of LSD through his books, was sentenced to ten years. Todd was identified as the "marketing manager" of the operation and jailed for 13 years. The other principle defendents received varying custodial sentences and those in the outer circle of the plot were given various suspended sentences, fines and probation orders.

When sentencing Kemp, Justice Park told him: "All this was done, it is said, in the pursuit of the ideal that LSD liberated people's minds and therefore your work would be beneficial to mankind. That was, I think, a false ideal." Acknowledging the intellectual calibre of those he had sentenced, Park commented: "I regret very much ... that severe sentences are to be passed on people with excellent characters, excellent professional qualifications, and others in possession of very considerable scientific skill." That so many highly educated people could be involved with LSD manufacture and distribution clearly rattled the fourth estate, as it was a theme noticed repeatedly in the media reports about the trial.[32]

The editorial in *The Times* on the day after sentences had been passed announced they were "severe, but rightly so". Several column inches were taken up in justifying the sentences by using the same weak and unproven arguments about the alleged deleterious effects of LSD on the personality.[33]

After sentencing had taken place, on 11 March, twenty-one members of the Julie team attended Bristol Crown Court where Mr. Justice Park publicly commended them. Several of the officers were wearing their Operation Julie tie designed by Detective Constable Alun Morgan. The tie featured a silver circle of 11 clasped hands, representing the 11 forces from which the team was drawn. In the centre of the circle was an ear of rye, the cereal from which ergotamine tartrate, the basis of LSD, is obtained.

As the prison doors slammed shut on those convicted and sentenced for their part in the Operation Julie conspiracy the cries of protest from their customers were notable by their absence. Not only had the acidheads allowed the Julie trial to proceed without any form of organised defence or outcry, they also failed to express their anger at the sentences. Only hippie newspaper *International Times* attempted to put the dénouement of the trial in context.

The article "Lysergic Love Criminals" railed against the ignorance of the prosecution and judges and was dismayed by the selective mechanism of justice: "And the world said: consciousness expanding is anathema. Just as anatomists were considered anathema in Savonarola's time. They were delving illicitly into God's world. Cutting people open was regarded as similar to eating them ... And by the same token the tools for the examination of consciousness are regarded by the powers that be as a threat to the desultory scraps of consciousness over which they preside. ... No comparison can be made between the violence of smack dealing and the pacific nature of acid exchanges. No comparison can be made between the crimes, or lack of them, induced by acid and the crimes which are impresarioed, with society's less than tacit consent, by alcohol and a plethora of other noxious Class A substances, both psychic and chemical that few bother or dare to impugn ... Imagination is to wear grey again this season. The unexhilerated brains of Parliamentary draughtsman have decided that acid is 'evil' and the higher echelons of the Judiciary have seen fit to describe it as '*the* evil.'"[34]

With the principal conspirators now serving prison sentences the police finally had the time to examine the success and failures of Operation Julie in detail. Even though the operation had been a resounding success, it had its critics in the police who didn't like the idea of cross-force policing and the creation of special units. This underlying current of ill will made itself felt at a meeting of the Association of Chief Police Officers on 18 December 1978 when one officer referred sarcastically to Operation Julie as "the longest running show after *The Mousetrap*" and said he thought it should now be brought to a close and officers reunited with their home forces.[35]

It must have been incredibly difficult for officers who had spent months living undercover as hippies or in the cramped conditions of a surveillance post to go back to the humdrum, workaday routine of general policing. The feeling of belonging to a special elite for over a year and then being unceremoniously returned to the backbiting canteen culture of regional policing was too much for some. Others were resented by the forces they returned to; a resentment driven by jealousy that their colleagues had been involved in such an historic investigation.

Detective Constable Allan Buxton commented: "Operation Julie was so successful I thought the squad would be kept together. Instead, everyone was sent back to their own forces and treated like lepers. When I got back I was told, 'you've had your holiday and earned some money and now you can come back and do some police work.'"[36] Other officers were given menial police duties almost as though their part in Operation Julie had to be punished in some way.

The result of this dissatisfaction was that within a year of the arrests, six of the Operation Julie squad planned to resign from the police force. The first to go was Detective Chief Inspector Dick Lee. Prior to handing in his resignation Lee paid a visit to psychiatrist Ronnie Laing and Steve Abrams. He revealed to them that they had both been under suspicion in the early stages of the Julie investigation because of Laing's friendship with Solomon and Abrams' public espousal of drug use. A bizarre night of heavy drinking ensued, Lee arguing the police version of events that Laing and Abrams countered with the psychoanalytical and counter culture position on acid. Lee left the flat and allegedly handed in his resignation that same day.[37]

Prison gives people time for reflection and some of the Julie conspirators began to think about the assets that had been confiscated from them. Having had their initial appeal to the Court of Appeal rejected, Henry Todd and Brian Cuthbertson submitted a further appeal to the House of Lords, claiming that their assets, comprising cash, stocks, gold, krugerrands and stamps, amounting to over £500,000 was unlawfully forfeited. Seizures of cash and other assets is allowed under the Misuse of Drugs Act, but the appellants argued that as they had only been convicted of conspiracy the law did not apply in their case. The Law Lords determined that Justice Park acted illegally and the assets should not have been seized, but refused to order them to be returned.

The appellants threatened to sue the Director of Public Prosecutions, Sir Thomas Harrington, QC, but he stated he would not return any assets unless there was a legal challenge. Giving assets back to convicted criminals was something the legal and political establishment wished to avoid at all costs, not least for the message it would send through the criminal underworld. Discussions took place between the DPP and the Attorney General and Inland Revenue staff as they tried to find a way not to have to return assets to Todd and Cuthbertson. A decision was finally reached which maintained the status quo. The Inland Revenue issued large tax claims against the Julie conspirators, effectively ending any claim for their assets to be handed back to them.[38]

A body of folklore sprang up in the wake of the Operation Julie trial. Some elements of this are too far-fetched for serious consideration while parts occupy the plausible middle ground between fact and fiction, becoming accepted fact purely by repetition. These rumours do two things; they hint at the unexplored areas of the Operation Julie conspiracy and demonstrate how the microdot gang has influenced popular culture. The acid in the water supply was patently nonsense but the following rumours appear to have at least some truth in them.

In the welter of theory and speculation following the 1977 arrests, one national Sunday newspaper printed: "Seventy-one people were arrested. And a detective said last night that when the matter comes to court well-known names will be mentioned including a friend of the Royal Family."[39] Surprisingly this allegation was not followed up and nothing more was heard of the story in the papers. Nevertheless, after the trial rumour began to spread among Britain's LSD users that a friend of Princess

Margaret's was questioned about allegations he had bought 30,000 doses of LSD on behalf of the Queen's sister.

Princess Margaret is known to have liked the high life and there have been allegations that she smoked cannabis and took other drugs. She certainly enjoyed hanging out and having fun, whether at her retreat on the tropical island of Mustique, or closer to home, at Glen House in Scotland, where, on one New Year's Eve, she danced and sang *Jumping Jack Flash* with the Incredible String Band's Robin Williamson.

In February 2007, a BBC Wales website published an article containing: "Rumour has it that Princess Margaret was involved with one of the main suspects and that the police hierarchy delayed the swoop until she was well out of the way." The author of the article was Lyn Ebenezer, a journalist who covered the Operation Julie events as they happened in 1977. Ebenezer claims he was told about the rumour by one of the Operation Julie undercover police officers.[40]

Another well-known name that has become inextricably linked with Operation Julie lore is that of Francis Crick, the discoverer of DNA. In 2004, the *Daily Mail* quoted a friend of Richard Kemp's who claimed Crick knew Kemp and Solomon and had taken LSD to help untangle the mysteries of DNA. Supporters of LSD seized on this tall tale and the story spread uncritically throughout the media and on over 14,000 internet sites. The article, based on a thirdhand source, is highly dubious. LSD first arrived in Britain during September 1952 and for several years was available only to a few psychotherapists. It is highly unlikely Crick, who discovered DNA in 1953, would have had access to the drug at that time.[41]

However, Crick, a Cambridge resident until 1977, was known to have used LSD later in his life. Crick's biographer, having spoken to his widow, ascertained that although Crick did not know Kemp and Solomon he did know Henry Todd, who introduced him to LSD in 1967. Crick was apparently: "… fascinated by its effects – by how he became confused about what familiar objects were for, and by the way it seemed to alter the passage of time." He took LSD several times but no factual evidence has yet appeared that indicates he was more closely connected with the drug's manufacture or distribution.[42]

Operation Julie has gone down in counter culture folklore. Even today, acidheads know of the case and in Britain "Operation Julie acid" is mentioned with the same reverence American LSD acidheads use for Owsley's psychedelic produce of the Sixties. Kemp's LSD, tabletted from a large consignment of pure LSD which was taken out of the country just before the raids, was circulating well into the Nineties and it's possible that some people still have their own stash of Julie acid, lovingly salted away for a special occasion.

Operation Julie has now become a legend and popular culture has frequently referred to the event. Punk band The Clash, veterans of the early free festival scene in their guise as the 101ers, recorded the track "Julie's Working for the Drug Squad" on their 1978 album *Give 'Em Enough Rope*: "An' then there came the night of the greatest ever raid, they arrested every drug that had ever been made."[43] Other bands such as the obscure Drug Squad have also alluded to the conspiracy on their 1980 single "Operation Julie".

The cat and mouse, police versus the acid intellectuals, game that Operation Julie became resulted in the story being dramatised for ITV in 1985. The three part mini series wasn't a hit with the public though. It was low on action and high on dialogue and character, intrigued the critics but failed to ignite the public's imagination. The name and the myth live on; as recently as August 2007 some internet discussion groups were taking seriously the possibility that there may be LSD and money still buried deep in the Welsh hillsides.

Those imprisoned for their part in the Operation Julie events served their prison sentences without incident and were released on various dates during the Eighties. There were no fanfares in the mainstream or alternative media. After release some of the conspirators kept in touch with each other, the rest vanished. Kemp and Bott's relationship survived their incarceration but they parted shortly after their release and both disappeared. Rumours abound as to their whereabouts; Kemp has been seen in Goa, Bott is thought to have lived simply for many years as a smallholder in southwest Ireland. David Solomon died in April 2007, and of Andy Munro, nothing has been heard. None of the principal conspirators has ever expressed any interest in telling the story from their point of view, either to make money or to give their side of the story. Their lives have moved on but their names will be forever linked to Operation Julie.

Since their release from custody, only one of the Julie gang has been in the public eye. On his release from prison, Henry Todd had returned to one of his passions, mountaineering, opening a business supplying oxygen cylinders to climbers. In May 1999, Michael Matthews, at twenty-two the youngest Briton to have summited on Everest, died on the descent from problems with his oxygen supply. Todd's company had supplied the oxygen and Matthews' father pursued a private prosecution for manslaughter. Todd was suddenly thrust into the news and his connection with Operation Julie exhumed. He was exonerated of any blame but the adverse publicity he received because of his Operation Julie connections affected his business, which closed.[44]

The defendants in the Operation Julie trial did more to promote LSD in Britain than anyone before or since. Whether or not they caused a psychedelic evolution, as Kemp intended, is debatable. It certainly wasn't a public revolution. But the changes in worldview their LSD brought to countless thousands of people have had a more subtle effect in society. There are now people in their fifties and sixties who occupy key roles in industry, science, the armed forces, the police, and numerous authors, who have taken their Operation Julie vision into the heart of the establishment and tried to change things from the inside.

Kemp and his associates were, whatever their motivations, activists. Unlike most who espouse the hippie dream they made it happen, facilitating consciousness change for anyone who wanted it, and paid the price for doing so. Their supporters contend that the purity of Kemp and Munro's LSD radically changed the consciousness of thousands of people. They claim the Julie acid caused its users to examine and refine their lifestyles, relationships, personalities and spiritual goals. More abstractly, it could be argued Kemp and Munro's LSD helped fuel the free festival movement of the 1970s, providing the energy and lysergic shimmer for those surreal events.

Their detractors believe Kemp and Munro's acid was the product of an organization driven by vicious, uncaring greed, responsible for the moral degradation and damage to the mental health of thousands of young people. Unlike the pro Julie view there was little, if any, evidence for the claims of the prosecution and, if Martin Mitcheson's data were correct, evidence to the contrary. But the people who write history, make history. The mainstream media and the police have written the only histories of the Operation Julie microdot gang and so it is the establishment's view that is put forward.

The tenacity with which the police pursued the Operation Julie LSD conspiracy has rarely been equalled. It could be asked why, if the police, on a tight budget, could smash the LSD ring, they could not do the same for the heroin trade. Heroin has killed more Britons every year than LSD has done since it was first synthesised. Heroin destroys lives and families, the acquisitive crime it breeds making areas unsafe to walk or park in and puts a shoplifting premium on the cost of retail goods. LSD does none of this. But heroin is not a tool for examining consciousness, nor does it, or those who manufacture and distribute it, seek to transform the user to be able to see through the drudgery of western materialism and redundant Judeo-Christian spirituality. Heroin dulls individuals and communities, giving police and politicians an easy enemy to blame social ills upon. LSD energised individuals and helped create communities, new modes of living and the temporary autonomous zones of the free festival.

The conclusion drawn by the counter culture about the Operation Julie saga is simple. The British establishment, that thousand-year-old interlocking web of legislated power, law, status and wealth seems unable to countenance anyone who wishes to expand their consciousness with LSD but is content to allow widespread abuse of heroin, barbiturates and alcohol.

Detective Chief Superintendent Dennis Greenslade, head of Operation Julie, summed up the battle of ideology and lifestyle choice represented by the Operation Julie events: "We were up against the intelligentsia – and we won."[45]

Greenslade was correct. The battle might have been won, but the war was not over yet. Despite the prosecution's claim that Operation Julie had wiped out LSD in Britain, and what was available could only be obtained at a premium, that was not the case. Shortly after the trial, Release told the *New Musical Express* the "bulk price was now £40 for 4,000 (10p a tab) with a street price at £1". They also claimed that LSD, far from drying up, is now "almost as easily obtainable as cannabis".[46]

12 COMING DOWN AGAIN

> How about a positive LSD story? Wouldn't that be newsworthy, just the once? To base your decision on information rather than scare tactics and superstition and lies? I think it would be news-worthy.
>
> Bill Hicks[1]

For LSD users who became involved with the drug in the heady days of the Swinging Sixties or the Operation Julie acid-drenched Seventies, the prospect at the dawn of the Eighties looked bleak. Attempts at fermenting the psychedelic revolution through communal living, festivals and LSD philosophy and spirituality had been tenuous at best, risible at worst. The original acid generation now stood blinking in the cold light of Margaret Thatcher's new Conservative government. Tolerance for any form of drug use was at its lowest and young people saw the counter culture lifestyle as anachronistic and outmoded. There was a new spirit of raw, entrepreneurial, dog-eat-dog capitalist culture in the air. The LSD generation was up against the me generation and suddenly everything looked very different.

The drug scene was changing fast too. In the Sixties and Seventies certain types of drugs were primarily taken by clearly defined subcultures; acid and cannabis by hippies, amphetamines by punks, cocaine by the wealthy, heroin and barbiturates by people who craved oblivion, and so on. Of course, this is a generalization but it was largely the case. The advent of punk in the late Seventies was the beginning of the end for clearly defined drug user groups. They still existed, but all kinds of drugs were now so widespread and cheap by the Eighties, that the barriers between tribal groupings and their chemical predilections began to merge.

One of the first casualties of this fragmentation of LSD culture was the closure of Lee Harris' *Home Grown* magazine. Harris had done an excellent job in reporting on psychedelic culture and the magazine was one of the few publications to support the Operation Julie defendants. Now, minimal profits, a dwindling market and apathy made the magazine unviable and the enterprise folded. Harris retained Alchemy, his Portobello Road "head shop", which remains a focus and gathering point for alternative Londoners to the present day.[2]

The successive musical genres of Punk, New Wave and the New Romantics drew on radically different aspirations to the early LSD counterculture and required different drugs to fuel their cultures. LSD was still widely available, despite the aftermath of Operation Julie, but was now viewed differently by the next generation of drug users, many of whom were now taking LSD more for the sheer weirdness of its effects rather than for its spiritual insights. As ever, musicians continued to use LSD and the drug continued to be the motivating factor in some musical scenes. In the early Eighties, pop star Julian Cope of the Teardrop Explodes was a fervent advocate of LSD and its use slowly permeated the late Seventies and early Eighties Liverpool musical scene.

During that period, the music scene in the Beatles' hometown had centred round a club called Eric's. The club was notorious, as much for the drugs which could be obtained there as it was for the new music emanating from its tiny stage. Journalist, Andrew Hussey remembered Eric's and the role LSD played as: "The atmosphere was exciting, often drenched in LSD (then the most unfashionable drug in the UK)."[3]

Unfashionable or not LSD, as it had done with so many other musicians, provided Cope with a muse. As the single "Reward" inched its way up the pop charts Cope was rehearsing his band for a tour of America's East Coast. In the studios, "rehearsals came to a stop, as Gary and I would be overcome by the power of the acid that we constantly ingested." During these sessions the Teardrop Explodes were summoned to appear on *Top of the Pops*, Britain's most prestigious music showcase. On the way to the show Cope took LSD: "The acid made us happy and nice. We gushed around the place like inbreds at a New England dinner party." Cope repeated the Pops-on-acid routine with his next single, "Passionate Friend", once again managing to perform live magnificently whilst tripping heavily.[4]

In January 1982, Cope met a young American teenager called Courtney Love, the daughter of Hank Harrison, one of the Grateful Dead's inner circle, and future wife of doomed Nirvana front man, Kurt Cobain. Love was no stranger to LSD, having taken it when she was four years old. Knowing Cope's liking for acid, she had her father send large quantities of the drug through the post from America. "About six packages of acid and MDA, each package containing 200 tablets had arrived at my home with my name on the envelopes ..."[5]

The form in which LSD appeared was also changing. Although LSD soaked on blotting paper had been available since the Fifties, by the Seventies the preferred form of the drug tended to be microdot. Operation Julie chemists Richard Kemp and Andy Munro had refined the production of potent microdot LSD to a fine art and other chemists followed in their wake. Microdot LSD had many advantages. It was easy to store and transport, in bottles, bags or between layers of sellotape and it did not easily degrade by repeated handling. But changes in manufacturing techniques and the 1986 American law, which linked sentences for LSD to the weight of the carrying agent, meant that LSD on blotting paper – much lighter than microdots – became the most widely available form of the drug.

Blotter LSD was initially available on plain or coloured sheets, hand ripped into doses. Enterprising LSD manufacturers developed the process, each production run of LSD soaked on to sheets of perforated blotter printed with a different design. A full sheet of blotter contained approximately a thousand doses.

However, blotter LSD was difficult to store and transport and constant handling and exposure to sunlight could easily degrade the LSD content.

The free festival movement, building on its success in the Seventies was, in the early Eighties, massive and going from strength to strength. There was now an established circuit of annual events and it was possible for the committed traveller to start in late spring with the May Hill festival and spend the entire summer at festivals or parties, culminating in September with the Psilocybin Fair in mid-Wales. If the much-vaunted LSD revolution was anywhere it lay at the heart of free festival culture whose anarchy, acceptance and desire to live a life not defined by laws or materialism seemed to be the living embodiment of the psychedelic experience.

LSD was widely available at all these events and was becoming more widespread. People were now going to free festivals as much to stock up on LSD as to take it for pleasure. Many of the free festival veterans were living permanently on the road and for some, selling drugs defrayed the costs of their itinerant lifestyles. Small groups and bands who formed the core of the festivals, such as the Tibetan Ukranian Mountain Troupe (TUMT), a Prankster-like surreal hippie travelling circus, were certainly involved in the distribution of LSD at festivals. Arriving at Stonehenge in 1981 their Book of the Road notes: "I've just gone for a little walk round the site and sold out of lysergic gasket paper."[6] The term "lysergic gasket paper" referred to the fact that "the acid would arrive on site as plain A4 sheets of impregnated dark green cartridge paper that looked a bit like gasket paper so were stashed in the tool box with the spanners and such, the printed fascia sheets would come in with somebody else and the two would be stuck together on site."[7] Groups like the TUMT practiced what they preached and put enormous amounts of energy and effort into ensuring free festivals were places where the psychedelic lifestyle could be lived to the full.

But the halcyon days of taking acid at festivals were coming under threat and with it the original ethos of free festivals. These events, particularly the Stonehenge festivals, had represented a kind of hippie pilgrimage, with the taking of LSD a crucial part of the psychedelic quest. Now heroin, cocaine, amphetamines and barbiturates were becoming increasingly prevalent at festivals. The rapid spread of hard drugs within the free festival culture, 1982–84, gave the police a reason to prevent or to disrupt them. Older travellers did what they could to maintain the vision of the early festivals. But more and more unemployed young people, driven out of squats or bored with low paid jobs, were becoming attracted to the travelling life, squatting in the winter, going to festivals in the summer. Many of these new travellers were only interested in getting as stoned as possible in what they saw was an accepting environment. Free festival veterans did their best to be inclusive of these newcomers, many of whom were LSD users keen to become part of the traveller's subculture. But many others failed to understand the history and culture that the original hippie travelling community were rooted in and frictions inevitably arose.

The Operation Julie trial had alerted criminal elements to the potential for huge profits, with minimal risk, to be made from drug trafficking. They saw the free festivals as a ready-made unregulated market place in which to ply their trade. Don Aitken of Release reflected on the beginning of the end when he commented: "I think I first realised Stonehenge was doomed when (I think it was 1982) signs began to appear on the main drag advertising drugs in weight quantities. People weren't buying drugs to take to the festival – they were coming specifically to buy drugs to take back home to distribute."[8]

Although harder drugs were increasingly available, the ethos of producing high quality LSD continued. In some cases the attention to quality and detail extended even to the packaging the LSD arrived in. At the Stonehenge free festival in the mid-Eighties Glenda Pescado remembers, "the most beautifully packaged acid I'd ever seen turned up. Samurai acid, each 100 or so blotters came in its own matt black wallet with an embossed logo on it. Each blotter was different white print on black paper with a gold lining, wonderful stuff."[9]

Increasing numbers of people living on the road and moving between festivals, coupled with the constant harrying by the police led to hundreds of travellers' vehicles forming a convoy. This quickly became known as the Peace Convoy or the Hippie Convoy and attracted considerable media coverage and the opprobrium of local and national politicians. The British government invested considerable time and money in tracking and infiltrating the free festival movement with the intent of bringing it to a halt at any cost.

The 1984 Stonehenge festival represented the peak of the free festival movement and was the last major event before the police destroyed the Convoy. Over 100,000 people attended the month long happening, and signs advertising the price of different types of LSD were openly displayed on tents, caravans and buses. That Stonehenge and the free festivals were predicated on LSD use is reflected in a survey conducted among 500 festival attendees. Seventy per cent of respondents claimed to have regularly taken LSD and or magic mushrooms, and those who also described themselves as holding pagan beliefs had taken psychedelics most often. Half of those surveyed stated they intended to take LSD while at the festival.

The final, carefully planned, confrontation between state and travellers came on 1 June 1985. A large convoy attempting to establish camp at Stonehenge well in advance of the festival's start were shepherded by police, in paramilitary riot outfits, into a field about 11 km from the ancient monument. There they systematically attacked and beat the would-be festivalgoers, including pregnant women, and destroyed their vehicles. Independent Television Network journalist, Kim Sabido was present and was horrified at what he saw: "What we – the ITN camera crew and myself as a reporter – have seen in the last thirty minutes here in this field has been some of the most brutal police treatment of people that I've witnessed in my entire career as a journalist. The number of people who have been hit by policemen, who have been clubbed whilst holding babies in their arms, in coaches around this field, is yet to be counted ... There must surely be an enquiry after what has happened today."[10]

Veteran traveller, Sid Rawle believes the debacle could have been avoided if certain elements within the Peace Convoy had not been desperate to get the festival site, regardless of the consequences: "They all had to get the drugs in and buried."[11]

The event, known as the Battle of the Beanfield, caused the convoy to scatter. Many travellers moved abroad. Others, now deprived of their income, vehicles and community came off the road or became mired in filthy camps where hard drugs slowly corroded the last vestiges of the free festival vision Bill Dwyer, Wally Hope and Sid Rawle had worked so hard to bring to fruition.

A year later, on 3 June 1986, Home Secretary Douglas Hurd described the hippie Peace Convoy as: "A band of medieval brigands who have no respect for law and order and the rights of others."[12] A few days later Prime Minister Margaret Thatcher announced the Conservative government would be "only too delighted to do anything we can to make life difficult for such things as 'hippie convoys.'"[13] The glory days of the free festivals were over.

But the smashing of the hippie convoy did little to upset the manufacture and distribution of LSD. There was still a huge demand for the drug and it was working its unique magic on a new influx of young people who were fresh to the free festival scene. These individuals started off in the traditional counter culture but went on to develop their own alternative lifestyle, eventually assisting in bringing new and old LSD cultures together through new music and new drugs. The story of Monkey, from south London, illustrates perfectly how the new generation took to acid.

While at the Glastonbury festival in 1981, the teenaged Monkey paid £1.50 for his first LSD trip. It was on a small square of blotting paper depicting a black star on a red background. The low price, only five years after the events of Operation Julie, demonstrates how quickly new LSD manufacturers filled the gap left by Kemp and Munro. The authorities' claim they had smashed LSD distribution in Britain had proved to be a hollow boast. LSD appealed to Monkey and he continued to use it as his involvement with free festivals intensified. He began to buy larger quantities of LSD, mainly from one of the regular free festival bands who sold LSD to help finance their lifestyle: "Most of the travellers on the convoy financed their travelling by selling cannabis, speed and acid at the free festivals or from their squats during winter."[14]

Eventually, Monkey's personal use of LSD morphed into dealing. Through his contacts, Monkey was able to buy LSD in quantity, a thousand doses costing in the region of £600. He would occasionally sell trips single or in small numbers for £2–£5 each but mainly sold the LSD wholesale at £700 for 1000 doses of blotter LSD. This represented a 16 per cent mark up, hardly the sort of huge profits the media and police suggest is made by LSD dealers.

Selling LSD to others, whether in single doses or large quantities, carries with it a degree of moral responsibility. The LSD dealer knows he or she is selling a substance that can instantly change the course of someone's existence. Being aware of this, Monkey "… only sold to good friends who I knew could handle it. I never sold to strangers I did not know. If I sold in bulk, I did not feel any guilt. I thought I was doing a good service for all the people wanting acid. I had had bad trips and was still taking them." Monkey's personal belief about LSD is clear, his reason for making the drug widely available was motivated by more than just profit: "Acid is something everyone should experience at least once in their life."[15]

Monkey's firsthand experience of how LSD was used and distributed at free festivals underscored the significance and centrality of the drug to that movement: "Acid was for sale at every free festival I went to, the music was very acid orientated. Most of the free festivals were probably financed through acid sales the bands and people involved made. The bands who I knew played for nothing but made their money from selling acid. Acidheads like me knew which bands to approach for acid at the free festivals."[16]

With free festivals almost driven out of existence and many hippie travellers having now relocated to the more liberal countries of France and Spain, the media and government needed a new moral panic to replace LSD. They soon found it, but so did tens of thousands of Britain's young people. The "new" drug, Ecstasy, was actually older than LSD, having been first synthesised in 1912. It was used initially as a slimming drug, and eventually found favour, as did LSD, as an effective tool in psychotherapy. From the early Eighties it had been widely used as a recreational drug in America, with increasing amounts being brought back to Britain.

Ecstasy made its appearance on the free festival scene long before it became a favourite with young people in clubs and raves. The Tibetan Ukranian Mountain Troupe's Glenda Pescado recalls: "In 1982 someone turned up at Stonehenge festival with an A4 sheet of pink blotters with little flying saucers on them, saying this is synthetic mescaline, MDMA, of course the term Ecstasy hadn't been coined at that point."[17]

Ecstasy, also known as E and MDMA, the initials of its chemical formula (3, 4-methylenedioxy-N-methylamphetamine hydrochloride) is a mild psychedelic. Characteristically Ecstasy causes feelings of empathy, love and compassion in those who use it. However, Ecstasy lacked the spiritual, numinous dimension that LSD often engendered, and adherents of Ecstasy were much more interested in dancing all night than probing the mysteries of the universe. Ecstasy also had many advantages over LSD for those who wanted a taste of psychedelia but did not want to go all the way. Ecstasy was much less intense and bad trips were almost unknown. Where LSD often caused people to become quiet as they journeyed deep into their mind, Ecstasy invariably made its users garrulous, happy to talk, socialise and above all, dance. Additionally, Ecstasy appealed to women in a way that LSD had not. The result was that the emergent Acid House culture was a much more sexually equitable one than had been the Sixties psychedelic explosion.[18]

The media hysteria surrounding Ecstasy culture and Acid House music was even more lurid than that which had attended the emergence of LSD in the Sixties. Tabloid newspapers ran with headlines such as: "Shoot these evil acid barons" "Ban acid cult that killed our girl" and "Hell of acid kids". In their rush to judgement, the tabloids had ignored one crucial fact; the term "acid house" was not derived from the slang term for LSD, but referred to the style of music preferred by Ecstasy users. Its etymology in that context is vague but all commentators agreed that the acid in Acid House was not LSD.

Gradually Ecstasy and Acid House music took over the remnants of the free festival scene. Monkey recalls the transition: "I took a mini sound system to Glastonbury in 1989 and played acid house music. We got a lot of complaints from the Gong, Hawkwind fans etc. A few people liked it and some had heard it before. We were on Es all that weekend. By 1989 several larger sound systems had taken to house music and were playing at free festivals. Also the acid house parties had moved outside and took over the free festivals."[19]

Free festival and rave cultures, despite their differences, merged. This was a marriage of convenience, two tribes flung together by the outlaw status imposed on them by society and a shared liking for music, dance and drugs, especially LSD and Ecstasy. Most Ecstasy users were perfectly happy with the drug's effects and didn't want more. It was an easy drug to take at the weekend, have a fantastic time and be back at work on Monday no worse for wear. Nevertheless, suggesting that individuals seek out the drugs that provide the experience they need, some people quickly tired of Ecstasy and wanted something more meaningful.

Mark Harrison, one of the prime movers behind the radical dance music collective Spiral Tribe, summed up this sense of dissatisfaction, saying: "MDMA has its place, but once you've taken it a couple of times, its lessons are learned very quickly and it becomes unnecessary … From what I've seen, I don't think it has very much to show you, whereas I don't think you can go wrong with LSD and magic mushrooms. They are much more important … LSD and magic mushrooms have a much more creative influence, not just on raves, but on life, on one's understanding of oneself and the world around."[20]

Harrison's shift in perspective from Ecstasy to LSD took place at the 1991 Longstock free festival. Harrison continues: "Up until that point I thought ley lines, solstices and all that mumbo-jumbo was just hot air, I had no belief in it. Suddenly all that changed." Spiral Tribe had rediscovered the native British spirituality, the impetus behind the free festival movement that LSD had once revealed to the earlier hippie travellers.[21]

Spiral Tribe went on the road, a techno version of Ken Kesey's Merry Pranksters, providing relentless hard core techno for raves in woods, quarries and empty buildings. Now dance and drug evangelists they turned people on to their wavelength using the Spiral method, defined as the "rewiring of neural circuits through the use of LSD-25, a reconditioning of consciousness as old notions dissolve in the acid surge".[22] LSD, now having an effect on the organisers of raves, also still exerted its influence over musicians. Bands such as Psychic TV and Coil had always hinted acid was their drug of choice and in 1991, Coil released their *Love's Secret Domain* CD. The initials of the CD were, perhaps, a clue. One of the singles from the CD, "Windowpane", was named after a powerful form of LSD that came on small gelatin squares.

The Criminal Justice and Public Order Act 1994, gave police a slew of new powers. The right to free speech was eroded and Section five of the Act brought in laws criminalizing previously civil offences including the ability of police to prevent gatherings that featured "repetitive beats". Clearly aimed at the Acid House rave, squat, road protest and other outdoor counter culture activities, free festivals became even scarcer and even more risky. This Act led to a series of primarily London based club nights springing up to cater for the vestiges of hippie culture. Megatripolis – the name speaks for itself – was begun in 1993 by psychedelic veteran Frasier Clark. Its festival-like ambience together with a series of guest speakers such as Allen Ginsberg, Terence McKenna, Howard Marks and Baba Ram Dass made it a popular venue for users of LSD and other psychedelics. Rave and dance music mixed with tribal drumming and light shows reminiscent of the Sixties. Although many just went for the dancing, others saw Megatripolis and others like it as part of a developing psychedelic movement.[23]

The cultural impact of Acid House spurred novelist Irvine Welsh to write a book of the same name, containing an eponymous story that played with ideas of how LSD can affect concepts of identity. Coco Bryce, the story's protagonist, perhaps unwisely, takes two doses of LSD alone at night in the middle of an electrical storm. Cosmic serendipity steps in; Bryce is struck by lightning as an ambulance containing a pregnant woman passes by and his consciousness switches places with her newborn baby.[24] That LSD was now beginning to appear in mainstream fiction in 1994 was testament to the depth to which it was embedded in British culture. And it was still massively popular, for instance in October 1995 over 41,000 LSD tablets were discovered by police under a street in Darwen, Lancashire.

Albert Hofmann, the discoverer of LSD, was now retired and an elderly man. At the 1996 Worlds of Consciousness Conference in Germany, he reflected on LSD and the steps in his life that led him to discover it. Age appeared to have mellowed his views about LSD and he now seemed to be espousing many ideas about LSD initially held by the counter culture.

Firstly he expounded the idea that LSD had not been synthesised by accident: "… considering the discovery of LSD in the context of other significant discoveries or our time in the medicinal and technical field, one might arrive at the notion that LSD did not come into the world accidentally, but was rather evoked in the scope of some higher plan." Hofmann contrasted the discovery, in the 1940s, of the tranquillisers, which covered up psychic problems whereas LSD revealed them. Were these the comments of a scientist whose mental faculties were deserting him or of someone who now had no professional reputation to maintain and who could say exactly what he wanted about the substance he had discovered? Hofmann also referred to the "coincidence" of the effects of LSD being discovered at the same time as the atomic bomb was under development, echoing a belief held by many in the early counter culture.[25]

The advent of blotter acid, with its brightly coloured, culturally relevant images, caused misunderstanding among the authorities. The prevalence on blotters of cartoon characters such as Mickey Mouse generated the unsubstantiated belief that blotter manufacturers were somehow targeting children. They weren't, but in the early Eighties, the authorities' ignorance led to an LSD urban legend sweeping America and eventually taking root in Britain.[26]

In a typical example, a public institution such as a school, hospital or police station would receive a photocopied flyer warning that LSD "tattoos" are being given to local children. The police referred to blotters as a tattoo because they resembled children's stick-on tattoos, the New Jersey police issuing the statement, "... children may be susceptible to this type of cartoon stamp believing it a tattoo transfer." The implication of these tales is that drug pushers are aggressively marketing these LSD laced tattoos to children in an attempt to get them hooked. The flyer often claims the LSD can be absorbed directly into a child's skin merely by touch alone and that many children have already died from the tattoos.

Of course, the information on the flyers was rubbish; pushers were not marketing LSD to children and nor could LSD be easily absorbed through the skin from a blotter. LSD is not addictive and there is not one report of a child dying as the result of LSD use. Yet despite this, and despite some police forces refuting the hoax, the "acid tattoo" urban legend spread, promulgated by those who failed to heed official information or chose not to for their own ends. The legend gathered momentum as recipients of the flyers photocopied and distributed them to their friends, creating viral marketing for a product that did not exist. The acid tattoo urban legend joined the ranks of other LSD scare stories such as the students who took LSD and stared at the sun until they went blind.

"Peril of the LSD Cartoon Stamps" screamed the headline to an article in a November 1985 edition of tabloid newspaper the *Daily Star*. The legend had come to Britain! Joe Clancy faithfully reported how "stamps laced with LSD are being sold to schoolchildren – and just one lick could kill". Clancy's inability to separate fact from fiction was matched only by that of police at New Scotland Yard who warned: "The stamps are potentially lethal. A youngster could throw himself under a bus or off a building after taking this drug."[27]

Just as it had in America, the urban legend took root in Britain and has circulated in one form or other ever since. In 1991 a major wave of the legend was seen with duplicated acid tattoo flyers being distributed in Merseyside, north Wales, Hampshire, Somerset and the West Midlands. One of the flyers was pinned to a notice-board at BICC Cables in Wrexham and claimed: "A young child could happen upon these tattoos and have a fatal trip." Wrexham drug squad officer John Atkinson told the local paper:

"These are just stupid chain letters that cause nothing but alarm." Other police officials weren't as enlightened and in September 1991 West Midlands police actually issued a letter of their own, warning parents and schools about the evil tattoos.[28]

The acid tattoo urban legend once again demonstrated how little real awareness the police had about LSD culture. The story had been quashed several times but kept re-appearing, uncritically spread by the media and believed purely because it had appeared in print. In the new millennium, the paper flyer has been superseded by a hoax email message, ensuring the legend's longevity as it mutates to keep up with changing forms of information distribution.

The acid tattoo scare was just one of a number of urban legends circulating in Britain. In 1997, Nestlé came up with an ingenious marketing strategy, selling the "holes" from the popular confectionary item Polo mints. The "holes" were small, round pieces of mint that vaguely resembled LSD microdots. Nestlé couldn't possibly have imagined what would happen next. The *Daily Express* ran an article entitled "Hole Lot of Hassle". "Teachers all over the country are alarmed by a new-look Polo mint. It's not the mint with the hole that is worrying to them but the 'hole from the mint' produced by Nestlé Rowntree. The classroom menace is a small, white pill-shaped sweet, each marked with a P, L, or O. Teachers are confiscating hundreds of them fearing they might be drugs. One was convinced that the L on one 'hole' was short for LSD. So the new sweet has been added to toxicology identity lists." Fortunately, this particular urban legend did not catch the public's imagination and disappeared as quickly as it had arisen.[29]

LSD had heavily influenced art and design from the Sixties onwards, producing the characteristic multicoloured paisley and swirl patterns that were used in fashion, advertising and publishing. Now, LSD itself had become a vibrant form of folk art and exhibitions of sheets of blotter art began to appear. Individual sheets, free of LSD, obtained from the blotter manufacturers or specially designed purely as art became very popular and auction sites such as eBay offer many examples for sale to the collector.

The images printed on blotter LSD can be of anything, but often reflect the present culture or some aspect of LSD's history. Albert

Hofmann, Walt Disney characters, film stars, music iconography, politicians and contemporary cultural images such as flying saucers, all have been used as LSD blotter images. "These are symbols of a secret society," claims Mark McCloud, an American who has made it his life's work to collect and chronicle the hundreds of designs produced. McCloud has been arrested, and his collection confiscated, several times by the Drug Enforcement Agency, but he only collects inert sheets of blotter, donated by LSD chemists and dealers.[30]

Blotter art collecting is now a rapidly growing market in the UK. One of the leading blotter art dealers is Paul Guest, who runs the BlotterArt.co.uk website. Sheets of blotter art signed by psychedelic luminaries such as Hofmann, Leary and psychedelic chemists Sasha and Ann Shulgin are highly collectable items. A sheet of blotter art signed by Albert Hofmann is currently valued in excess of £3000.[31]

As the millennium approached, people began to express serious doubts over the medical use of LSD in the Fifties and Sixties, when a group of former psychiatric patients announced they intended to seek compensation. Their action was driven by Wolverhampton MP, Ken Purchase who had taken an interest in claims that some of those who underwent LSD psychotherapy up to forty years earlier had subsequently suffered psychiatric problems as a result of their treatment.

"The more I looked into this, the more I was concerned about what happened to people," said Purchase, who had compiled a dossier containing over seventy cases. The MP approached Alexander Harris solicitors, who took the case on. Any claim would be made against the health authority responsible for the hospital where the therapy took place. The crux of any claim would be for the claimants' legal team to prove LSD was the cause of their problems and also that doctors were negligent in how they had administered the treatment.[32]

Media publicity brought over three hundred other complainants forward and headlines such as "Did LSD Kill My Father?" and "LSD Wrecked My Life" soon began to appear. Some of the stories related in the newspapers were a far cry from the positive impression given by the LSD psychotherapists of the Fifties and Sixties.

One of the claimants, Valerie Bateson of Radcliffe, in Lancashire recalled how she was given LSD for post natal depression in 1964. “It was like a bad dream. I drank it the first time and I just blacked out and I was paralysed. It took twenty-four hours before I got the feeling back into my body. I was so frightened. I used to take Holy Communion in the hospital chapel before a treatment as I really did not think I would live another day.”[33]

Bateson had six treatments of the drug, but claims after being discharged she developed monophobia, the fear of being alone, as well as panic attacks that prevented her taking medication or starting employment. Similar accounts came from patients who were treated at all the major LSD psychotherapy centres in the Fifties and Sixties, including Powick, the hospital in Worcestershire where LSD therapy began in 1953.

The investigation lasted until 29 February 2000 and Ronnie Sandison, who pioneered the psychotherapeutic use of LSD at Powick Hospital in Worcester, became involved in going through the files of many former patients. In 2006, reflecting on what he called a “sensitive” time for him, Sandison commented: “The really sad thing was revealed when I read the notes on some of the patients, from which it was evident that their doctors subsequent to their LSD treatment had all made every possible effort to help these unfortunate patients, condemned as most of them were, to a lifetime of mental disturbance, often cloaked as physical disorder.”[34]

It’s hard to know just how many of the claims represented genuine problems caused by LSD therapy and how many were either just extensions of the initial illness or problems developed independently of the treatment. Both sides were aware of this, Vizard Oldham of the solicitors acting for the NHS stating: “We are defending the action and are gathering expert evidence. The difficulty with the case is that these things are alleged to have happened thirty or forty years ago, and not all the NHS staff involved are still alive.”[35] Head of the NHS litigation authority, David Towns, was more bullish: “Investigations and expert evidence led the authority to believe that there were no legal liability and the claims were defended."[36]

The NHS knew it would be difficult for the claimants to conclusively prove LSD therapy had caused their alleged problems. But they also knew they had no defence when it came to less abstract matters including whether patients were told what drug they were taking and what its effects would be. In most cases this either didn't take place or the patient wasn't asked to sign a consent form.

After five years of legal and medical argument, by November 2000, only forty-six claims were still outstanding. Despite their earlier stance the NHS decided to make an out of court settlement of £195,000 to the remaining claimants. David Towns still believed the litigation authority at the NHS could have won the legal argument but said the NHS had decided on a settlement to save the taxpayer a protracted and expensive court battle.

The legal conclusion to the experimental LSD psychotherapy of the Fifties and Sixties cast a long shadow over the achievements and breakthroughs made by people like Ronnie Sandison; their sincere attempts to free people from mental imprisonment thrown back in their faces. Thus, the new century began with LSD again at the centre of a media furore. Sixty-seven years after Albert Hofmann's serendipitous discovery his "problem child", as he referred to the drug, was still causing difficulties, still an answer in search of a question.

13
REVOLUTION IN THE HEAD

> It is my wish that a modern Eleusis will emerge, in which seeking humans can learn to have transcendent experiences with sacred substances in a safe setting.
>
> Albert Hofmann[1]

In the years that have passed since Swiss chemist Albert Hofmann first synthesised LSD in November 1938, the drug has passed through a number of distinct phases in Britain. The medical and military establishments' use of LSD was initially sanctioned by the government, with high hopes that this new chemical would be the key to unlocking the secrets of the subconscious. But support for investigating LSD's potential quickly halted once the young people started to use the drug and it became one of the driving forces responsible for the cultural changes of the Sixties. As a result, LSD was made illegal in October 1966.

No robust medical or legal argument was offered as to why LSD should be illegal. The government's decision was not based on controlled medical tests, or evidence from the military or medical experiments with the drug. It appeared that legislators were swayed more by the opinion and influence of the British media, as well as the lurid horror stories about LSD emanating from America, as the scientific facts. Hansard, the official journal of parliamentary record, shows the legislative process was conducted in an atmosphere of flippancy, with parliamentarians displaying ignorance and disinterest in a drug they apparently knew nothing about.

At the time LSD was outlawed, only a few thousand members of the public in Britain, at most, had used the drug. At a conservative estimate, at least a million British citizens have tried LSD in the fifty-nine years since the first record of its recreational use. Bad practice at Porton Down and the failure of psychotherapists to inform patients about the drug they were taking aside, few seem to have been forced or coerced into using the drug. Indeed, the evidence suggests the reverse is true; people have gone out of their way to obtain, use and to pass on a drug that they believed has consciousness enhancing properties.

Of those who have taken LSD, a small percentage developed mental health problems. Opinion is divided whether these individuals had a pre-existing or latent illness, which LSD exacerbated, and whether or not the problem would have emerged had they never taken LSD. This has proved an impossible question to answer, but the negative personal effects of LSD cannot be overlooked, as it is this aspect of the psychedelic experience employed most often in media or political debate. But the numbers of those affected are small, and must be balanced against the multitudes of people who suffer serious physical and mental problems from the use of legally sanctioned drugs such as alcohol and tobacco.

Of those who have taken LSD, some have tried it once and found the experience to be so awe-inspiring they did not feel the need to repeat it, but are glad they tried it. This is often the origin of the maxim "everyone should take LSD once in their life". Others found it to be a drug worth taking repeatedly, if only for the dazzling trip into the synaesthesic wonderland it provided. For them it was a drug to be used to have the most intense mental and physical fun imaginable.

At the other end of the spectrum, some LSD users have had the course of their lives permanently changed for the better by LSD. These changes are as varied as are the individuals themselves but the insights offered by LSD have stimulated tens of thousands of people into a radical change in lifestyle, broadly involving some form of religious or spiritual practice. In and among these extremes, the majority of those who have taken LSD have found the drug to be a mixture of these primary reactions. For these, the psychedelic foot soldiers, LSD proved to be a signpost to a novel way of perceiving the world, a new way of living and, as they incorporated the drug into their lives, an entrée into the social grouping we broadly refer to as the counter culture. And it is the counter culture's use of LSD which has been the main focus of this book.

The counter culture's overarching conclusion about LSD, drawn from published sources and interviews, is that it is a powerful, mind-expanding drug. Acid is viewed within the counter culture as a sacred substance whose careful use will result in a permanent change in the consciousness of the user. Few who have used LSD believe its use should be restricted by law and most believe that it should be the choice of each individual whether or not they wish to use the drug.

At the start of the twenty-first century, public interest in LSD was at an all time low. Free festival culture had been all but legislated out of existence and Ecstasy and its analogues were the drug of choice among young people. LSD was scarce and what there was tended to be of low quality. Young people, it seemed, no longer wanted a drug that required a degree of discipline to reap its optimum effects, and dance culture tended to favour LSD of a weaker dosage, enough to provide the motivating power for endless dancing but not enough for the user to experience the full psychedelic effect.

This downturn in LSD's fortunes was echoed in Home Office statistics, which revealed that in 2000, the proportion of people committing crimes involving LSD was less than one quarter of one per cent of total drug offences. Seizures of the drug had plummeted too, from 1859 (representing 143,000 doses) in 1990, to 292 (representing 25,000 doses) in 2000. The Home Office commented: "The popularity of LSD appears to have been waning in recent years …"[2]

LSD was further made unpopular in the public eye by the very public results of legal action taken by former NHS patients and former military personnel. Almost abandoned by the counter culture and vilified by the legal and medical professions, in the early years of the new millennium LSD appeared to be yesterday's drug, a once powerful agent for personal change whose time had passed, a relic of headier, more liberal days.

But there was still an enormous groundswell of interest in and demand for LSD. That the counter culture had moved on to other drugs was only partly because of the Acid House and Ecstasy movements. The fact was, if good quality LSD was not available then it could not be taken. The combination of time, money and scientific knowledge required to manufacture LSD was available only to a very small number of people. Add to that the high risk of arrest and imprisonment and it is easy to see why usage of LSD was at an all time low. LSD manufacture relies on highly motivated individuals or small groups. Its production tends to go in cycles, when major laboratories are put out of business a period of time elapses before another evangelical chemist steps forward to fill the gap.

Signs of a new cycle in illicit British LSD manufacture and use became evident in February 2004 when police arrested Casey Hardison at Ovingdean, near Brighton. Acting on a tip off from American customs officials, who had found Ecstasy in a parcel, Hardison, an American citizen, was placed under surveillance for several months prior to his arrest. When enough evidence was gathered to suggest he was involved in making drugs the police raided his rented house, discovering the most complex illicit drug laboratory since Kemp's in 1977. They also found 146,000 doses of blotter based LSD as well as quantities of the psychedelic drugs DMT and 2CB. The police were so concerned about the amount of chemicals in the lab they sealed the street off and a large team of specialists clad in protective clothing was sent in to gather evidence and dismantle the laboratory. Hardison was escorted from the premises wearing a hooded boiler suit, as the police believed there might be a serious risk of contamination from his clothes and body.[3]

During his ten-week trial at Lewes Crown Court, Hardison revealed he had made £125,000 from his illegal activities. But money, he said, useful though it was to fund his activities, was not the motivating factor for making psychedelic drugs. His defence was, like the Operation Julie chemists, he was driven to make LSD for ideological reasons. Although caught red-handed, Hardison refused to plead guilty and told the judges that being arrested and imprisoned for making LSD denied him autonomy over his body. He argued that the manufacture and use of psychedelic drugs was a victimless crime and he appealed to the jury to find him innocent.

Prosecutor Richard Barton told the jury Hardison had come to Britain "... in order to set up and run illegal laboratories manufacturing Class A drugs, and to put his beliefs about these drugs being readily available and widely distributed into effect in this country." This was countered by Hardison's defence who claimed: "His actions were not motivated by greed. He didn't do it to buy a villa in Spain but in order to acquire further experience to continue to push forward the frontiers of knowledge."[4]

In his summing up, Judge Niblett refuted Hardison's claims that he had little interest in making a profit, saying, "You realised the potential profit was huge, running possibly to millions of pounds. I am quite satisfied that was your goal." In LSD manufacturing trials, the judiciary has always stressed to the jury and the media the potential profits. In most cases, they have been far off the mark of the real amounts involved, using multiples of street prices to extrapolate what an LSD chemist could, in theory receive for his troubles.[5]

It is self evident that profit can be made from making and selling any form of drug. Yet even when it is obvious, as with Richard Kemp in the Seventies and now Hardison, that the drug is being made primarily for ideological reasons the judiciary refute this explanation. Prior to his arrest in Britain, Hardison was known in America as a psychedelic pioneer, having published several articles attesting to his search for knowledge through psychedelics. However, the judiciary effectively represents the views of the Establishment and not the counter culture. If judges were to accept ideology as the reason for the use of psychedelic drugs it would feed the wrong message to the public. Consequently, their reasoning goes, the only reason anyone can have for manufacturing LSD is to make a profit, the inference being that those who take LSD are in some way manipulated by the manufacturers and distributors. As the previous chapters have demonstrated, nothing could be further from the truth. Those who take LSD do so because they have chosen of their own free will.

Hardison was sentenced to twenty years imprisonment in December 2004. As he was led from the dock, he shouted: "You would think I was a terrorist." His appeal in 2006 failed, the judges once again dwelling on the financial potential. Mr. Justice Keith told the court: "This was not an amateurish operation in a garden shed. It was a sophisticated and calculated attempt to introduce synthetic drugs in the UK market, which could have reaped great financial rewards." Adding that he though Hardison deserved every day of his sentence.[6]

The sentence Hardison received exemplifies the inconsistencies in court disposals for LSD manufacturing in Britain. In 1978, during a decade when LSD use was at its zenith, responsible for the development of a visible counter culture, Richard Kemp was sentenced to thirteen years. That was a long enough sentence, yet twenty-six years later, with LSD use at its lowest, Hardison was imprisoned for twenty years and is due to be released in 2014, after which he will be deported to the U.S. despite having married a UK citizen. In both cases, the defence was ideology and it is tempting to suggest the heavy sentences were handed down as much to punish the temerity displayed as for the crimes committed. Murderers, paedophiles and armed robbers are rarely given sentences of twenty years and inconsistent sentencing that can be interpreted as an attack on personal freedom and lifestyles diminishes respect for the law as a whole.

Two years into his sentence, Hardison wrote from prison affirming his beliefs, "I am an ideologue who wanted to embrace and experience Albert's problem child!" He went on to explain how his libertarian values were forged by his upbringing "… in a barn, a boat and a school bus at various times and places, raised by a family who had homesteaded in the Depression in the mountains of Montana and Idaho. Told by them that I could do anything I damn well please provided I put my mind to it and harmed no one in the process."[7]

Kemp's musings in *Microdoctrine* notwithstanding, it's rare we have the opportunity to hear from an LSD chemist on why they devote their lives to creating the potent psychedelic. In Casey Hardison's case it had its origins in personal and family experiences with the addictive qualities of alcohol and drugs, which he transcended through AA's Twelve Step programme. An early experiencee with LSD showed him:

"... a rare glimpse of the power of the human mind to shape reality. I saw that my limited neurotypical consciousness was only one plane, level or aspect and that there were infinite new things to discover. I found new perspectives on birth, death, and the nature of mind and consciousness as the field of creation. The experience of the oneness of all things replaced the myth of separation. Perennial wisdom dawned and my heart burst forth in praise, gratitude and love, rooted in a mindset of compassion for self and other."

Personal experience with LSD, and how the psychedelic community was treated by the government and its agencies also led Hardison to seriously question the 'War on Drugs' as it relates to psychedelics. He concluded that the 'War on Drugs' was fundamentally concerned with those in positions of authority (the 'Establishment') being hell-bent on maintaining control of psychedelic substances to prevent people changing their consciousness:

"... the so-called 'war on drugs' is not a war on pills, powder, plants, and potions, it is war on mental states — a war on consciousness itself — how much, what sort we are permitted to experience, and who gets to control it. More than an unintentional misnomer, the government-termed 'war on drugs' is a strategic decoy label; a slight-of-hand move by government to redirect attention away from what lies at ground zero of the war — each individual's fundamental right to control his or her own consciousness."

These thoughts are hardly of someone who manufactures LSD purely for profit and greed as the trial judge suggested. Hardison made an Ideological commitment to himself to synthesise LSD and eventually, after trial and error with other psychedelics, he did just that. Further clarifying why he took the path he did, Hardison was brutally honest:

"There is no single pat answer. The simplest: my love of learning. The veiled: for my ego, for the attention, to feel special, to be loved. The flippant: because I could. Semi-consciously: civil disobendience, academic and religious freedom in the study of the mind, and an expression of equal rights. The most accurate: my desire to share entheogenesis with others, to wake humanity up from the penumbral dream-world of materialist delusion, to help end the blatant injustice and rape of human dignity that occurs with the context of a 'War on (some) drugs', to seize the world stage and help to create a forum for the cooperative and conscious stewardship of Mother Earth and all her relations."[8]

Kemp and Hardison's involvement in manufacturing, distributing and taking LSD for ideological reasons may be seen as an act of civil disobedience; the conscious breaking of a law because it is believed to be unworkable or immoral. Their actions were conscious and in full knowledge of the way the law treats those who create substances that alter consciousness. An "us and them" situation between LSD users and the authorities has always existed, two sides each with radically different beliefs and aspirations.

This "us and them" situation has led politicians, the media and the judiciary to frame the attacks on LSD and other psychedelics as part of an ongoing "war on drugs". "War on Drugs" looks meaningful when delivered in oration from the lectern of a party political conference, or screaming from a newspaper headline. It is, however, a meaningless phrase, a political catch-phrase used to manipulate opinion against a nebulous enemy, doublespeak to disguise the fact that what lies behind a war on drugs is actually a war on the people involved with them.

The history of LSD in Britain shows this to be not just a war on the personal freedoms of individuals who wish to alter their consciousness, but also a war on the lifestyles connected with particular drugs, such as LSD. This has been shown by the draconian treatment meted out to hippie travellers and the Acid House party scene to give but two relevant examples. At a time when politicians are stressing anti-discrimination, diversity and equality of opportunity, large sections of society are being discriminated against solely because of their choice of drug and the lives they choose to lead based on that choice.

LSD is illegal; manufacture and distribution is a crime. But a crime against whom? In many ways, LSD is a victimless offence. Unlike drugs like heroin, cocaine, amphetamines and alcohol, LSD is not linked to acquisitive crimes, so there is no direct cost to society from shoplifting or theft. It is not a physically addictive drug, and any mental compulsion to take LSD repeatedly is soon rendered pointless due to the body's tolerance to the drug. Drug prevention and treatment services see few people who have had a problem with LSD and its use does not clog up substance misuse services. The more LSD is examined dispassionately, uncoupled from its political baggage and the media circus, the fewer reasons there are for its illegal status.

This view is shared by consultant psychiatrist Ben Sessa, at least for the use of LSD in a medical context. When he took an interest in the medical uses of LSD, Sessa reviewed the papers published by Ronnie Sandison who ran the LSD psychotherapy unit at Powick Hospital in the Fifties and Sixties. Sessa concluded that LSD did have relevance for use in therapy. He also discovered that a degree of revisionism had taken place within the medical establishment. "Scientists, psychiatrists and psychologists were forced to give up their studies for socio-political reasons," he remarked in January 2006. For instance when he was a medical student the textbooks claimed there was no medical use for the drug. "It was as if a whole generation of psychiatrists have had this systematically erased from their education. But for the generation who trained in the 50s and 60s, this really was going to be the next big thing. Thousands of books and papers were written, but then it all went silent. My generation has never heard of it. It's almost as if there has been an active demonization."[9]

The government, Sessa contends, has not banned the use of morphine in hospitals because its derivative, heroin, is used and trafficked by criminals. This is a compelling argument, illustrating that the medical ban on LSD stems more from the fact that the potential for using it in psychotherapy has not yet been fully explored. Richard Horton, editor of the medical journal *Lancet*, added weight to Sessa's case in April 2006, saying "the demonization of psychedelic drugs as a social evil" had helped suppress useful medical research that would lead to a better understanding of how the brain functions as well as treatments for a wide variety of mental conditions such as depression.[10]

Sessa and Horton's attempts to persuade the medical establishment to look again at LSD's potential paled when compared to the findings of a two-year study commissioned by the Royal Society of Arts. The results, published in March 2007, called for the legal status of *all* drugs to be reclassified in line with their potential for actual harm. The study found that the current drug classification, introduced under the Misuse of Drugs Act 1971, was irrational, arbitrary and lacking in consistency. One of the authors, Professor Colin Blakemore, said the object had been "... to bring a dispassionate approach to a very passionate issue ... Some conclusions might appear to be liberal in stance, but that was not our starting position. We intend to reach conclusions that were evidence based."[11]

Twenty drugs were selected for the study, including tobacco and alcohol. They were each ranked on a combination of factors including their potential for physical harm, their tendency to cause dependence and their social impact on families, communities and society. Two separate groups of experts worked on giving an overall harm score to each drug. The results were that heroin was top with a score of 2.8, while LSD came fourteenth with a score of 1.3, well below the currently legal alcohol and tobacco. Blakemore noted: "We hope that policy makers will take note of the fact that the resulting ranking of drugs differs substantially from their classification in the Misuse of Drugs Act and that alcohol and tobacco are judged more harmful than many illegal substances."[12]

The study's conclusions were taken a step further in October 2007 when Richard Brunstrom, one of Britain's most senior police officers called for all drugs to be legalised. Brunstrom, then Chief

Constable of North Wales, issued a fully referenced paper detailing why drug prohibition had not been and will not ever be effective. Brunstrom concurred that the present system of classifying drugs as outlined in the Misuse of Drugs Act was unfit for purpose and should be radically overhauled. Prohibition, he claimed, was harmful in itself, causing five key harms; increasing crime, causing a crisis in an already overloaded criminal justice system, economic harm, undermining public health, the destabilization of countries producing drugs and the undermining of civil rights.

Commenting on the hierarchy of harm from earlier in the year, Brunstrom noted that tobacco and alcohol were both ranked higher than many currently illegal substances. He commented, "No one is seriously proposing that alcohol and tobacco become banned substances; for these very harmful drugs our society has already settled upon a regime of control and regulation, rather than proscription, albeit with rather mixed results to date. The big question is therefore this: if that is our preferred option for these drugs then why do we treat other, demonstrably less harmful, substances so differently?"[13]

The Chief Police Officer's conclusions were stark and controversial. His first point summed up what he saw as the problems inherent in drug prohibition. "Current UK drugs policy is based upon an unwinable 'war on drugs' enshrined in a flawed understanding of the underlying UN conventions and arising from a wholly outdated and thoroughly moralistic stance based on rhetoric and dogma rather than a rational (and more ethical) philosophy." Brunstrom's solution is for the Misuse of Drugs Act to be scrapped, and all drugs to be legalised, with the proviso that the "careful regulation of substances of abuse" is undertaken via a new "Substance Misuse Act".[14]

Just what would comprise such an Act, Brunstrom does not expand on, and any such Act would take years of political finessing before it came to fruition. For the legalization and appropriate regulation of drugs to take place society would firstly have to stop being in denial about the reality of drugs and the redundancy of prohibition. A comprehensive programme of drug education would need to be in place and a system would be needed by which good quality, reasonably priced, substances could be made available. This would be a complicated process but there are existing models to build on such as the way the Dutch cannabis cafés are licensed.

Whatever one thinks about the conclusions drawn by the Medical Research Council and Richard Brunstrom, they are based on scientific medical fact and long years of police experience. If fact and experience are to be ignored over ignorance and prejudice then society will continue to reap the dubious rewards of a disenfranchised youth who know from their own experience that, if used carefully, most drugs are not particularly dangerous.

Any discussion about the right to use LSD, or any other drug, hinges on the relationship between government and the individual. A government's function should not be to limit personal freedoms, but to encourage its citizens to live as free a life as possible. It is necessary for the government to legislate and protect against individuals causing any form of harm or harassment to others but interference in the lives of its citizens should not extend to deciding which drugs they are at liberty to take. In matters concerning drugs, the law should only be involved if someone's *behaviour* causes problems. This is the situation alcohol enjoys now. Anyone is free to become intoxicated and provided their behaviour is acceptable, they are free to enjoy themselves with their chosen drug. Why should this not be the case with all drugs?

If all drugs, not just LSD, were treated in this way, rapid and dramatic changes would take place in society. In 2007, it was estimated that fifty per cent of all crime in Britain was committed to acquire money or goods that could be exchanged for drugs such as heroin and crack cocaine. Legalizing all drugs would drastically cut this figure. If drugs were available through legitimate outlets there would be no issues of contamination or fluctuating strength, thus immediately reducing health problems and risk of overdose. The often-dangerous criminals behind the drug trade would swiftly move to other areas of illegality, and each year thousands of people would be spared the indignity of being criminalised purely because of their choice of intoxicant.

Last, but not least, the government would be able to levy taxes on all presently illegal substances, as it does now on tobacco and alcohol.

In 2005, the British government's projected spend on drug treatment and prohibition services was approximately £1,483,000,000. The real figure is actually much higher as it does not include, for example, the wider expenditure involved in processing drug cases through the criminal justice system. Should so much be spent, year after year, when prohibition demonstrably does not work? If drugs were legalised, and the government remained concerned about levels of drug use, some of the vast sums of money set aside each year for prohibition and treatment would be far more effectively spent on drug education.[15]

In one twelve-month period, Sessa, Horton and Brunstrom opened a serious debate, not just about the future of LSD, but the future of all intoxicants in society. Whether or not any political party has the will to take up the challenge presented and revolutionise the public's perception and society's treatment of drugs and drug users remains to be seen.

In October 2007, the *Daily Telegraph*, a daily newspaper on the right of the political spectrum, published the results of a poll to find the world's top 100 living geniuses. The poll was jointly topped by Albert Hofmann (discoverer of LSD) who shared the honours with Sir Tim Berners-Lee (inventor of the World Wide Web). Nigel Clarke, speaking for poll administrators Synectics UK & Europe, said: "I think that Albert Hofmann and Tim Berners-Lee have this in common with the great geniuses of the past. Both of them have, in their own way, turned the world that we live in upside down."[16]

Despite this fresh interest in LSD by psychotherapists, despite a high-ranking policeman's views and and despite the respect given to Hofmann, the legal position in Britain looks less likely than ever to change. In 2009 a significant event took place which left anyone with sympathies toward LSD in no doubt that those who hold political power have no intention of ever making psychedelic drugs legally available. Moreover, the event made clear the governmental thought processes which underlie the restriction of all personal freedoms around drug use.

In late October 2009, Professor David Nutt, the government's chief drug advisor, published a research paper which ranked drugs in order of their harm to individual and society. In many ways this was similar to the 2007 study mentioned previously but Nutt went a step further, criticising politicians for "distorting" and "devaluing" the research evidence in the debate over illicit drugs. Nutt also produced evidence that Ecstasy and LSD were less dangerous than alcohol and tobacco. "Alcohol ranks as the fifth most harmful drug after heroin, cocaine, barbiturates and methadone. Tobacco is ranked ninth… Cannabis, LSD and ecstasy, while harmful, are ranked lower at 11, 14 and 18 respectively."[17]

Nutt's claims prompted swift and draconian reaction. Despite his assertions being based on sound research, the idea that substances such as LSD could be less harmful than legal, taxable drugs such as alcohol and tobacco was abhorrent to the government. Home Secretary Alan Johnson immediately wrote to Professor Nutt, asking for his resignation as chair of the ACMD (Advisory Council on the Misuse of Drugs). Nutt resigned but refused to be silenced and was outspoken in his criticism of the government's attitude, "Politics is politics and science is science and there's a bit of a tension between them sometimes."[18]

The director of the Centre for Crime and Justice also came out in support of Professor Nutt, pointing out that Nutt's paper showed what a realistic drugs policy could look like if it was actually based on scientific research rather than "political or moral positioning". Garside said: "I'm shocked and dismayed that the home secretary appears to believe that political calculation trumps honest and informed scientific opinion. The message is that when it comes to the Home Office's relationship with the research community honest researchers should be seen but not heard. The home secretary's action is a bad day for science and a bad day for the cause of evidence-informed policy making."[19]

Both the results of the 2007 study and Nutt's 2009 research proved scientifically that LSD and psychedelic drugs were less harmful to the individual and to society than many commonly accepted legal ones. This evidence was ignored. That a government – any government – will ignore scientific evidence to suit their own political ends, should give any thinking member of the electorate cause for concern. In the case of drugs it means an elected body can, based purely on the beliefs and prejudices of that political party, suppress and legislate against the individual's right and freedom to change their consciousness at will by the agent of their choice. Applied to other areas of society, the consequences of ignoring evidence-based research could easily lead to the development of an authoritarian government where the restriction of individual freedoms becomes the norm. If a government can control personal freedoms to the extent that they have power over what substances an individual can or cannot take, then we are but a step away from every aspect of our lives being controlled. The freedom to change consciousness must be paramount in any genuinely free society. Framing these controls as a 'war on drugs', as has been the case, is nonsense. This is nothing less than a war against people and lifestyles and against certain states of consciousness.

Alan Johnson's attitude also demonstrates extreme and callous social cynicism. If any government really wanted to prevent harm from drugs in any meaningful way they would immediately outlaw alcohol and tobacco, substances which each year kill, maim and destroy thousands of human bodies and lives, families and communities. Yet because these drugs are the drug of choice by those in government, and the bulk of society, and because they yield millions in tax, they are deemed acceptable. The corporations who manufacture them are allowed to advertise their product as being life-enhancing and, in the case of alcohol in particular, heavy and binge drinking is encouraged among young people in the clubs, pubs and bars of every high street in Britain. What is wrong with a society which glorifies, encourages and profits from drugs which enslave people, yet chooses to persecute drugs such as LSD which members of the psychotherapeutic profession and a subculture of millions believe are agents of personal and social transformation?

The government's uncompromising anti-psychedelic drug message was further hammered home in their 2010 Drug Strategy consultation paper. Home Secretary Theresa May wrote, "This government does not believe that liberalisation and legalisation are the answer". In other words, scientific evidence and the rights of the individual are subservient to political belief. In the strategy all drugs were treated as being of equal harm and even so-called 'legal highs' were singled out for future legislation. The subtext of this Orwellian document was that any currently illegal drug which changed consciousness would, whatever the evidence to the contrary, remain illegal and drug users would be persecuted by the legal system for wishing to experiment with causing changes to their consciousness.[20]

Yet although there is a political and legal crackdown on LSD and other psychedelics, freedom of thought and expression is still an option. An authentic and vocal grass roots psychedelic movement has emerged over the past few years in Britain and is gathering strength and influence. In April 2011 at the University of Kent, a three day event called Breaking Convention took place. Subtitled "A Multi Disclipinary Conference Exploring Psychedelic Consciousness", the event attracted over six hundred delegates from Britain and elsewhere to listen to lectures from more than sixty leading figures in the field of psychedelic research. Many of the speakers were scientists, academics and authors. Most had experienced the transformative power of LSD or other psychedelics. All were passionate in their belief that psychedelic drugs need to be brought back into society where they can be used for a variety of personal and psychotherapeutic reasons without fear of legal or social recrimination.

Some academics are now being given space to discuss psychedelics in the serious media. One such is Dr Sue Blackmore. Her views on psychedelics are clear and based not only on her personal experience but on her scientific research into consciousness. Her article for the *Sunday Telegraph*, "I Take Illegal Drugs For Inspiration", made it clear that she believed LSD and other psychedelics were useful tools for examining consciousness, "drugs, such as LSD, psilocybin, DMT or mescaline, that undermine everything you take for granted. These are psychedelics that threaten our ordinary sense of self, and that is where they touch most deeply on my scientific interests." Those in political power who seek to keep psychedelics illegal may seize on statements such as this and ask just why anyone would want to question their ordinary sense of self. Yet this question of who we are and what we exist for is one of the central questions of religion and philosophy. Governments, as we have seen in the crackdown on Britain's psychedelic culture, and outspoken LSD chemists such as Richard Kemp, simply do not want people asking what are essentially spiritual questions, questions to which the answer may require living and thinking in ways which fundamentally undermine western modes of consumerist thinking.[21]

More recently Blackmore poses the question, "Is LSD a great spiritual teacher? Or indeed a teacher at all?" In an article for *The Guardian* she concluded that it was the "ultimate psychedelic", although not one to be taken lightly, "This drug, above all, confronts you with yourself. The flickering flowers can turn into scenes of horror and desperation, the coloured-streaked sky into a theatre of unwelcome memories and shame... You have to face it. And this is, I think, what makes it the ultimate psychedelic. There is no hiding with LSD. You have to face whatever comes up or be overwhelmed by it." Some may dismiss this as do it yourself psychotherapy, but for Sue and thousands of other LSD users the results are worth any risks involved.[22]

In view of the sacking of Professor Nutt and Theresa May's drug strategy, there appears to be no room for manouvre or compromise between the beliefs of the political administration and those who believe LSD is a valuable tool for exploring consciousness. This impasse suggests that people will choose the route of civil disobedience and follow in the footsteps of Richard Kemp, Andy Munro and Casey Hardison, manufacturing and using psychedelic drugs without regard for laws which they feel restrict their individual liberty.

Irrespective of any medical or legal argument, LSD is now firmly embedded in the social and cultural fabric of Britain. Every adult has at least a vague idea of what LSD is, most either know someone who has used the drug or have experimented with it themselves. The phrase "on acid" is frequently used as cultural shorthand, to denote an experience that is surreal, weird, or highly unusual. For example, in a December 2007 edition of the *Observer* magazine, columnist Kate Muir wrote of her visit to the film premiere of *The Golden Compass* "... and to the after-party which was surreal, 'like an ice-dancing royal wedding on acid', I heard someone say". Advertising and fashion make free with the patterns, shapes and colour combinations originating from the LSD vision and musicians are currently enjoying a revival of psychedelic based sounds. It is clear that the psychedelic experience, real and imagined, still pervades Albion's dream.[23]

LSD is a highly contentious tool for consciousness change and is here to stay. It cannot be uninvented or legislated out of existence. It is human nature to take intoxicants of one form or another and LSD is just one of many psychedelic substances humans have sought out and used for millennia. In most cultures, these substances have been understood and accepted as consciousness expanding tools, to be used carefully at certain times and with the appropriate set and setting. It is western civilization's insistence on repressing the human need for transcendence that has led to the problems society perceives it faces from drug use and specifically the problems some LSD users have experienced.

At the start of this book, reference was made to the possibility that at various times the history of LSD has been infiltrated with conspiracies. However, despite the extent of his research, the author has found nothing to indicate that any organised conspiracy has taken place. But the question needs to be asked: why has the British government spent so much time, money and effort persecuting LSD manufacturers, suppliers and users, as well as disrupting the counter culture the drug helped create? The author's view is that if there is a conspiracy, it is an unspoken one, enacted by the British Establishment; that matrix of political, legal, economic, religious, and social forces committed to maintaining the status quo. It is a conspiracy of whispers, borne out of the misunderstanding, ignorance, prejudice and fear that LSD has engendered in society.

Political and media scaremongers have persistently highlighted the mental health problems that LSD can cause, citing this as the reason for the drug's vilification. The real "dangers" of LSD however are not to the individual, but to the status quo itself. This book has shown that the insights people have gleaned from LSD, peyote, mescaline and similar psychedelic drugs all seem to be antithetical to the materialistic, consumer driven lifestyle currently led by the majority of the civilised world.

Reports from the majority of those who have used the drug suggest that LSD shatters their worldview causing them to look deep within themselves, to reflect on and challenge their lifestyles, values and relationship with the environment. At its most potent, LSD gives the user no option but to examine and challenge all accepted notions of perception, thought, identity, culture and the nature of reality. The danger, to the Establishment, must be that if enough people used LSD, there might, as chemist Richard Kemp hoped, be a revolution that could threaten how life in Britain is lived.

Of course, Kemp's much vaunted LSD revolution was not realised. At least not in the way he envisaged. But an ongoing, subtle, psychedelic revolution did take place. It took place in the mind of everyone who ever took LSD, and its effects have been far reaching.

This revolution in the head initially bore fruit in upheavals in the relatively ephemeral, but highly visible, areas of music, fashion and art. At the next level, it stimulated interest in ecological and environmental matters, causing people to reevaluate how they lived, what they ate, what their actions were doing to the planet. Because of LSD's effect on perceptions of identity and society, people were inspired to try new ways of living outside the nuclear family structure, in communes, communities, squats and mixed relationships. The drug triggered interest in alternative therapies such as yoga and homeopathy, all virtually unknown in Britain prior to the Sixties. On the deepest level, LSD gave spiritual, religious and numinous experiences, imbuing the user with feelings of love and a oneness with humanity and the universe. It is an enduring irony that LSD, pursued so eagerly by the British and American military for martial purposes, became the major catalyst for the love and peace generation. All these ideas and experiences have caused manifestly real changes in individuals and society, and they continue to do so.

In April 2007, as if to echo the insights millions of people have drawn from their LSD experiences, Albert Hofmann wrote his clearest statement to date of his beliefs about LSD: "Alienation from nature and the loss of the experience of being part of the living creation is the greatest tragedy of our materialistic era. It is the causative reason for ecological devastation and climate change. Therefore I attribute absolute highest importance to consciousness change. I regard psychedelics as catalyzers for this. They are tools which are guiding our perception toward other deeper areas of our human existence, so that we again become aware of our spiritual essence.

"Psychedelic experiences in a safe setting can help our consciousness open up to this sensation of connection and of being one with nature. LSD and related substances are not drugs in the usual sense, but are part of the sacred substances, which have been used for thousand of years in ritual settings."[17]

On Tuesday, 29 April 2008, Albert Hofmann died aged 102. His death generated worldwide media coverage, with the British broadsheets devoting several pages to obituaries and features dealing with LSD and its effect on society and culture. People from all walks of life came forward to give the media soundbites about how LSD had influenced their lives and, rather than being vilified as the creator of a drug which destroyed minds, Hofmann was, by and large, lauded as the catalyst behind a minor cultural revolution, the echoes of which are still reverberating through the lives of everyone who came into contact with his "problem child".

Albion Dreaming has shown that Britain has been a crucible for LSD culture, every bit as socially relevant as the American experience of the drug. It is hoped that this book will stimulate further research into just how influential the British LSD experience has been on the development of psychedelic culture worldwide. Whether you believe LSD is an escape from reality or a trip to the heart of it, the hidden history of the most potent and undefinable drug known to humankind is only just being unearthed. LSD is a valuable tool for consciousness change, the understanding of which is still in its infancy.

Millions of psychedelic voyagers have tried to articulate the purpose of their LSD experiences, but few have been effective in doing so. Perhaps the best verbalization, and the final word in this book, comes from philosopher Aldous Huxley in a letter to LSD's discoverer, Albert Hofmann. Although specifically about LSD, Huxley's comments could refer to the purpose of any transcendent human experience, whether accessed through natural or chemical means:

> Essentially this is what must be developed: the art of giving out in love and intelligence what is taken from vision and the experience of self-transcendence and solidarity with the universe.[24]

THANKS!

A few key people are responsible for this book's existence. I would like to thank Martin Liu and Chris Newson of Marshall Cavendish for taking it on and to Pom Somkabcharti for bringing it to fruition. My editor, Sarah Abel tightened, tweaked and queried the text until it was in a fit state for your eyes. Thanks too to Adrian Whittaker and Deena Omar for their encouragement and constant attention to detail. And of course to my wife, Gaynor Roberts who endured the highs and lows of the research and writing process.

The following people gave freely of their time, experiences and insights, providing the background hum of authenticity necessary for a book such as this. If I have omitted anyone, please accept my apologies.

Steve Abrams, Nigel Ayers, Brian Barritt, Bear, Joseph Berke, Sue Blackmore, William Bloom, Walter Brock, David Brunskill, Chris Case, Bob Campbell, David Clarke, Maureen Clyne, Dave Cunliffe, Neil Cuttriss, Ray Daniel, Age Delbanco, Paul Devereux, Jeff Dexter, Jeremy Dunn, Dice George, Lyn Ebenezer, Chris Faiers, Max Freakout, Robert Forte, Christopher Gibbs, Eric Gow, Great White Shark, Paul Guest, Adrian Haggard, Michael Haggiag, Casey Hardison, Amira Harris, Lee Harris, Dave Henniker, Charles Herwin, Vanessa Hollingshead, Paul Hollister, Stewart Home, Luke Hopkins, Hoppy, Philip Hogg, Jean Houston, Roger Hutchinson, Ronald Hutton, Alan Ibbotson, Mike Jay, Andrew Kerr, Stephen Kirkpatrick, David Larcher, Martin Lee, Nigel Lesmoir-Gordon, Adrian Laing, Julie-Anne Lowe, Oliver Mandrake, Tom Maschler, John May, Toni Melechi, Pete Mellor, Penny Mellor, Patricia McCann, Mark McCloud, John Michell, Vin Miles, Monkey, Andy Munro, Steve Mynott, Chris Newson, Deena Omar, Neil Oram, Stephen O'Neill, Julian Palacios, Christopher Partridge, Kath Porteus, Sid Rawle, Matt Ridley, Tim Rundall, Rick Rutkowski, Ben Sessa, Craig Sams, Ronnie Sandison, Jonathan Schoch, Paul

Sieveking, Peter Simmons, Lionel Snell, Mark Stahlman, Allan Staithes, Carl Stickley, Dominic Streatfeild, Liz Spencer, Dave Tomlin, Tom Vague, Roman Vasseur, Julian Venables, Justin Warman, Ian Wilson, Adrian Whittaker, Gary Woodcock, and Rowdy Yates.

CONTACT

The author is interested in hearing from anyone who reads *Albion Dreaming*. Comments, criticism and information I have missed are all welcome at: meugher@gmail.com

RECOMMENDED WEBSITES

The internet is increasingly the best way to find up-to-the-minute information about psychedelic drugs. I highly recommend the following sites:

http://www.lsdbritain.com
http://www.maps.org
    Multidisciplinary Association for Psychedelic Studies
http://www.hofmann.org
http://www.beckleyfoundation.org
http://www.susanblackmore.co.uk
http://psypressuk.com
http://www.erowid.org
http://www.blotterart.co.uk
http://www.blotter.com
http://www.ukrockfestivals.com

PERMISSIONS

Permission to use the photos in the plate section has been granted from the following sources:

Photos 1, 2, 6, 7, 8, 16, 18, 25, 26, 30: Author's collection
Photo 3: Ronald Sandison
Photos 4, 5: Maxwell Hollyhock; the *New Scientist*
Photo 9: Marianne Clancy
Photo 10, 13, 14: John Hoppy Hopkins; www.hoppy.be
Photo 11: Crown Copyright, the National Archives
Photo 12: Jonathan Schoch
Photo 15: Tom Maschler
Photo 17: Gabi Nasemann Pape
Photo 19: Hampshire Constabulary History Society; http://www.hants.org.uk/hchs/
Photo 20: Vin Miles
Photo 21: Julie-Anne Lowe and Stephen Kirkpatrick
Photo 22: Jeremy Dunn
Photo 23: Ray Daniel
Photo 24: Dave Henniker
Photos 27, 28, 29: D.C. Neil Cuttriss; copyright the Chief Constable of Sussex Police

REFERENCES

1. TURN ON, TUNE IN, DROP OUT

1. http://www.m-w.com/dictionary/LSD
2. www.lycaeum.org/~sputnik/Tattoo/
3. Cam Cloud, *Acid Trips and Chemistry,* Ronin Press, Berkeley, 1999
4. http://comment.independent.co.uk/commentators/article338622.ece
5. Paul Devereux, *The Long Trip*: *a prehistory of psychedelia*, Penguin Arkana, London, 1997
6. Thomas Szasz, *Ceremonial Chemistry: the ritual persecution of drugs,* RKP, London, 1975
7. Jay Stevens, *Storming Heaven*, Heinemann, London, 1988

2. HOFMANN'S POTION

1. Albert Hofmann, *LSD: my problem child*, McGraw-Hill, New York 1980, p 61
2. ibid, p ix
3. Mary Kilbourne Matossian, *Poisons of the Past*, Yale University Press 1989, pp 113–22
4. Hofmann, 1980, op cit, p 14
5. ibid, p 15
6. ibid, p 19
7. Albert Hofmann, "LSD: from problem child to wonder drug", speech given at Basel, Switzerland, 13–15 January 2006, quoted in http://undergrowth.org/lsd_problem_child_and_wonder_drug
8. The *Guardian*, 8 August 2002, "A dose of madness"

9. Hofmann, 1980, p 38
10. *Omni*, July 1981, vol 3 no 10, "Interview with Albert Hofmann", p 70
11. ibid
12. Hofman, 1980, op cit, p 47
13. George Andrews, *Burning Joy*, Trigram Press, London, 1966, "Amsterdam Reflection" p 33
14. John Marks, *The Search For The Manchurian Candidate*, Allen Lane, London, 1979, p 53

3. LSD: THE CURE OF SOULS?

1. Peter Stafford, "Re-creational uses of LSD", *Journal of Psychoactive Drugs*, vol 17(4), Oct–Dec 1985, p 221
2. Ronald Sandison, *A Century of Psychiatry, Psychotherapy and Group Analysis*, Jessica Kingsley, London 2001
3. Interview with Ronnie Sandison, 3 February 2007
4. Sandison, 2001, op cit, p 20
5. Thomas Ling and John Buckman, *Lysergic Acid and Ritalin in the Treatment of Neurosis*, Lambarde Press, London, 1963, p 14
6. Interview with Ronnie Sandison, 3 February 2007
7. Sandison, 2001, op cit, p 38
8. Interview with Ronnie Sandison, 3 February 2007
9. R.A. Sandison, A.M. Spencer and J.D.A. Whitelaw, "The therapeutic value of Lysergic Acid Diethylamide in mental illness", *The Journal of Mental Science*, no 100, 1954, pp 491–507
10. ibid, p 500
11. Interview with Ronnie Sandison, 3 February 2007
12. *The Journal of Mental Science*, op cit, p 505
13. The *Sunday Mercury*, 23 August 1954, "Mrs. Brown comes out of the shadows"; The *News Chronicle*, 17 June 1954, "Science had Alice-in-Wonderland drug"
14. *The Journal of Mental Science*, op cit, p 507
15. Email from Joel Elkes, 22 June 2007

16. Letter from Joel Elkes, *Lancet*, no 268, 1955
17. Email from Ronnie Sandison, 29 May 2007
18. Interview with Ronnie Sandison, 3 February 2007
19. Sandison, 2001, op cit, p 42
20. *The Journal of Mental Science*, op cit, p 503
21. Email from Ronnie Sandison, 10 June 2007
22. Interview with Ronnie Sandison, 3 February 2007
23. Graham McCann, *Frankie Howerd: stand-up comic*, Harper Perennial, London, 2005, pp 186–9
24. http://www.contemporaryconcepts.co.uk/horsley-millman/chapter_2.htm
25. Adrian Laing, *R.D. Laing: a life*, Sutton Publishing, London, 2006, p 102
26. ibid, p 62
27. ibid, p 115
28. *Scotland on Sunday*, 21 May 2006, “Licence to trip: when 007 met Dr in the know”
29. Nick Kent, *New Musical Express*, 13 April 1974, Syd Barrett feature
30. A.G. Malleson, N.H. Rathod, P. Bruggen and C.E. Salter, “Withdrawal of LSD”, *British Medical Journal*, no 1, 1966, p 1483

4. LSD: A CURE FOR THE COMMON COLD?

1. http://news.bbc.co.uk/1/hi/uk/4745748.stm
2. The National Archives, Abreactive Drugs, DEFE 10/35
3. http://www.mod.uk/DefenceInternet/AboutDefence/WhatWeDo/HealthandSafety/PortonDownVolunteers/
4. The National Archives, Enzyme Panel of the Chemical Defence Advisory Board, Crown Copyright, 1953
5. Letter from Kim Galloway, Corporate Secretariat, Porton Down, 17 October 2007
6. Human studies with incapacitating agents, http://www.mod.uk/DefenceInternet/AboutDefence/CorporatePublications/Healthand SafetyPublications/PortonDownVolunteers/

7. The *Guardian,* 22 January 2005
8. Email from Eric Gow, 15 November 2007
9. Coroner's Report, Extract from autobiography of Dr. Collumbine, 7 September 2004, p 5
10. Peter Wright with Paul Greengrass, *Spycatcher*, Dell Publishing, New York, 1987, p 202
11. The *Guardian*, 14 March 2002, "Drugged and duped"
12. The National Archives, Abreactive Drugs, op cit
13. ibid
14. The National Archives, Screening tests prior to administration of psychomimetic drugs in human subjects, September 1960, WO 195/14637
15. Rob Evans, *Gassed: British chemical warfare experiments on humans at Porton Down*, House of Stratus, London, 2000, p 235
16. Dr. W.M. Hollyhock, Weapons Against The Mind, *New Scientist*, 22 April 1965
17. Human studies with incapacitating agents, op cit
18. Film held at The Imperial War Museum, *Trial of an incapacitating drug*, London, MGH 4464
19. James S. Ketchum M.D., *Chemical Warfare: secrets almost forgotten*, Chembooks Inc., Santa Rosa, 2006, p 156
20. Dr. W.M. Hollyhock, 1965, op cit
21. Letter from Val Hollyhock, 5 September 2007
22. Minutes of Applied Biology Committee meeting, Porton Down, 24 November 1965, WO 195/16161
23. Human studies with incapacitating agents, op cit
24. ibid
25. Philip Hoare, *Spike Island: the memory of a military hospital*, Fourth Estate, London, 2002, p 367
26. Email from Ronnie Sandison, 29 May 2007
27. *The Times*, 26 May 1964, "British defence against germ warfare"
28. The *Guardian*, 15 October 1968, "Protest over troops' tests with LSD"
29. www.wiltshire.police.uk/antler
30. *Hansard*, 4 April 2005

31. http://www.leighday.co.uk/doc.asp?cat=852&doc=929
32. The *Guardian*, 23 January 2005, "MI6 ordered LSD tests on servicemen"
33. ibid
34. The *Guardian*, 14 March 2002, "Drugged and duped"
35. http://news.bbc.co.uk/1/hi/uk/4745748.stm
36. ibid
37. The *Daily Record*, 1 March 2006, "LSD test man will not sue"
38. The *Guardian,* 22 January 2005

5. THE JOYOUS COSMOLOGY

1. Bob Dylan, "It's all right ma, I'm only bleeding", In: *Bringing it all back home*, 1965
2. Nicholas Murray, *Aldous Huxley: an English intellectual*, Abacus, London, 2002. A comprehensive overview of all aspects of Huxley's life
3. Martin Lee and Bruce Shlain, *Acid Dreams*, Grove Weidenfeld, New York, 1992, p 45
4. Email from Ronnie Sandison, 25 May 2007
5. Lee and Shlain, 1992, op cit, p 45
6. See chapter 1 no 7, p 45
7. Murray, 2002, op cit, p 399
8. Aldous Huxley, *The Doors of Perception*, Vintage, London, 2004. Gives a full account of Huxley's first mescaline experience
9. ibid, p 50
10. Michael Horowitz and Cynthia Palmer (eds), *Moksha*: *Aldous Huxley's classic writings on psychedelics & the visionary experience*, Park Street Press, Rochester, 1999, p 69
11. http://web.ukonline.co.uk/sotcaa/sotcaa.html?/sotcaa/hidden/mayhew01.html
12. Horowitz and Palmer, op cit, 1999, p 107
13. ibid, p 107
14. ibid, p 107
15. ibid, p 81

16. ibid, p 86
17. ibid p 86
18. Alcoholics Anonymous, *Pass it On: the story of Bill Wilson and how the A.A. message reached the world*, 1986, pp 368–77
19. BBC interview with Aldous Huxley, 7 and 11 July 1961
20. Aldous Huxley, *Island*, Chatto and Windus, London, 1962, pp 32 and 145
21. Jeff Dexter interview, 6 October 2007
22. Murray, 2002, op cit, p 454
23. Email from Vanessa Hollingshead, 20 January 2007
24. ibid
25. Michael Hollingshead, *The Man Who Turned On The World*, Blond & Briggs, London, 1973, p 7
26. ibid, p 9
27. ibid, p 10
28. www.hofmann.org/lsd/index.html
29. Ram Dass, *Fierce Grace,* Zeitgeist Video, 2001
30. Robert Greenfield, *Timothy Leary: a biography*, Harcourt Inc., New York, 2006, p 164
31. Timothy Leary, *High Priest*, Ronin Publishing, Berkeley, 1995, p 244
32. ibid, p 246
33. ibid
34. ibid, p 249
35. Jeff Dexter interview, 6 October 2007
36. David Solomon (ed), *LSD: the consciousness expanding drug*, G.P. Putnam, New York, 1964
37. ibid, 1964, p x

6. THE FOGGY RUINS OF TIME

1. See chapter 5 no 25, p 33
2. Letter from Dave Cunliffe, 31 October 2006
3. ibid
4. ibid
5. The *Guardian,* August 8 2003, "Mean streets"

6. Brian Barritt, *The Road of Excess: a psychedelic autobiography,* PSI Publishing, London, 1998, p 4
7. ibid, p 4
8. The *Guardian*, 17 April 1983, "Tory peer tells of her LSD 'trip'"
9. *The Times*, 19 February 1963, "M.O.H. took drug as hobby"
10. See chapter 5 no 31, p 246
11. See chapter 3 no 25, p 83
12. http://okneoac.com/m/chs/ch11.html
13. See chapter 5 no 25, p 142
14. V. Vale and A. Juno, *RE/Search: Pranks*, RE/Search Publications, San Francisco, 1988, p 78
15. *Mojo*, November 2000, "The leper messiah", pp 58–63
16. Julian Palacios, *Lost in the Woods*, Boxtree Ltd, London, 1998, p 30
17. Interview with Nigel Lesmoir-Gordon, 26 January 2007
18. op cit
19. The *Observer*, 16 July 2006, "An eternal summer with Syd"
20. http://www.mp3lyrics.org/d/donovan/sunny-south-kensington
21. http://arts.independent.co.uk/books/features/article314324.ece
22. Interview with Dave Tomlin, 30 October 2006
23. See chapter 5 no 25, p 144
24. http://www.noah.org/trepan/people_with_holes_in_their_heads.html
25. Joey Mellen, *Bore Hole*, Glucocracy, London, 1975
26. ibid
27. Letter from Trocchi to Hollinsghead, 8 December 1965
28. Michael Hollingshead's Christmas card in author's collection

7. STRANGELY STRANGE, BUT ODDLY NORMAL

1. Ivan Pawle, "Sign on my Mind", In: *Heavy Petting*, REPUK 1045, 2005
2. See chapter 2 no 13

3. John Michell, *The Flying Saucer Vision*, Abacus, London, 1974, p 22
4. Email from Amanda Fielding, 28 November 2006
5. Postcard from Hollinsghead to Trocchi, Gstaad, 31 January 1966
6. See chapter 3 no 25, p 115
7. *The Times*, 11 May 1966, "Drug case said to be 'trend setter'"
8. *London Life*, 19 March 1966, "The drug that could become a social peril"
9. ibid
10. The *People*, 20 March 1966, "The men behind 'LSD' – the drug that is menacing young lives"
11. The *News of the World*, 20 March 1966, "Menace of the 'Vision of Hell'"
12. Bob Dylan, "Ballad of a Thin Man", In: *Highway 61 Revisited*, Columbia 4609532, 1965
13. The *News of the World*, 20 March 1966, "Now – the morning glory kick"
14. The *Guardian*, 15 April 1966, "Morning glory seeds still banned"
15. *The Times*, 7 April 1966, "'Vision of hell' drug charges"
16. The *Daily Telegraph*, 30 April 2006, "Jagger's dealer sells his stash"
17. The *People*, 17 April 1966, "BBC in a wild 'drug party' sensation"
18. *The Times*, 11 April 1966, "Drug case said to be 'trend setter'"
19. *The Times*, 28 April 1966, "LSD drug charges man convicted"
20. See chapter 5 no 25, p 170
21. ibid, p 177
22. Email from Owsley, 4 November 2006
23. Terry Taylor, *Baron's Court, All Change*, Four Square, London, 1965, p 99
24. Johnny Dolphin, *Journey Round an Extraordinary Planet*, Synergetic Press, Tuscon, 1990, p 5
25. Emails from Stewart Home, son of Julia Callan-Thompson, 2007
26. "Effects of LSD", *British Medical Journal*, 1966, no 1, pp 1495–6

27. The National Archives, CUST49/5590
28. The *Guardian*, 5 August 1966, "Hallucinations of L.S.D."
29. *British Medical Journal*, 1966, no. 2, p 49
30. Alan Bestic, the *Sunday Times*, undated press cutting
31. CUST49/5590, op cit
32. The *Evening Standard*, 8 September 1966, "To LSD and back again"
33. The *Independent*, 11 October 2006, "Psychedelia: paying homage to its origins"
34. Mick Farren, undated/unnamed book extract
35. Barry Miles, *Paul McCartney: many years from now*, Secker & Warburg, London, 1997, p 376
36. http://www.applecorp.com/aditl/origins.htm
37. Joe Boyd, *White Bicycles: making music in the 1960s*, Serpent's Tail, London, 2005, p158

8. SENSES WORKING OVERTIME

1. www.historytalk.org/Notting%20Hill%20History%20 Timeline/ timelinechap10.pdf
2. *Private Eye*, 23 December 1966, free flexi disc
3. The Pretty Things, "£.S.D.", In: *Get The Picture?*, Rep 4928 2002, Fontana TF 688, 1966
4. http://www.johncoulthart.com/feuilleton/?p=1748
5. Unnamed and undated newspaper cutting, January 1967, "Jury urges definition of LSD"
6. The *News of the World*, 29 January 1967, "Pop stars and drugs"
7. ibid
8. The *News of the World*, 5 February 1967
9. The *News of the World*, 12 February 1967, "Pop songs and the cult of LSD"
10. Jonathon Green, *Days In The Life: voices from the English underground 1961–71*, William Heinemann, London, 1988, p 175
11. The *News of the World*, 5 February 1967

12. Bill Wyman, *Stone Alone*, Penguin Books; London, 1991, pp 481–2
13. http://redlandsbust.blogspot.com
14. Email from Christopher Gibbs, 3 July 2007
15. http://redlandsbust.blogspot.com
16. ibid
17. The *News of the World*, 19 February 1967, "Drug squad raids at pop stars' party"
18. The *Sunday Times*, 21 September 2003, "Dancing for Mr B"
19. Simon Napier-Bell, *Black Vinyl, White Powder*, Ebury Press, London, 2002, p 107
20. Dave Tomlin, *Tales from the Embassy vol. 2*, Iconoclast Press, London, 2006, p 51
21. The *People*, 30 August 1967
22. Green, 1989, op cit, p 163
23. See chapter 6 no 16, p 144
24. ibid, p 143
25. The *News of the World*, n.d. 1967, "Beatle Paul says: I took LSD"
26. http://www.applecorp.com/aditl/origins.htm
27. Internal BBC memo from Roland Fox, assistant head of publicity, 29 May 1967, "The Beatles new L.P"
28. ibid
29. Internal BBC memo from Frank Gillard, director of Sound Broadcasting, 24 May 1967, "Gramophone Records"
30. Email from Augustus Owsley Stanley III, 26 August 2006
31. Iain Sinclair, *The Kodak Mantra Diaries*, Albion Village Press, London, 1971
32. ibid
33. http://www.allenginsberg.org
34. Allen Ginsberg, *City Midnight Junk Strain – selected poems 1947–1995*, Penguin, London, 2001, p 195
35. http://books.guardian.co.uk/review/story/0,12084,1434855,00.html
36. Internal BBC memo from Huw Wheldon, controller of television programmes, 28 July 1967, "Drugs"
37. Steve Marriott and Ronnie Lane, "Itchycoo Park", 1967

38. Email from Grahame Hood, Palmer's biographer, 6 November 2006
39. Note from examiners on *The Trip*, British Board of Film Censors, 13 October 1971
40. *International Times,* 5–20 October 1967, "The Acid Report", p 10
41. See chapter 7 no 37, p 154
42. All information regarding Victor Kapur from the National Archives, MEP02/1180
43. See chapter 7 no 37, p 162

9. ALL YOU NEED IS LOVE?

1. The *Sunday Times*, 21 October 2007, "LSD Article plays tricks on Huhne's mind"
2. The National Archives, MEP02/1180
3. The *People*, 21 September 1969
4. http://www.eelpie.org/epd.htm
5. ibid
6. ibid
7. Jonathan Raban, *Soft City*, Collins Harvill, London, 1974, p 176
8. ibid, p 177
9. http://www.chaos-works.com/index.html
10. ibid
11. Steve Marriott and Ronnie Lane, "Lazy Sunday Afternoon", In: *Ogdens' Nut Gone Flake*, Castle Communications, CLACT016, 1968
12. "Happy Days Toy Town", ibid
13. Interview with Mike Heron, 18 October 1994
14. Internal Home Office memo, 15 September 1969, "Dr. Timothy Leary"
15. Home Office, 17 September 1969, "Refusal of Leave to Land Report"
16. Memo from P.J.R. Norris immigration officer, 15 October 1969
17. Memo from B. Greenyer, 26 September 1969

18. Roger Hutchinson, *High Sixties*, Mainstream, Edinburgh, 1992, p 65
19. Interview with Jeff Dexter, 6 October 2007
20. ibid
21. ibid
22. *The Times* Saturday review, 28 February 1970, "Priest of the sugar lump"
23. Gandalf's Garden, Quintessence, issue 6, 1969
24. Divine Light Mission "Natural High" poster targeting University Students, http://www.prem-rawat-talk.org/forum/posts/20145.html
25. Interview with Andrew Kerr, 11 May 2007
26. http://www.prem-rawat-talk.org/forum/posts/20260.html
27. http://www.prem-rawat-talk.org/forum/posts/20283.html
28. http://www.prem-rawat-talk.org/forum/posts/20279.html
29. Dexter, 6 October, op cit
30. David Cunliffe, *Blackburn Brainswamp*, Redbeck Press, Bradford, 1991, p 16
31. Email from Pete Mellor, 9 December 2006
32. Dexter, 6 October, op cit
33. Interview with Pete Simmons, 25 March 2006
34. *The Times*, 24 March 1970, "LSD induces urge to kill"
35. Barry Cox, John Shirley and Martin Short, *The Fall of Scotland Yard*, Penguin, London, 1977, pp 84–131
36. ibid
37. ibid
38. Nigel Fielding, "Lucy Sent Down", *City Limits*, 1–7 November 1985
39. ibid
40. Bishop, the *Los Angles Free Press*, 25 February 1972, "We're a natural little community"
41. Email from an informant who requested anonymity, 5 March 2007
42. ibid
43. The *Observer* magazine, 3 June 1995, "Lights … camera"
44. *International Times*, 13–27 January 1971, "Dear brothers and sisters", p 3

45. *International Times*, 1972, p 5
46. http://drugs.homeoffice.gov.uk/drugs-laws/misuse-of-drugs-act
47. See chapter 5 no 30 p 452
48. Home Office Memo from Mr. B. Greenyer, 21 January 1973, "Claim for asylum by Mr. T.F. Leary"
49. The *Sunday Times*, 21 October 2007, "LSD article plays tricks on Huhne's mind"

10. BRING WHAT YOU EXPECT TO FIND

1. The *Western Telegraph*, 31 July 1975, "Hippy hundreds at Boncath festival"
2. *Festival Eye*, 1989, vol 1 no 4, "Stonehenge Festival"
3. http://www.ukrockfestivals.com/phun-vftmud.html
4. Hamish Miller and Paul Broadhurst, *The Sun and the Serpent,* Pendragon Press, Launceston, 1989, p 11
5. *Albion*, 1967, no 1
6. For comprehensive histories of the early Glastonbury Fairs see: Crispin Aubrey and John Shearlaw, *Glastonbury: an oral history*, Ebury Press, London, 2004. George McKay, *Glastonbury: a very English fair*, Victor Gollancz, London, 2000
7. Aubrey and Shearlaw, ibid, p 25
8. The *Observer*, 20 June 1971
9. McKay, 2000, op cit
10. Email from William Bloom, 9 August 2007
11. Aubrey and Shearlaw, 2004, op cit p 23
12. The *Observer* music magazine, June 2006, p 74
13. Interview with Andrew Kerr, 11 May 2007
14. http://www.mooncowhq.ch/Cornelius/Cornelius05.htm
15. Mick Farren, *Give the Anarchist a Cigarette*, Jonathan Cape, London, 2001, p 302
16. Richard Barnes, *The Sun in the East: Norfolk and Suffolk fairs*, RB Photographic, Norfolk, 1983
17. Bill Dwyer's defence notes. http://www.takver.com/history/aia/aia00034.htm

18. ibid
19. Email from "Jill", 20 November 2006
20. http://www.parliament.nsw.gov.au/prod/PARLMENT/hansArt.nsf/V3Key/LC19961126031
21. Interview with Sid Rawle, 15 April 2007
22. George McKay, *Senseless Acts of Beauty*, Verso, London, 1996, p 16
23. Interview with Roger Hutchinson, 20 October 2006
24. ibid
25. http://www.ukrockfestivals.com/windsor-74-release.html
26. Interview with Allan Staithes, 4 March 2007
27. http://www.ukrockfestivals.com/windsor-74-release.html
28. http://www.ukrockfestivals.com/acidia-lightshow.html
29. Email from Nigel Ayres, 20 August 2007
30. Email from Pat Conlon, 18 August 2007
31. http://www.prem-rawat-talk.org/forum/posts/20130.html
32. http://www.grahamhancock.com/supernatural/article_01.html
33. http://freepages.genealogy.rootsweb.com/~colinsgenealogy/Udevsite/notonly2.pdf
34. Penny Rimbaud, *The Last of the Hippies*, Flowerpot Press, London, n.d.
35. http://www.freenetpages.co.uk/hp/mjbou/travellers/wallyhope.html
36. Email from Nigel Ayres, 9 September 2006
37. The *Guardian*, 26 November 1974, "Man gave LSD to son, aged 9"
38. http://freepages.genealogy.rootsweb.com/~colinsgenealogy/Udevsite/notonly1.pdf
39. C.J. Stone, *Fierce Dancing: adventures in the underground*, Faber & Faber, London, 1996
40. *The Times*, 28 June 1978
41. Interview with Sid Rawle, 15 April 2007
42. Windsor Freep, August 1974
43. Martyn Pritchard and Ed Laxton, *Busted! The sensational life-story of an undercover hippie cop*, Mirror Books, London, 1978

44. Dick Lee and Colin Pratt, *Operation Julie*, W.H. Allen, London, 1978, p 54
45. http://www.ukrockfestivals.com/trentishoe-73.html
46. ibid
47. http://www.ukrockfestivals.com/trentishoe76.html
48. http://www.ukrockfestivals.com/meigan-75-menu.html
49. The *Western Telegraph*, 31 July 1975, op cit
50. http://www.ukrockfestivals.com/meigan-75-menu.html
51. http://www.ukrockfestivals.com/zorch.html
52. http://www.herenow.be/herenowpages/vaultsyourtales2.htm
53. http://www.aural-innovations.com/issues/issue7/nukli.html

11. THE MIND ALCHEMISTS

1. The *Evening Standard*, 27 February 1978, "The Brotherhood of LSD"
2. The *Guardian,* 3 January 1972, "Pinhead LSD 'a killer'"
3. Tim Lott, *The Scent of Dried Roses*, Penguin Books, London, 1977, p 177
4. ibid
5. The National Archives, HO 319/315
6. ibid
7. ibid
8. ibid
9. Stewart Tendler and David May, *The Brotherhood of Eternal Love*, Cyan Books, London, 2007, p 208
10. Interview with 'Operation Julie' defendant who requested anonymity, July 2007
11. HO 319/315, op cit
12. ibid
13. ibid
14. ibid
15. ibid
16. ibid
17. Tendler and May, 2007, op cit
18. HO 319/315, op cit

19. *International Times*, December 1978, "Insult to injury"
20. See chapter 10 no 44, p 290
21. HO 319/315, op cit, plus information supplied under guarantee of anonymity from one of the Operation Julie defendants
22. HO 319/315, op cit
23. See chapter 9 no 38
24. Letter from D. Solomon to L. Harris, 29 April, 1977
25. ibid
26. The *Daily Express*, 9 March 1978
27. ibid
28. *The Times*, 18 February 1978, "Doctor in LSD case denies having been a 'banker'"
29. *The Times*, 2 March 1978, "Drug abuse experts says LSD causes little injury"
30. The *Guardian*, 2 March 1978, "LSD case judge refuses doctor's expert evidence"
31. *Cambrian News*, 17 March 1978, "Microdoctrine"
32. The *Evening Standard*, 8 March 1978, "22 Years For LSD Lovers"
33. *The Times*, 9 March 1978, "Severe, but rightly so"
34. *International Times*, n.d., "Lysergic Love Criminals"
35. HO 319/315, op cit
36. The *Western Mail*, 11 October 1978, "Operation Julie detectives quit force in anger"
37. Interview with Steve Abrams, 9 May 2007
38. *The Times*, 13 June 1980, "Gang's drug fortunes unlawfully seized" and *The Times*, 12 November 1980, "Tax claims over 'Julie' case"
39. The *News of the World*, 27 March 1977, "Drugnet: 71 held in drug raids"
40. http://www.bbc.co.uk/wales/mid/sites/tregaron/pages/julie_lyn.shtml
41. The *Mail on Sunday*, 8 August 2004, "Nobel Prize genius Crick was high on LSD when he discovered the secret of life"
42. Matt Ridley, *Francis Crick: Discoverer of the Genetic Code*, Harper Collins, New York, 2006, p 156
43. http://azlyrics.us/52525

44. *The Times*, 21 July 2006, "Father's anguish as men cleared of Everest killing"
45. The *New Musical Express*, 18 March 1978, "Operation Julie"
46. ibid

12. COMING DOWN AGAIN

1. http://thinkexist.com/quotes/bill_hicks/4.html
2. Alchemy, 261 Portobello Road, London, W11 1LR
3. http://www.newstatesman.com/200306160035
4. Julian Cope, *Head-On/Repossessed*, Thorsons, London, 1994 pp 112–3
5. ibid, p 168
6. http://www.ukrockfestivals.com/henge-history-80-82.html
7. Email from Glenda Pescado, 5 February 2008
8. Don Aitken, undated/unnamed book extract
9. Email from Glenda Pescado, 1 February 2008
10. Andy Worthington, *Stonehenge: celebration and subversion*, Alternative Albion, Wymeswold, 2001, p 130
11. Interview with Sid Rawle, April 2007
12. Peter Gardner, *Medieval Brigands*, Redcliffe, Bristol, 1987, p 7
13. ibid, p 7
14. Email interview with Monkey, 27 December 2007
15. ibid
16. ibid
17. Email from Glenda Pescado, 1 February 2008
18. Nicholas Saunders and Rick Doblin, *Ecstasy: dance, trance and transformation*, Quick Trading Co., San Francisco, 1996
19. Email interview with Monkey, op cit
20. Matthew Collin, *Altered States: the story of Ecstasy culture and Acid House*, Serpent's Tail, London, 1998, pp 214–5
21. ibid
22. http://www.network23.org.uk/node/15
23. http://www.parallel-youniversity.com/fraser/
24. Irvine Welsh, *The Acid House*, Jonathan Cape, London, 1994
25. Albert Hofmann, speech delivered to the Worlds of

Consciousness Conference, Heidelberg, 1996
26. http://www.lycaeum.org/drugs/other/tattoo/
27. The *Daily Star*, 15 November 1985, "Peril of the LSD cartoon stamps"
28. Paul Sieveking, *Fortean Times,* no 63, "Acid tattoo scare"
29. The *Daily Express*, 6 January 1997, "Hole lot of hassle"
30. http://www.sfweekly.com/1995-08-30/news/acid-house/full
31. www.blotterart.co.uk
32. "Patients given LSD may be able to claim compensation", *British Medical Journal*, 4 November 1995, 311(7014), pp 1185–6
33. The *Lancashire Evening Telegraph*, 3 December 1999, "LSD wrecked my life – Gran"
34. Email from Ronnie Sandison, 29 May, 2007
35. The *Guardian*, 17 November 1999, p 2
36. The *Worcester News*, 24 April 2002, "LSD trio set to discuss payout"

13. REVOLUTION IN THE HEAD

1. http://www.psychedelic.info/index_2_eng.html
2. http://www.homeoffice.gov.uk/rds/pdfs2/hosb402.pdf
3. The *Argus*, Brighton, 25 January 2005
4. The *Argus*, Brighton, 19 March 2005
5. The *Argus,* Brighton, 21 January 2005
6. The *Argus,* Brighton, 26 May 2006
7. C. Hardison, personal communication, 7 November 2006
8. http://www.erowid.org/culture/characters/hardison_casey/hardison_casey_2007_motivation_of_an_entheogenic_chemist.pdf
9. The *Guardian*, 11 January 2006, "Psychiatrist calls for end to 30-year taboo over use of LSD as a medical treatment"
10. http://www.guardian.co.uk/science/2006/apr/14/medicalresearch.drugs
11. The *Independent*, 23 March 2007, "Tobacco and alcohol 'are more dangerous than LSD'"

12. ibid
13. http://www.edocr.com/doc/61/drugs-policy-radical-look-ahead
14. ibid
15. ibid
16. The *Daily Telegraph*, 30 October 2007
17. http://www.crimeandjustice.org.uk/estimatingdrugharmspr.html
18. http://www.independent.co.uk/news/uk/politics/drug-adviser-sacked-over-lsd-claims-1812091.html
19. http://www.guardian.co.uk/politics/2009/oct/30/drugs-adviser-david-nutt-sacked
20. http://www.homeoffice.gov.uk/publications/alcohol-drugs/drugs/drug-strategy/drug-strategy-2010
21. http://www.susanblackmore.co.uk/journalism/telegraphdrugs.htm
22. http://www.guardian.co.uk/commentisfree/belief/2011/mar/22/lsd-acid-trip-self-knowledge
23. The *Observer* Magazine, 15 December 2007
24. http://www.psychedelic.info/index_2_eng.html
25. http://www.hallucinogens.com/hofmann/child8.htm

BIBLIOGRAPHY

Daevid Allen, *Gong Dreaming,* SAF, London, 2007.

George Andrews, *Burning Joy*, Trigram Press, London, 1966.

Crispin Aubrey and John Shearlaw, *Glastonbury: festival tales*, Ebury Press, London, 2004.

Richard Barnes, *The Sun in the East: Norfolk and Suffolk fairs*, RB Photographic, Norfolk, 1983.

Brian Barritt, *The Road of Excess: a psychedelic autobiography,* PSI Publishing, London, 1998.

David Black, *Acid: A New Secret History of LSD*, 2nd edn, Vision, London, 2003.

Joe Boyd, *White Bicycles: making music in the 1960s*, Serpent's Tail, London, 2005.

William V Caldwell, *LSD Psychotherapy*, Grove Press, London, 1968.

Cam Cloud, *Acid Trips and Chemistry*, Ronin Press, Berkeley, 1999.

Sidney Cohen, *Drugs of Hallucination*, Paladin, London, 1973.

Matthew Collin, *Altered State: the story of Ecstasy culture and Acid House*, Serpent's Tail, London, 1997.

Caroline Coon and Rufus Harris, *The Release Report*, Sphere, London, 1969.

Julian Cope, *Head-On/Repossessed*, Thorsons, London, 1999.

Barry Cox, John Shirley, and Martin Short, *The Fall of Scotland Yard,* Penguin, London, 1977.

Richard Crocket, R.A. Sandison and Alexander Walk (eds), *Hallucinogenic Drugs and their Psychotherapeutic Use,* H.K. Lewis, London, 1963.

David Cunliffe, *Blackburn Brainswamp*, Redbeck Press, Bradford, 1991.

Johnny Dolphin, *Journey Round an Extraordinary Planet*, Synergetic Press, Tuscon, 1979.

Jane Dunlap, *Exploring Inner Space*, Scientific Book Club, London, 1961.

Rob Evans, *Gassed: British chemical warfare experiments on humans at Porton Down*, House of Stratus, London, 2000.

Mick Farren, *Give the Anarchist a Cigarette*, Jonathan Cape, London, 2001.

Monica Furlong, *Genuine Fake*, Unwin, London, 1986.

Allen Ginsberg, *Selected Poems 1947–1995*, Penguin, London, 1996.

Allen Ginsberg, *Wales: A Visitation*, Cape Goliad Press, London, 1967.

Tony Gould, *Inside Outsider*, Allison & Busby, London, 1993.

Jonathon Green, *Days in the Life: voices from the English Underground, 1961–71*, William Heinemann, London, 1988.

Robert Greenfield, *Timothy Leary: a biography*, Harcourt Inc., New York, 2006.

Christoph Grunenberg (ed), *Summer of Love*, L.U.P., Liverpool, 2005.

Roger Harris, *The LSD Dossier*, Compact Books, London, 1966.

Phillip Hoare, *Spike Island: the memory of a military hospital*, Fourth Estate, London, 2002.

Albert Hofmann, *Insight Outlook*, Humanics, Atlanta, 1989.

Albert Hofmann, *LSD: my problem child*, McGraw-Hill, New York, 1980.

Michael Hollingshead, *The Man Who Turned On The World*, Blond & Briggs, London, 1973.

Stewart Home, *Tainted Love*, Virgin Books, London, 2005.

Gordon Honeycombe, *Adam's Tale*, Hutchinson, London, 1974.

Michael Horowitz (ed), *Children of Albion: poetry of the Underground in Britain*, Penguin Books, London, 1969.

Michael Horowitz and Cynthia Palmer (eds), *Moksha: Aldous Huxley's classic writings on psychedelics & the visionary experience*, Park Street Press, Rochester, 1999.

Roger Hutchinson, *High Sixties*, Mainstream, Edinburgh, 1992.

Aldous Huxley, *Island*, Vintage, London, 2005.

Aldous Huxley, *The Doors of Perception*, Vintage, London, 2004.

Robert Irwin, *Satan Wants Me*, Bloomsbury, London, 2000.

Gary Lachman, *Turn Off Your Mind*, Macmillan, London, 2001.

Adrian Laing, *R.D. Laing: a Life*, Sutton, London, 2006.

Timothy Leary, *Flashbacks*, G.P. Putnam, New York, 1990.

Timothy Leary, *High Priest*, Ronin, Oakland, 1995.

Timothy Leary, *Psychedelic Prayers*, Ronin, Oakland, 1997.

Martin Lee and Bruce Shlain, *Acid Dreams*, Grove Weidenfield, New York, 1992.

Dick Lee and Colin Pratt, *Operation Julie*, W.H. Allen, London, 1978.

Donovan Leitch, *The Hurdy Gurdy Man*, Century, London, 2005.

Shawn Levy, *Ready, Steady, Go!*, Fourth Estate, London, 2002.

Thomas Ling and John Buckman, *Lysergic Acid and Ritalin in the Treatment of Neuroses*, Lambarde Press, London, 1963.

Tim Lott, *The Scent of Dried Roses*, Penguin, London, 1997.

Tom Lyttle (ed), *Psychedelics*, Barricade Books, New York, 1994.

John Marks, *The Search for the Manchurian Candidate*, W.W. Norton & Co., New York, 1991.

Christopher Mayhew, *Time to Explain*, Hutchinson, London, 1987.

George McKay, *Glastonbury: a very English fair*, Gollancz, London, 2000.

George McKay, *Senseless Acts of Beauty*, Verso, London, 1996.

Toni Melechi (ed), *Psychedelia Britannica*, Turnaround, London, 1997.

Barry Miles, *Ginsberg: a biography*, Virgin, London, 2000.

Barry Miles, *Paul McCartney: many years from now*, Secker & Warburg, London, 1997.

Nicholas Murray, *Aldous Huxley*, Abacus, London, 2003.

Simon Napier-Bell, *Black Vinyl, White Powder*, Ebury, London 2002.

Elizabeth Nelson, *The British Counter Culture 1966–73*, Macmillan, London, 1989.

Richard Neville, *Playpower*, Paladin, London, 1970.

Constance Newland, *My Self and I*, Frederick Muller, London, 1963.

Christopher Partridge, *The Re-Enchantment of the West*, (vol 2), T&T Clark, London, 2005.

Martyn Pritchard and Edward Laxton, *Busted! The sensational life-story of an undercover hippie cop*, Mirror Books, London, 1978.

Jonathan Raban, *Soft City*, Collins Harvill, London, 1988.

Matt Ridley, *Francis Crick*, Harper Collins, New York, 2006.

Penny Rimbaud, *Shibboleth*, AK Press, Edinburgh, 1988.

Penny Rimbaud, The Last of the Hippies, Flowerpot Press, London, n.d.

Ronnie Sandison, *A Century of Psychiatry, Psychotherapy and Group Analysis*, Jessica Kingsley, London, 2001.

Nicholas Saunders and Rick Doblin, *Ecstasy: dance, trance and transformation*, Quick Trading Co., San Francisco, 1996.

Nicholas Schaffner, *Saucerful of Secrets*, Sidgwick & Jackson, 1992.

Iain Sinclair, *The Kodak Mantra Diaries*, Albion Village Press, London, 1971.

David Solomon (ed), *LSD: the consciousness expanding drug*, G.P. Putnam, New York, 1964.

Peter Stafford, *LSD in Action*, Sidgwick & Jackson, London, 1970.

Peter Stafford, *Psychedelics Encyclopedia*, Ronin, Berkley, 1992.

Jay Stevens, *Storming Heaven*, Heinemann, London, 1988.

C.J. Stone, *Fierce Dancing: adventures in the underground*, Faber & Faber, London, 1996.

Dominic Streatfeild, *Brainwash*, Hodder & Stoughton, London, 2006.

Stuart Tendler and David May, *The Brotherhood of Eternal Love*, Cyan Books, London, 2007.

David Tomlin, *Tales from the Embassy Vol. II*, Iconoclast Press, London, 2006.

Julian Vayne, *Pharmakon*, Mandrake Press, Oxford, 2006.

Alan Watts, *The Joyous Cosmology*, Vintage Books, New York, 1970.

Fay Weldon, *Auto da Fay*, Flamingo, London, 2003.

Irvine Welsh, *The Acid House*, Jonathan Cape, London, 1994.

Andy Worthington, *Stonehenge: celebration and subversion*, Alternative Albion, Wymeswold, 2004.

Andy Worthington (ed), *The Battle of the Beanfield*, Enabler Publications, Teignmouth, 2005.

Peter Wright, *Spycatcher*, Dell, New York, 1988.

INDEX